Read this book online today:

With SAP PRESS BooksOnline we offer you online access to knowledge from the leading SAP experts. Whether you use it as a beneficial supplement or as an alternative to the printed book, with SAP PRESS BooksOnline you can:

• Access your book anywhere, at any time. All you need is an Internet connection.
• Perform full text searches on your book and on the entire SAP PRESS library.
• Build your own personalized SAP library.

The SAP PRESS customer advantage:

Register this book today at *www.sap-press.com* and obtain exclusive free trial access to its online version. If you like it (and we think you will), you can choose to purchase permanent, unrestricted access to the online edition at a very special price!

Here's how to get started:

1. Visit *www.sap-press.com*.
2. Click on the link for SAP PRESS BooksOnline and login (or create an account).
3. Enter your free trial license key, shown below in the corner of the page.
4. Try out your online book with full, unrestricted access for a limited time!

Your personal free trial **license key**
for this online book is: **7iry-mbs4-g3ja-2cku**

ABAP™ Data Dictionary

 **PRESS**

Günther Färber, Julia Kirchner
ABAP Basics (2nd Edition)
2011, app. 500 pp.
978-1-59229-369-8

Karl-Heinz Kühnhauser
Discover ABAP
2008, app. 500 pp.
978-1-59229-152-6

Horst Keller, Sascha Krüger
ABAP Objects (2nd Edition)
2007, app. 1000 pp.
978-1-59229-079-6

Horst Keller
The Official ABAP Reference (2nd Edition)
2005, app. 1200 pp.
978-1-59229-039-0

Tanmaya Gupta

ABAP™ Data Dictionary

Galileo Press

Bonn • Boston

Galileo Press is named after the Italian physicist, mathematician and philosopher Galileo Galilei (1564–1642). He is known as one of the founders of modern science and an advocate of our contemporary, heliocentric worldview. His words *Eppur si muove* (And yet it moves) have become legendary. The Galileo Press logo depicts Jupiter orbited by the four Galilean moons, which were discovered by Galileo in 1610.

Editor Kelly Grace Harris
Developmental Editor Laura Korslund
Copyeditor John Parker
Cover Design Graham Geary
Photo Credit iStockphoto.com/shulz
Layout Design Vera Brauner
Production Manager Kelly O'Callaghan
Assistant Production Editor Graham Geary
Typesetting Publishers' Design and Production Services, Inc.
Printed and bound in Canada

ISBN 978-1-59229-379-7

© 2011 by Galileo Press Inc., Boston (MA)

1st edition, 2011

Library of Congress Cataloging-in-Publication Data
Gupta, Tanmaya.
 ABAP data dictionary / Tanmaya Gupta. — 1st ed.
  p. cm.
 Includes index.
 ISBN-13: 978-1-59229-379-7
 ISBN-10: 1-59229-379-4
 1. ABAP/4 (Computer program language) I. SAP AG. II. Title.
 QA76.73.A12G87 2011
 005.13'3—dc22
 2011000239

Contents at a Glance

1   Introduction   19

2   Data Types   27

3   Domains   39

4   Data Elements   59

5   Tables   77

6   Views   169

7   Table Maintenance Dialog   205

8   Complex Data Types: Structures and Table Types   263

9   Search Helps   285

10   Lock Objects   325

11   Database Utility   349

Dear Reader,

Welcome to *ABAP Data Dictionary*! This book will answer all your questions about the central repository of information for ABAP data. You'll learn basic background information, as well as details about the specific functionality of Data Dictionary elements (domains, tables, views, etc.), both of which will help you enhance your programming skills.

After spending the last few months working with Tanmaya on this book, I am confident that the content contained in these pages will meet, and likely even exceed, all expectations. Tanmaya's strict attention to the organization and structure of the book are evident throughout, and his commitment and hard work are apparent in his thorough explanations and detailed screenshots. After witnessing the time and care that went into the preparation, writing, and editing of this manuscript, I can truly say that Tanmaya is one of the most dedicated authors I've ever had the pleasure of working with. I consider myself lucky to have had the opportunity to be his editor.

We appreciate your business, and welcome your feedback. Your comments and suggestions are the most useful tools to help us improve our books for you, the reader. We encourage you to visit our website at *www.sap-press.com* and share your feedback about this work.

Thank you for purchasing a book from SAP PRESS!

Kelly Grace Harris
Editor, SAP PRESS

Galileo Press
Boston, MA

kelly.harris@galileo-press.com
www.sap-press.com

Contents

1   Introduction **19**

1.1   Systems, Applications, and Products in Data Processing (SAP) 19
1.2   Advanced Business Application Programming (ABAP) 21
1.3   Data Dictionary 22
        1.3.1   Data Dictionary Tasks 23
        1.3.2   Objects in the Data Dictionary 24
1.4   Summary 25

2   Data Types **27**

2.1   Data Types 27
        2.1.1   Built-In Elementary Data Types 28
        2.1.2   User-Defined Data Types 32
2.2   Mapping of the Data Types 35
2.3   Summary 38

3   Domains **39**

3.1   An Introduction to Domains 39
3.2   Attributes of Domains 41
        3.2.1   Short Description 42
        3.2.2   Properties Tab 42
        3.2.3   Definition Tab 43
        3.2.4   Value Range Tab 50
        3.2.5   Documentation 52
3.3   Creating Domains 52
3.4   Changing Domains 55
3.5   Deleting Domains 56
3.6   Summary 57

4   Data Elements **59**

4.1   An Introduction to Data Elements 59
4.2   Attributes of Data Elements 59
      4.2.1   Short Description 60
      4.2.2   Attributes Tab 60
      4.2.3   Data Type Tab 61
      4.2.4   Field Label Tab 63
      4.2.5   Further Characteristics Tab 64
      4.2.6   Documentation 69
4.3   Creating Data Elements 71
4.4   Deleting Data Elements 75
4.5   Summary 76

5   Tables **77**

5.1   An Introduction to Tables 77
      5.1.1   Transparent Tables 77
5.2   Components of a Table 82
      5.2.1   Table Fields 84
      5.2.2   Includes 89
      5.2.3   Foreign Key 92
      5.2.4   Technical Settings 112
      5.2.5   Indexes 122
      5.2.6   Enhancements in Tables (Append Structures
              and Customizing Includes) 127
      5.2.7   Delivery Class 133
      5.2.8   Activation Types 135
      5.2.9   Data Browser/Table View Maintenance 136
5.3   Creating Tables 137
      5.3.1   Options when Creating Tables 140
      5.3.2   Maintaining Technical Settings 143
      5.3.3   Creating Foreign Keys 144
      5.3.4   Creating Secondary Indexes 147
5.4   Changing Tables 149
      5.4.1   Inserting New Fields 150
      5.4.2   Deleting Existing Fields 152
      5.4.3   Changing Existing Fields 153
      5.4.4   Changing Table Category 154

	5.4.5	Moving Fields	155
	5.4.6	Copying Fields from Another Table	156
5.5	Deleting Tables		158
5.6	Creating Other Dictionary Objects		159
	5.6.1	Creating Table Pools	159
	5.6.2	Creating Table Clusters	162
	5.6.3	Creating Pooled Tables/Cluster Tables	164
5.7	Deleting Other Dictionary Objects		166
5.8	Summary		167

6   Views 169

6.1	An Introduction to Views		169
6.2	Attributes of Views		170
	6.2.1	Join	170
	6.2.2	Relationship between Foreign Keys and Join Conditions	173
	6.2.3	Projection	173
	6.2.4	Selection	174
	6.2.5	Maintenance Status	175
6.3	Types of Views		176
	6.3.1	Database Views	177
	6.3.2	Projection Views	179
	6.3.3	Append Views	179
	6.3.4	Help Views	180
	6.3.5	Maintenance Views	181
6.4	Creating and Deleting Views		182
	6.4.1	Creating Database Views	183
	6.4.2	Creating Projection Views	189
	6.4.3	Creating Append Views	191
	6.4.4	Creating Help Views	194
	6.4.5	Creating Maintenance Views	198
	6.4.6	Deleting Views	204
6.5	Summary		204

7   Table Maintenance Dialog 205

| 7.1 | Table Maintenance Dialog: Initial Screen (Transaction: SE54) | 206 |
| 7.2 | Table Maintenance Generator | 208 |

	7.2.1	Components of Table Maintenance Generator	208
	7.2.2	Creating the Table Maintenance Generator	218
	7.2.3	Modifying the Table Maintenance Generator	221
7.3	Maintaining Authorization Groups		239
7.4	Maintaining Function Group		243
7.5	View Variants		245
7.6	View Clusters		250
	7.6.1	Structure of a View Cluster	250
	7.6.2	Creating View Clusters	251
	7.6.3	Testing View Clusters	259
7.7	Summary		261

8   Complex Data Types: Structures and Table Types 263

8.1	Structures		264
	8.1.1	Types of Structures	264
	8.1.2	Creating Structures	266
8.2	Table Types		271
	8.2.1	Access Mode	272
	8.2.2	Key Definition	273
	8.2.3	Key Category	274
	8.2.4	Generic Table Types	275
	8.2.5	Correlation between Table Types and Internal Tables	276
	8.2.6	Creating Table Types	276
	8.2.7	Ranges Table Types	279
	8.2.8	Creating Ranges Table Types	280
8.3	Deleting Data Types		283
8.4	Summary		283

9   Search Helps 285

9.1	Introduction to Search Helps		285
9.2	Types of Search Help		286
	9.2.1	Elementary Search Help	287
	9.2.2	Collective Search Help	294
	9.2.3	Search Help Exit	297
9.3	Creating Search Help		300
	9.3.1	Creating Elementary Search Helps	300

9.3.2   Creating Collective Search Helps 305

9.4   Value Transport for Input Helps 311

9.4.1   Parameterizing the Import Parameters 311

9.4.2   Returning the Values from the Hit List 312

9.5   Search Help Attachment 312

9.5.1   Search Help Attachment to a Data Element 313

9.5.2   Search Help Attachment to a Check Table 316

9.5.3   Search Help Attached to a Table or Structure Field 318

9.5.4   Search Help Attached to a Screen Field 320

9.5.5   Hierarchy of the Search Help Call 322

9.6   Summary 324

10   Lock Objects 325

10.1   An Introduction to Locks 325

10.2   Lock Mechanisms and Their Attributes 327

10.2.1   Lock Objects 327

10.2.2   Lock Arguments 328

10.2.3   Lock Mode 329

10.2.4   Lock Server 330

10.2.5   _SCOPE Parameter 333

10.2.6   Lock Table 334

10.2.7   Local Lock Containers 336

10.2.8   Function Modules for Lock Requests 337

10.2.9   Foreign Keys in Lock Objects 341

10.2.10   Lock Mechanism 342

10.3   Creating Lock Objects 343

10.4   Deleting Lock Objects 347

10.5   Summary 348

11   Database Utility 349

11.1   An Introduction to the Database Utility 349

11.2   Processing Types 351

11.2.1   Direct 352

11.2.2   Background 352

11.2.3   Enter for Mass Processing 353

11.3   Storage Parameters 363

	11.3.1	Storage Parameter for a Table	364
	11.3.2	Maintaining Storage Parameters	364
11.4	Runtime Objects		367
11.5	Activation		370
	11.5.1	Mass Activation	370
	11.5.2	Background Activation	373
11.6	Adjusting Database Structures		374
11.7	Conversion		376
	11.7.1	Conversion Process	376
	11.7.2	Conversion Problems	380
	11.7.3	Continuing Terminated Conversions	381
	11.7.4	Finding Terminated Conversions	383
11.8	Editing Dictionary Objects in the Database		383
	11.8.1	Editing Tables	384
	11.8.2	Editing Views	389
11.9	Summary		394

The Author		395
Index		379

Introduction

The ABAP Data Dictionary is the central repository for data used in all ABAP-based SAP systems. It allows you to manage definitions for all object types (tables, views, types, domains, lock objects, etc.) that are used in ABAP programs and SAP components. In other words, instead of re-defining objects every time you use them in various programs or components, you can simply define them once, in the ABAP Data Dictionary, and the object definitions are then called by these programs or components as necessary. By serving as a central location for object definitions, the ABAP Data Dictionary ensures data consistency and eliminates data redundancy. As a core element of all ABAP-based SAP programs, it is used by all ABAP developers.

Purpose and Objective of the Book

The purpose of this book is to answer any and all questions an ABAP developer might have about the ABAP Data Dictionary. By providing both basic background information and details about the specific functionality of ABAP Data Dictionary elements, the book enables readers to enhance both their general understanding and their specific programming abilities. This book is a one-stop resource for all the information needed by a developer on the ABAP Data Dictionary, from basic information to advanced technical concepts.

Audience for this Book

This book is written for all ABAP developers and consultants, whether they are beginners or experienced. It not only explains the concepts behind the Data Dictionary to beginners, but also enhances the knowledge of experienced ABAPers. This book serves as a complete guide for all users.

Structure of the Book

This book is structured to make it very easy to understand. There are 11 chapters, the contents of which we'll now describe.

▶ **Chapter 1**
Chapter 1 gives you a general introduction and provides you an overview of SAP, ABAP, and the ABAP Data Dictionary. This chapter also tells you about various objects present within the ABAP Data Dictionary.

▶ **Chapter 2**
This chapter focuses on data types. It provides an overview of the categories of data types present in the ABAP Data Dictionary. This chapter also informs you about the classification of data types into built-in and user-defined data types and the mapping of Data Dictionary types with ABAP data types.

▶ **Chapter 3**
This chapter introduces you to the concept of domains and explains their attributes. We also discuss creating, changing, and deleting domains.

▶ **Chapter 4**
This chapter introduces you to the concept of data elements and their attributes. We also discuss creating, changing, and deleting data elements.

▶ **Chapter 5**
This chapter focuses on tables, which is one of the most important topics in ABAP. This chapter starts with a general introduction to tables and their classification into transparent, pooled, and cluster tables. We also discuss various components of tables, such as table fields, table includes, foreign keys, technical settings, indexes, and enhancements such as append structures, customizing includes, delivery classes, and activation types. We also discuss how to create, change, and delete tables.

▶ **Chapter 6**
This chapter focuses on the concept of views. This chapter starts with a general introduction to the topic. Next, it informs you about various attributes such as joins, projections, selections, and the maintenance status of views. This chapter also discusses types of views: database views, projection views, help views, and maintenance views. You also learn about the creation and deletion of views.

▶ **Chapter 7**
Chapter 7 provides knowledge about the Table Maintenance Generator (also

known as the Table Maintenance Dialog). This chapter explains Transaction SE54 and Transaction SM30. It also explains important concepts such as authorizations, view variants, and view clusters. We also discuss the creation of the table maintenance dialog, view variants, and view clusters.

▶ **Chapter 8**
Chapter 8 focuses on user-defined complex data types. This chapter deals with structures, types, and creation. You also get the details about table types and their attributes, such as access modes, key definitions, and key categories. You also learn about ranges, table types, and the creation of table types and ranges table types.

▶ **Chapter 9**
Chapter 9 gives an overview, introduction, and detailed information about search helps. In this chapter, you also learn about the classification of search helps into elementary and collective search helps. You also get to know about append search helps, search help exits, creating search helps, and attaching these search helps with various ABAP objects such as data elements, check tables, table fields, and screen fields.

▶ **Chapter 10**
Chapter 10 introduces the concept of lock mechanisms and lock objects. This chapter discusses various attributes of lock mechanisms and the creation and deletion of lock objects.

▶ **Chapter 11**
Chapter 11 focuses on database utilities. This chapter starts with a general introduction. You learn about processing types, storage parameters, runtime objects, activations, and adjusting database structures. This chapter also explains the conversion process, common problems, and finding and continuing terminated conversions. In this chapter, you also learn how to edit dictionary objects such as tables, views, pools, and clusters in the database.

This book shows how to solve problems in practical ways, with examples for each and every concept. Beyond the overview, it describes the detailed functionality of every component of the ABAP Data Dictionary. The reader can reap many benefits for programming and can enhance his or her understanding of how this central repository of SAP ABAP works and how it links to other ABAP objects. Because this book is full of diagrams, programs, examples, and screen shots, it should act as a complete guide and reference for all those who work in ABAP development.

Before we begin, I want to add a few lines of my own:

> *When your willingness is great and desires are passionate,*
> *No one can obstruct you to accomplish and innovate;*
> *Impart your knowledge to others and motivate,*
> *Inspire everyone to achieve, succeed, and celebrate.*

Tanmaya Gupta
Allahabad, Uttar Pradesh, India

Acknowledgments

Before we get into the thick of things, I would like to add a few heartfelt words for the people who were part of this book and who gave me unending support right from the day the book idea was conceived.

I would like to dedicate this book to my late grandparents, parents, and the rest of my family. There are times in such projects when the clock beats you time and again, and as you run out of energy you just want to finish it once and for all. My parents helped me endure such times with their unfailing blessings and warm wishes. I express my gratitude for their constant love, faith, inspiration, and motivation, without which this book would not have come into existence. They made me see the silver lining in every cloud.

I would like to thank my friends Ankit Khandelwal, Rajan Mishra, Rocky Agarwal, and Piyush Jain for their encouragement and support. I deeply express my gratitude to my best friend Ritika Varshney for her inspiration, suggestions, motivation, and support.

I am also thankful to Galileo Press, Publishing Director Florian Zimniak, Heather Smotrich, John Parker, Laura Korslund, and others for their efforts to make this book as good as it is and for publishing this book in such a beautiful format and on schedule. Special thanks to my editor Kelly Harris, who has been constantly engaged with this work with full enthusiasm and support. She has always been there beside me in case of any need, help, suggestions, or questions, and has always responded in no time.

I would like to thank all my friends, mentors, the team from Galileo Press, and everyone directly or indirectly associated with this book.

Tanmaya Gupta

SAP, the world's largest enterprise software company, uses its proprietary programming language ABAP/4 for customization. It has a very large data model with more than 13,000 database tables. These tables and their metadata are managed and maintained by SAP's own data dictionary known as the ABAP Data Dictionary.

1   Introduction

In this chapter, we briefly discuss the history of SAP. We start our discussion with a general introduction to Systems, Application, and Products in Data Processing (SAP) by examining when, why, and by whom SAP was founded. We will discuss various functional components that SAP provides, and offer an overview of Advanced Business Application Programming (ABAP), which is the proprietary language of SAP, and which enables it to be so highly customizable. Later in the chapter, we offer an introduction to the ABAP Data Dictionary, which acts as a central repository of information and centrally describes and manages all the data definitions used in the system and the database. Various objects like tables, views, domains, types, search helps, lock objects are present in the ABAP Data Dictionary, and we provide an overview of these objects.

1.1   Systems, Applications, and Products in Data Processing (SAP)

SAP is the world's largest enterprise software company and the world's third largest independent software supplier. SAP was founded in 1972 as *"Systemanalyse und Programmentwicklung"* ("System Analysis and Program Development") by five former IBM engineers (Dietmar Hopp, Hans-Werner Hector, Hasso Plattner, Klaus E. Tschira, and Claus Wellenreuther) in Mannheim, Baden-Württemberg. This acronym was later changed to stand for *"Systeme, Anwendungen und Produkte in der Datenverarbeitung"* ("Systems, Applications, and Products in Data Processing"). *SAP AG* became the company's official name after the 2005 annual general meeting. AG is short for *Aktiengesellschaft,* a term that refers to a corporation that is limited by shares; i.e., one that is owned by shareholders and may be traded on a stock market. SAP was started with the intention of helping companies to optimize their business by seeing, thinking, and acting clearly—and thus closing the gap between strategy and execution.

In 1987, SAP began developing R/3, which can be used in the decentralized, non-mainframe computing environment known as client-server. In client-server arrangements, data is processed not by a single costly mainframe but by many cheaper networked "server" computers, which display their data on flexible PCs called "clients." R/3 was designed to allow a business to view its entire business operation as a single integrated process in which data entered into any single application in the system would simultaneously be registered in every other.

SAP's R/3 is highly customizable through the use of its proprietary programming language, *ABAP/4*. SAP's R/3 is very versatile, as it operates on different platforms, including UNIX, Windows NT, and OS/400. It also runs on several databases, including Oracle, ADABAS D, Informix, DB2 for UNIX, DB2/400, and Microsoft's SQL Server 6.0. SAP's R/3 is available in 14 different languages (including German, English, and Spanish). SAP has a very large data model with more than 13,000 database tables. To manage these tables and their metadata, SAP maintains its own dictionary. The *ABAP Data Dictionary* is stored in a relational database and can be used by application programs.

The SAP R/3 system provides the set of "functional components" (also known as "functional areas" or "application areas") that are written in the ABAP language. These application components can be used either alone or combined with other solutions. The integration capability of these components increases the benefits delivered for any company. Some of these components are Materials Management (MM), Production Planning and Control (PP), Sales and Distribution (SD), and Financial Accounting (FI).

While information is entered separately for each component, the components are fully integrated and provide real-time applications. This means that data entered into one component is automatically updated and reflected in all other components. When an event occurs in one component, another event is automatically triggered in another component.

Let's learn more about ABAP and its functionality in SAP R/3.

1.2   Advanced Business Application Programming (ABAP)

ABAP, or ABAP/4, was originally abbreviated from *"Allgemeiner Berichts autbereitungs prozessor,"* which in English means "generic report preparation processor." It was developed in the 1980s and was later renamed *"Advanced Business Application Programming."* ABAP was first introduced in SAP R/2 as a report language. Now ABAP is widely used by SAP developers to develop SAP R/3 objects and by SAP customers to enhance SAP applications. Customers can develop custom reports and interfaces with ABAP programming. ABAP/4 is a proprietary language of SAP.

All ABAP programs reside under the SAP Database. Unlike Java or C++, where programs are stored in a separate external file, ABAP programs are stored inside the SAP database. Source code and generated code are two forms of ABAP code that exist in the database. Source code can be viewed, created, and edited with the ABAP Workbench tools, whereas generated code is a binary representation of source code, similar to Java bytecode. ABAP programs are executed under the control of a runtime system. A runtime system is an important component of the SAP kernel. It is responsible for processing ABAP statements, controlling the flow logic of screens, and responding to events, etc. The ABAP runtime system converts database-independent ABAP statements ("Open SQL") into database-dependent statements ("Native SQL"). Some of the features of ABAP are as follows:

▶ **Data sharing**
SAP has a large, centrally located database, and different users can access the same data with the help of database. This data sharing helps users to access data from anywhere.

▶ **Data integrity**
As discussed, SAP R/3 consists of various components. These components are highly integrated. Data entered into one component is automatically updated and reflected in all other components. When an event occurs in one component, another event is automatically triggered in another component.

▶ **Enhancements**
This feature enables you to enhance the functionality of the programs, function modules, and global classes. With the help of user exits and BAdIs (Business Add-Ins), you can enhance the standard objects.

▶ **Data persistency**
Data is permanently stored in the relational database of the SAP R/3 system. This data can be accessed from the database any time later.

1.3 Data Dictionary

The Data Dictionary, also known as a *metadata repository*, is a central repository of information about data. Such information can contain a variety of details; for example, a data's meaning, its relationship to other data, its origin, its usage, and/ or its format. The ABAP Data Dictionary centrally describes and manages all the data definitions used in the system and the database. It is completely integrated in the ABAP Development Workbench. All the other components present in the Workbench actively access the definitions stored in the data dictionary.

The ABAP Data Dictionary supports the definition of user-defined types (i.e., data elements, structures, and table types). These types are used in ABAP processors and ABAP programs. They also define the structure of database objects (i.e., tables, views, and indexes). These database objects are created automatically in the underlying database with their Data Dictionary definitions when the objects are activated. The ABAP Data Dictionary also provides editing tools like *Search help* and locking tool like *lock objects*. Thus, objects present in the ABAP Data Dictionary are tables, views, types (data elements, structures, and table types), domain, search helps, and lock objects (see Figure 1.1).

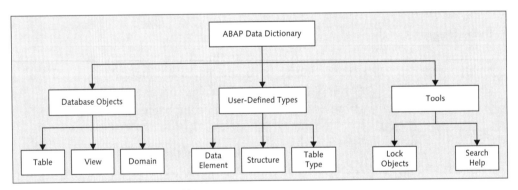

Figure 1.1 Data Dictionary Objects

1.3.1 Data Dictionary Tasks

ABAP Data Dictionary achieves the following with the help of its objects:

► Enforces data integrity

► Manages data definitions without redundancy

► Integrates tightly with rest of the ABAP/4 Development Workbench

Let us discuss these points in more detail.

Data Integrity

Enforcing data integrity ensures that data entered into the system is logical, complete, and consistent. Because of data integrity rules, the system automatically prevents the entry of invalid data. Defining the data integrity rules at the dictionary level means they only have to be defined once, rather than in each program that accesses that data. Examples of a lack of data integrity are:

► A DATE field with more than 31 days

► An order assigned to a customer with an invalid customer number

Data Definitions without Redundancy

Managing data definitions without redundancy is the process of linking information to their corresponding data elements. For example, the equipment number present in an equipment master table is used and accessed by several tables at different places. However, the equipment number is defined in only one central place. This central definition is defined for each instance of the equipment number, wherever it is used.

Integration with ABAP Workbench

The ABAP Data Dictionary is integrated with the rest of the ABAP Workbench. For this reason, ABAP programs automatically recognize the name and characteristics of dictionary objects. This functionality also provides easy navigation between the ABAP objects and dictionary objects. If you double-click on the dictionary object from the program code, the system takes you to the definition of that object in the Data Dictionary. Whenever the dictionary object is changed, the program code referring to that object always refers to the new version of that dictionary object. Because ABAP is an interpreted language, its interpreter sees only internal representation of

Data Dictionary objects. These internal representations are adjusted automatically when the system finds that changes have been made in the ABAP Data Dictionary. Because of this adjustment, screens, input help, database interface, and development tools always access current data. Inactive ABAP Data Dictionary objects have no effect on the runtime system. Inactive objects can also be activated together when all the changes are done. For example, Listing 1.1 declares Table EQUI_1 (an internal table) as a table type of EQUI. All the entries of Table EQUI are selected and copied to internal Table EQUI_1. Here in the program only internal Table EQUI_1 is declared but all other information like field names, data types, and field lengths is copied from Table EQUI, which is defined in the ABAP Data Dictionary.

```
Data: equi_1 type table of equi.
Select *
from equi
into table equi_1.
```
Listing 1.1 Integration of ABAP Data Dictionary with ABAP Workbench

Now let us discuss the objects of the ABAP Data Dictionary.

1.3.2   Objects in the Data Dictionary

Objects created in the ABAP Data Dictionary are created in the underlying relational database using the data definitions. The ABAP Data Dictionary thus describes the logical structure of the objects used in the application development and shows how they are mapped to the underlying relational database in tables or views. The most important object types in ABAP Data Dictionary are tables, views, types, domains, search helps, and lock objects.

Tables

Tables are defined independently of the database. First the table structure is created in the ABAP Data Dictionary, and then the table is created in the underlying database from this structure. You can learn about tables in Chapter 5, Tables.

Views

A view combines more than one table. The structure of the view is defined in the ABAP Data Dictionary. An application-dependent view can be defined that combines the data. You can learn about views in Chapter 6, Views.

Types

Types are generally used in ABAP programs and the ABAP Data Dictionary to define the structure of the fields, variables, constants, tables, etc. Types can be further classified as *built-in* and *user-defined* types. Data elements, structures, and table types are the type categories under user-defined data types. You can learn more about data types in Chapter 2, Data Types.

Domains

A domain is a central object that defines the technical attributes of a field. *Technical attribute* refers to data type, length, fixed value, and interval of a field (field of the table, structure, table type, etc.). A domain is assigned to the data element, which in turn is assigned to the table fields or structure fields. Consequently, all the fields that use the data element have the technical settings defined by the domain. You can learn about domains in Chapter 3, Domains.

Search Helps

With search help, the user can display the list of all possible input values for a screen field. Whenever the F4 key is pressed on the screen field, a pop-up appears listing the entries that satisfy the search in that screen field. You can select the needed record. There are two types of search help, *elementary search help* and *collective search help*. You can learn about search help in Chapter 9, Search Help.

Lock Objects

In the R/3 system, multiple users can access the same object simultaneously. When one person is editing the program/transaction, locks are set so that no other person can make changes in that program at the same time. Function modules are generated automatically from the lock-object definition of ABAP Data Dictionary. These function modules are responsible to Enqueue or Dequeue the locks on the objects. You can learn about lock objects in Chapter 10, Lock Objects.

1.4   Summary

The SAP R/3 system provides a set of "functional components" or "application areas" that are written in SAP's proprietary language, ABAP/4. These application components can be used either alone or combined with other solutions. The ABAP

Data Dictionary—a data dictionary or *metadata repository*—centrally describes and manages all the data definitions used in the system and the database. A variety of objects are defined in the ABAP Data Dictionary, including tables, views, types, search helps, lock objects, and domains.

Types or *data types* can be divided into built-in and user-defined types. We discuss these data types in Chapter 2, Data Types.

Data types describe the structure and functional attributes of fields. Data types also define the actual type definition in a data dictionary. Data types can be divided into built-in and user-defined types.

2   Data Types

In the previous chapter, we introduced you to SAP, ABAP, and the ABAP Data Dictionary. We also discussed the objects present under the ABAP Data Dictionary. In this chapter, we discuss the concept of data types, including built-in and user-defined data types. Data types are the most elementary object in the ABAP Data Dictionary; whenever fields, variables, constants, etc. are defined, they have some predefined characteristics like numbers, characters, strings, integers, dates, and times. These groups of characteristics are known as *data types*. The data types of the ABAP Data Dictionary are different from data types in the ABAP language. In this chapter, you'll learn how ABAP Data Dictionary types are mapped to ABAP program types, and you'll also learn the concepts behind elementary, reference, and complex types, and about their division into data elements, structures, and table types.

2.1   Data Types

In memory, programs are represented as bytes of strings of data. These bytes of strings are known as *fields*, and consist of *name* and *type*. Types can be character-based or numeric; for example, a NAME field is a character type, and an AGE field is a numeric type. Every field has its own name and data types. These types can be defined globally in the ABAP Data Dictionary or locally in an ABAP program. These global data types can be used in an ABAP program via the `type` command. The data types of database tables are a subset of all possible types, namely flat structures. Thus, the data type in the ABAP Data Dictionary is the user's view of the data. ABAP data types can be further divided into two categories (Figure 2.1):

- Built-in elementary data types
- User-defined data types

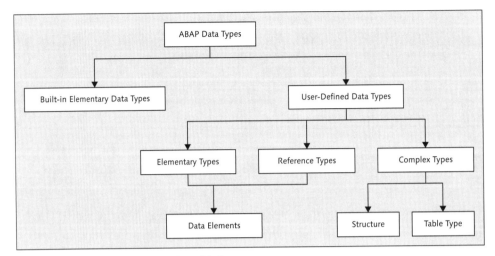

Figure 2.1 Data Types in ABAP Data Dictionary

2.1.1 Built-In Elementary Data Types

Some data types are already defined in the ABAP Data Dictionary. These data types are converted into their corresponding ABAP data types during runtime. In the following subsections, we describe these existing built-in data types.

ACCP: Posting Period

This data type has the length set to six places, and the format is YYYYMM. Because a point (".") is inserted between the year and month in input and output modes, the template of this data type has the form "____.__". For example, posting period 201004 is displayed as 2010.04.

CHAR: Character String

This data type can have a maximum length of 255 characters in tables. If longer character fields need to be used in tables, data type LCHR should be used. For example, CHAR data type must be used to represent any string such as name, address, etc.

CLNT: Client

Client fields always have three number spaces; for example, client 100, client 200, etc. This convention is used to make objects client dependent. If this field is not used in the object, then that object is considered client independent and can be used in all the clients.

CUKY: Currency Key

The currency key data type is used to refer to the fields of type CURR. The length of this data type is set to five places. For example, say a customer wants to pay 100 to a shopkeeper—obviously, the currency is incomplete without the currency field (i.e., whether it is 100 dollars, rupees, etc.). Here, 100 represents the currency field CURR, and $ or Rs. represents the currency key CUKY.

CURR: Currency Field

This data type represents the amount field with decimal places, sign, and commas separated into thousands. A field of this type must refer to a field of type CUKY. The maximum length for this data type is 31 characters.

DATS: Date Field

The length of this data type is eight places, and the output length can be defined within the user profile. The date is represented in YYYYMMDD format internally in the database. For example, the date 24 April 2010 appears as 20100424 internally and as 2010/04/24 if the date is separated by "/" in the output format of a user's profile.

DEC: Decimal Field

This data type represents the amount field with decimal places, sign, and commas separating thousands. It has a maximum length of 31 places. For example: the number -12345 is represented by this data type as -12,345 when displayed.

FLTP: Floating Point Number

This data type is used to represent floating point numbers. It can have a maximum length of 16 characters, including decimal places.

INT1: One-Byte Integer

This is a one-byte integer that can have values from 0 to 255 ($2^8 - 1$).The length is set to three places for this data type.

INT2: Two-Byte Integer

This is a two-byte integer that can have a value from -32767 ($-2^{16-1} -1$) to 32767 ($2^{16-1} -1$). This data type should only be used for length fields. These long fields are positioned immediately in front of a long field (type LCHR, LRAW). With `insert` or `update` on the long field, the database interface enters the length that was actually used in the length field. This data type can have its length set to five places.

INT4: Four-Byte Integer

This is a four-byte integer that can have a value from -2147483647($-2^{32-1} -1$) to 2147483647 ($-2^{32-1} -1$). This data type can have its length set to five places.

LANG: Language Key

This data type has its own field format for special functions. Its length is always set to one place. The field of this data type when stored in the database has one place, but has two places when displayed in the user interface. The conversion exit ISOLA converts the display at the user interface for the database and vice versa. This conversion exit is automatically allocated to a domain with data type LANG at activation. For example, the language English is represented as en in the user interface but stored as E in the database (Figure 2.2).

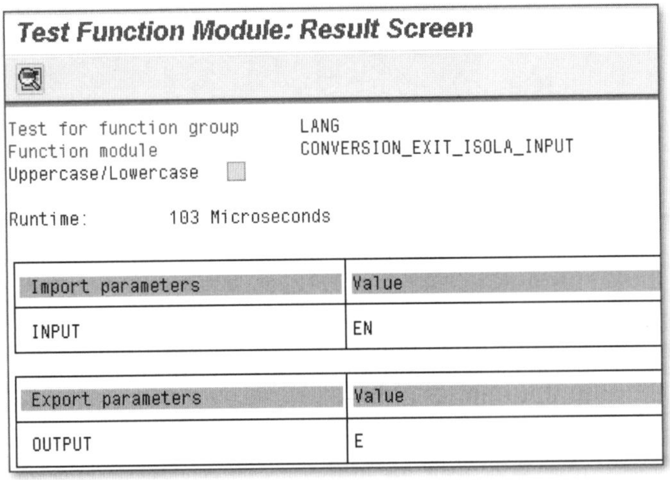

Figure 2.2 Representation of Language Field

LCHR: Long Character String

This data type represents the character string but with a minimum of 256 characters. This field should be preceded by a length field of type INT2. Fields of this type must be located at the end of the table. The length field must be filled with the actual required length while inserting or updating the record. You cannot use this field in the `where` condition of a `select` statement.

LRAW: Long Uninterpreted Byte String

This data type represents the uninterpreted byte string but with a minimum of 256 characters. This field should be preceded by a length field of type INT2. Fields of this type must be located at the end of table. The length field must be filled with the actual required length while inserting or updating the record. You cannot use this field in the `where` condition of a `select` statement.

NUMC: Numeric Text

This data type represents the long character field in which only numbers can be entered. The length of this field is set to a maximum of 255 places.

PREC: Accuracy Field

This field acts as an accuracy field of a QUAN field. The length is set to two places for this data type.

QUAN: Quantity Field

This data type represents the amount field with decimal places, sign, and commas separating thousands. A field of this type must refer to a unit field (UNIT). The maximum length for this data type is 31 places. For example, a customer purchases 100 units of sugar from the shopkeeper. This quantity is incomplete without specifying units (i.e., whether it is 100 grams or 100 kilograms). Here 100 represents the quantity field QUAN and grams and kilograms represent the unit field UNIT.

RAW: Uninterpreted Byte String

Fields of type RAW can have a maximum length of 255 in tables. If longer raw fields are required in tables, data type LRAW must be selected.

RAWSTRING: Uninterpreted Byte String of Variable Length

This data type can be used only in types (data elements, structures, table types) and domains. You cannot use it in database tables. In ABAP, this type is used as a reference to a storage area of variable size.

STRING: Character String with Variable Length

This data type has the same characteristics as RAWSTRING, discussed immediately before this.

TIMS: Time Field

This field is used to represent time. The length for this data type is set to six places, and the format is HHMMSS. The template has the form "__.__.__" for input and output. For example, 103045 is displayed as 10.30.45.

UNIT: Unit field

This data type refers to the fields of type QUAN. The length of this data type is set to two or three places. This data type is needed to specify the units or measurement involved, such as grams or kilograms. VARC: Character Field with Variable Length

From release 3.0 onwards, creation of new fields of this data type is not possible. However, existing fields with this data type can still be used. A field of this type cannot be used in the `where` condition of a `select` statement.

> **Note**
>
> You can assign a sign with the numeric data types CURR, DEC, FLTP, INT2, INT4, and QUAN. This sign is displayed on screen when assigned. The system automatically sets the comma separating thousands, along with decimal points, for data types CURR, DEC, QUAN; it also sets decimal points for data types DATS, ACCP, and TIMS.

2.1.2 User-Defined Data Types

User-defined data types can be defined and stored for all the programs in the ABAP Data Dictionary. These user-defined data types can be defined either globally in the ABAP Data Dictionary or locally in ABAP programs with the TYPES command. Both the declarations provide the same functionality for assigning the user-defined types according to business and program requirements. The types defined globally in the Data Dictionary can be accessed by ABAP programs to define data objects.

For example, suppose a variable `name` with a character type of length 30 is to be declared. As shown below, it can be declared locally in the program or a corresponding data element can be created, which in turn can be used in the program.

▶ `Data Name(30) type c.`
   This command declares the variable locally in the ABAP program.

▶ `Data Name type char30.`
   Here, `char30` represents the data element, which is referred to the domain `char30` having a data type as char and number of characters as 30.

User-defined data types can be further classified into three categories:

▶ Elementary data types

▶ Reference data types

▶ Complex data types

Let us now discuss these categories.

Elementary Data Types

Elementary types are part of the dual-level domain concept for fields in the ABAP Data Dictionary. The elementary type has semantic attributes such as data type, length, texts, value tables, or documentation. Elementary types are described with the help of data elements. Data type in a data element can be specified in two ways.

▶ **Directly assigning to a built-in ABAP Data Dictionary type**
   You can directly assign a built-in or predefined ABAP Data Dictionary type and a number of characters to an elementary type.

▶ **Assigning to a domain**
   The technical attributes are inherited from the domain. The domain specifies the technical specification of the data element. You can learn all about domains in Chapter 3, Domains.

Reference Data Types

Reference types describe the data objects that contain references (pointers) to other objects (data objects and ABAP objects). However, if there are no predefined references, references should be defined explicitly. The hierarchy of the reference types describes the hierarchy of objects to which these references can point.

Complex Data Types

Complex types are made up of other types. You can access complex data types either as a whole or by the individual component. Complex data types group semantically related data under a single name and manage and process them. There are no predefined complex data types defined in ABAP. They can either be defined in an ABAP program or in the ABAP Data Dictionary. Let us consider some examples of complex data types that are arranged in ascending order of complexity.

1. A structure consisting of a series of elementary data types of fixed lengths

2. An internal table whose line type is an elementary type

3. An internal table whose line type is a non-nested structure

4. A structure with structures as components

5. A structure containing internal tables as components

6. An internal table whose line type contains further internal tables

The following type categories can be defined in the ABAP Data Dictionary from Transaction SE11:

▶ **Data elements**
Data elements describe either an *elementary type* or *reference type*. Data elements are used to define the type of the table field, structure component, or the row type of a table type. All the semantic information about the meaning of the table field or structure component and information about editing the corresponding screen field can be assigned to a data element. You can learn all about data elements in Chapter 4, Data Elements.

▶ **Structures**
Structures define the complex types. *Structure types* describe the structure and functions of any structured data objects; that is, data structures with components of any type. Thus, a component can be a field of elementary type, reference type, or structure type. Tables and structures can also be considered and used as

components in a structure. A database table always has a structure and therefore is implicitly a structure type. However, a field of the database tables represents an elementary type. You can learn about structures in Chapter 8, Complex Data Types: Structures and Table Types.

▶ **Table types**

Table types define complex types. *Table types* describe the structure and functions of the internal tables used in the ABAP program. Table types are treated like construction blueprints for internal tables. When a table type is created, then line type, access type, and key need to be specified. Table types are covered in Chapter 8.

All the semantic information for a type can be entered in the type definition in the ABAP Data Dictionary. This includes text that is displayed for the F1 help, search helps, text used in screens, and technical documentation. Any complex types can be defined globally in the ABAP Data Dictionary and can be used in ABAP programs.

When the type is changed, all the objects that use this type automatically adjust to the change during activation. The central definition of types that are used more than once in the ABAP Data Dictionary changes centrally. These changes are made at all the relevant locations by the active ABAP Data Dictionary.

Note

All dictionary types lie in a common namespace. A data element, structure, and table type, therefore, cannot have the same name. However, a type defined in the dictionary and ABAP program may have the same name. If the names are identical, then local types get the preference over global types or the types defined in the type groups.

2.2 Mapping of the Data Types

The ABAP Data Dictionary and ABAP programming language have different data types. The ABAP Data Dictionary has more predefined or built-in types than the ABAP programming language. The data types are different because the predefined data types in the ABAP Data Dictionary have to be compatible with the external data types of the database tables supported by R/3. The ABAP processor uses the ABAP data types in the programs to define the variables, constants, work area of tables, structures, etc.

ABAP data types used in the ABAP Processor are as follows (see Figure 2.3):

- ▸ C: Character, used to represent character types
- ▸ D: Date, format YYYYMMDD
- ▸ F: Floating point number in DOUBLE PRECISION (eight bytes)
- ▸ I: Integer
- ▸ N: Numeric character string of arbitrary length
- ▸ P: Amount or counter field (packed; implementation depends on hardware platform)
- ▸ S: Time stamp, format YYYYMMDDHHMMSS
- ▸ T: Time of day, format HHMMSS
- ▸ V: Character string of variable length; length is given in the first two bytes
- ▸ X: Hexadecimal (binary) storage
- ▸ STRING: Character string of variable length
- ▸ XSTRING: Uninterpreted byte string of variable length

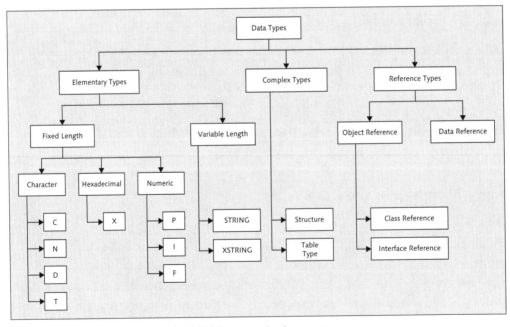

Figure 2.3 Data Types in the ABAP Programming Language

If a data element or a field of an ABAP Data Dictionary object (structure, table type, table, or view) is used in an ABAP program, the ABAP Data Dictionary data type is converted to the corresponding ABAP data type. Let us see how ABAP Data Dictionary types and ABAP processor data types are mapped together (see Table 2.1).

Dictionary Type	Meaning	Maximum Length n	ABAP Type
ACCP	Accounting period YYYYMM	6	N(6)
CHAR n	Character	1-255	C(n)
CLNT	Client	3	C(3)
CUKY	Currency key	5	C(5)
CURR n, m	Currency field	1-17	P((n+1)/2) DECIMALS m
DEC n, m	Calculation/amount field	1-31, 1-17 in tables	P((n+1)/2) DECIMALS m
DATS	Date	8	D(8)
FLTP	Floating point number	16	F(8)
INT1	Single-byte integer	3	X(1), Internal only
INT2	Two-byte integer	5	X(2), Internal only
INT4	Four-byte integer	10	X(4), Internal only
LANG	Language	Internal 1, External 2	C(1)
NUMC n	Numeric text	1-255	N(n)
PREC	Accuracy	2	X(2)
QUAN n, m	Amount	1-17	P((n+1)/2) DECIMALS m
RAW n	Byte sequence	1-255	X(n)
TIMS	Time HHMMSS	6	T(6)
UNIT	Unit	2-3	C(n)

Table 2.1 ABAP Data Dictionary Types and Processor Data Types

Dictionary Type	Meaning	Maximum Length n	ABAP Type
LRAW	Long byte sequence	256-max	x(n)
LCHR	Long character	256-max	c(n)
STRING	String of variable length	1-max	STRING
RAWSTRING	Byte sequence of variable length	1-max	XSTRING

Table 2.1 ABAP Data Dictionary Types and Processor Data Types (Cont.)

The characters used in Table 2.1 mean:

- *n*: number of places of the field in the ABAP Data Dictionary.
- *m*: number of decimal places of the field in the ABAP Data Dictionary.
- max: value of preceding INT2 field.
- Internal: length of the LANG fields represents its length in the dictionary.
- External: length of the LANG fields represents its length when displayed on the screen.

2.3 Summary

Programs are represented as bytes of strings of data known as *fields*. These fields are represented by name and data type. These data types can be defined in the ABAP Data Dictionary and can be used in ABAP programs via the type command. ABAP data types can be divided into built-in and user-defined data types. Built-in data types consist of predefined data types that are provided by SAP. These data types are converted into their corresponding ABAP data types during runtime. User-defined data types can be categorized further into elementary, referenced, and complex data types.

Before discussing elementary and referenced types, you should understand the concept of domains, which define the technical attributes of the table field. We discuss this in more detail in Chapter 3.

The domain is a crucial concept in the ABAP Data Dictionary, because it defines the technical attributes of a table field such as data types, lengths, decimal places, and conversion routines.

3 Domains

In this chapter, we explain the key concepts and activities related to domains in the ABAP Data Dictionary. We begin with a general introduction to the topic. Next, we discuss attributes of domains and how to create and change domains. We conclude the chapter with an explanation of how to delete domains.

3.1 An Introduction to Domains

A domain is a central object which defines the technical attributes of a field. The term technical attribute refers, among other things, to data type, length, decimal places, conversion routine, and value table. The domain is assigned to the data element, which in turn is assigned to the table fields or structure fields (Figure 3.1). So all the fields that use the data element have the technical settings defined by the domain. This means that the data element acts as a mediator or connector between domain and fields. One particular domain can be assigned to *N* number of data elements, and one particular data element can be assigned to *N* number of fields or components.

For example, domain MATNR (material number of type CHAR and length 18) is assigned to data elements such as MATNR, MATNN, MATNR_N, and MATNR_D, which in turn are assigned to many table fields and structure fields. You can also perform a where-used list using the WHERE-USED LIST button (⬚) on a domain and check the data element and package interface where that domain is used.

If the domain is changed, then all the assigned fields or components (which are assigned to the domain through the data element) also are changed. This ensures that the value ranges of fields or components are consistent. The value range of the domain is defined by specifying the data type and length. The number of decimal places can also be defined for numeric data types. Domains can also have fixed values or fixed intervals of values. Output length and conversion routines can also be defined for the domain. A conversion routine converts values from display format to internal format for the fields or components that refer to the domain.

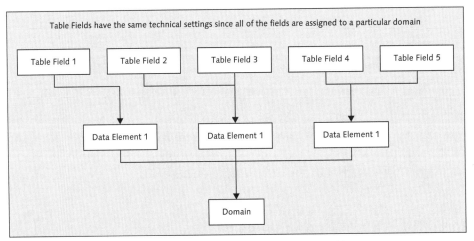

Figure 3.1 Relationship among Domain, Data Elements, and Table Fields

In SAP's ABAP, table field, variables, and constants are defined not only by predefined data types like character, number, float, and double but also by data element and domain. ABAP thus differs from other languages where table field, variables, and constants are defined by predefined data type only.

Fields are assigned to the data element, which in turn is assigned to the domain. These assignments to the data element and domain determine the other characteristics of the field such as its length, type, and values. This method of field definition is also known as the *two-level domain concept*.

For example, the EQUNR (equipment number) field of Table EQUI is assigned to the data element EQUNR, and this in turn is assigned to the domain EQUNR which is of type CHAR having length 18. This field is also present in other tables such as EQKT, EQBS, EQSE, etc. (Figure 3.2). Field EQUNR gets its semantic attributes from data element EQUNR and its technical attributes from domain EQUNR.

A variable of type of data element EQUNR can be defined in ABAP program with the statement:

```
DATA equnr11 TYPE equnr.
```

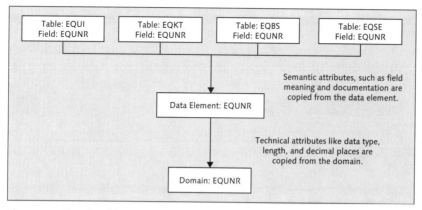

Figure 3.2 Two-Level Domain Concept

3.2   Attributes of Domains

Before discussing how to create a domain, we discuss its attributes in detail. In this section we learn about the tabs present in a domain, subscreens within those tabs, attributes within those subscreens, and their functionality. From Transaction SE11, you can create, change, or display the domain (Figure 3.3), and from Transaction SE12 you can display the existing domain.

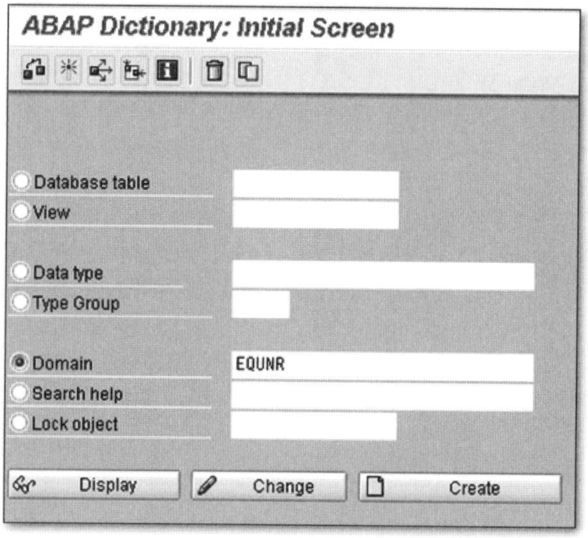

Figure 3.3   ABAP Dictionary: Initial Screen (Transaction: SE11)

Once you click on any of the buttons (CREATE, CHANGE, or DISPLAY), the maintenance screen of the domain appears. Within the maintenance screen, you can find screen elements such as DOMAIN NAME, SHORT DESCRIPTION; various tabs such as PROPERTIES, DEFINITION, and VALUE RANGE; and attributes within these tabs (Figure 3.4).

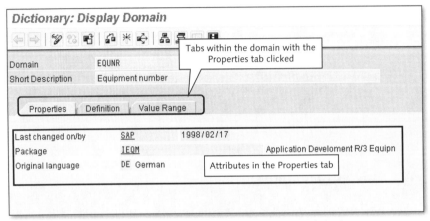

Figure 3.4 Maintenance Screen of Domain with Properties Tab Clicked

Now, we explain these tabs and other attributes of the domain in more detail.

3.2.1 Short Description

The first step in creating the domain is to create the short text description. This short text acts as the explanatory text when F1 help is generated. The short text also enables the developer to refer to its domain later on.

3.2.2 Properties Tab

The PROPERTIES tab defines the general properties of the domain. Attributes present within this tab are LAST CHANGED ON/BY, PACKAGE, and ORIGINAL LANGUAGE. These attributes get their values from the system and you cannot change them. These values automatically get updated when the domain is activated. We'll now discuss these attributes in more detail.

Last Changed On/By

This attribute displays the SAP user IDs of those who have changed the domain and the date when the domain was last changed.

Package

This attribute displays the name of the package inside which the domain is saved. A package is essentially the same as a folder. A folder is a location where different objects (such as files, images, etc.) of a particular business are saved, and a package is something where different objects such as the domain, data element, tables, programs, and screen are saved.

Original Language

This value displays the language in which the domain is created. The language-specific part of an object, such as its short description, is maintained in its original language. ABAP supports approximately 41 languages, including English, German, Spanish, French, and Danish.

3.2.3   Definition Tab

The DEFINITION tab defines the technical format of domains such as data type, number of characters and decimal places. It also defines output characteristics of the domain, such as output length, conversion routines, sign and lower case (Figure 3.5). We discuss these in more detail here.

Data Type

As already discussed in Chapter 2, a data type is the user's view on the data; i.e., the data format at the user interface. You can enter any of the existing data types for the data dictionary, such as ACCP, CHAR, CLNT, or NUMC.

No. of Characters

The number of characters defines the length that a data type can be.

Decimal Places

You can specify the number of decimal places for data type currency (CURR), decimal point (DEC), floating point (FLTP), and quantity (QUAN).

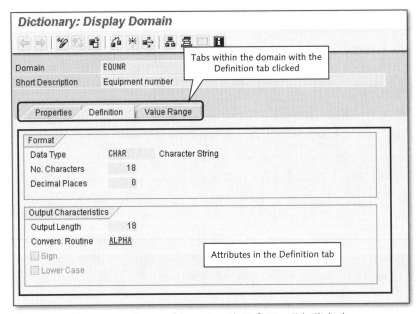

Figure 3.5 Maintenance Screen of Domain with Definition Tab Clicked

Output Length

This specifies the maximum field length. It also includes editing characters such as commas and decimals for inputting and outputting values. This value is generally computed automatically from the specifications of the data type, number of characters, and decimal places. But the user can also adjust the output length. For example: domain DATS, which is associated with the data type DATS (date), has its No. CHARACTERS as 8, and its OUTPUT LENGTH as 10 (Figure 3.6). This means that the date of April 21, 2010 will have the internal format of 20100421 (length 8) and output format as 2010/04/21 (length 10). This is because the No. CHARACTERS attribute does not include character "/" but the OUTPUT LENGTH attribute does include it.

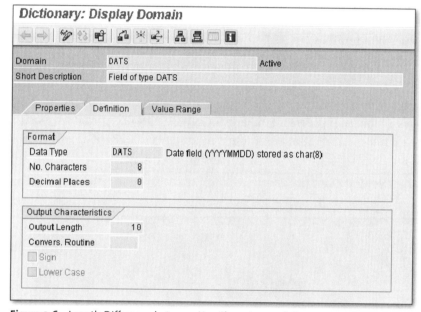

Figure 3.6 Length Difference between No. Characters and Output Length

Conversion Routine

Depending on the data type of the field, conversion takes place internally where the contents of a screen field are converted from display format to SAP internal format and vice versa. This conversion can be overwritten in the underlying domain with the help of a conversion routine. Conversion routines are identified by five-place names and are stored as a group of two function modules. These function modules have the following fixed naming conventions.

▶ CONVERSION_EXIT_XXXXX_INPUT

▶ CONVERSION_EXIT_XXXXX_OUTPUT

The INPUT function module converts the value of the field from display format to SAP-internal format, and the OUTPUT module converts the value of the field from SAP-internal format to display format. If the screen field refers to a domain with the conversion routine, then this conversion routine is executed automatically whenever an entry is made in this screen field (CONVERSION_EXIT_XXXXX_INPUT) or whenever values are displayed with this screen field (CONVERSION_EXIT_XXXXX_OUTPUT).

You can check the existing conversion routines in Transaction SE37 (FUNCTION BUILDER: INITIAL SCREEN). Go to Transaction SE37, enter "CONVERSION_EXIT_*_INPUT/CONVERSION_EXIT_*_OUTPUT" and press F4 . You will see the list of existing conversion routines.

For example, the domain EQUNR is associated with conversion routine ALPHA (Figure 3.7). CONVERSION_EXIT_ALPHA_OUTPUT converts the SAP-internal-format number 0000123456 into screen-display-format number 123456 (Figure 3.8); i.e., it deletes all the leading zeros. Similarly, CONVERSION_EXIT_ALPHA_INPUT converts the number 123456 into SAP internal format 0000123456.

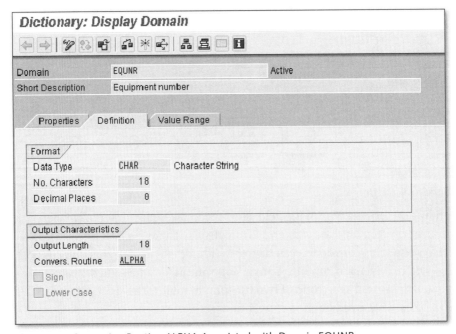

Figure 3.7 Conversion Routine ALPHA Associated with Domain EQUNR

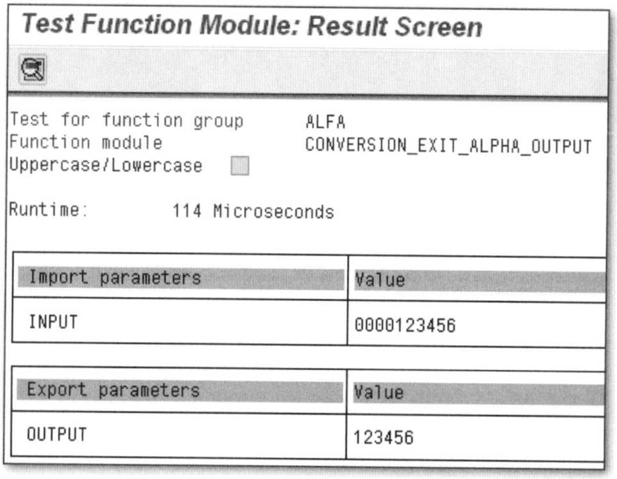

```
Test Function Module: Result Screen

Test for function group     ALFA
Function module             CONVERSION_EXIT_ALPHA_OUTPUT
Uppercase/Lowercase   ☐

Runtime:        114 Microseconds

┌─────────────────────────┬─────────────────┐
│ Import parameters       │ Value           │
├─────────────────────────┼─────────────────┤
│  INPUT                  │ 0000123456      │
└─────────────────────────┴─────────────────┘

┌─────────────────────────┬─────────────────┐
│ Export parameters       │ Value           │
├─────────────────────────┼─────────────────┤
│  OUTPUT                 │ 123456          │
└─────────────────────────┴─────────────────┘
```

Figure 3.8 Result Screen of CONVERSION_EXIT_ALPHA_OUTPUT

Sign

This attribute is required if the data type contains a negative value. If this flag is set, the first position of the output is reserved for a sign. If the flag is not set but the domain contains negative values, then problems might occur during screen output. This attribute can be maintained for data types currency (CURR), decimal point (DEC), floating point (FLTP), and quantity (QUAN).

Lower Case

This indicator enables you to distinguish uppercase and lowercase characters when values are entered with screen masks. Otherwise all the entries are converted to uppercase when you enter values with screen masks. This attribute can be maintained only for data types CHAR and LCHR.

We'll now use different scenarios to explain the concepts of output length, number of characters, decimal types, and signs.

1. Let us assume that the No. CHARACTERS field is 5, the DECIMAL PLACES fields is after 2 characters, and SIGN is not checked. When you press ⌈Enter⌋, the system automatically generates output. In this case, the output length is 6 (Figure 3.9). For example, the number 123.45 includes 5 digit places and 1 decimal, so the total output length is 6.

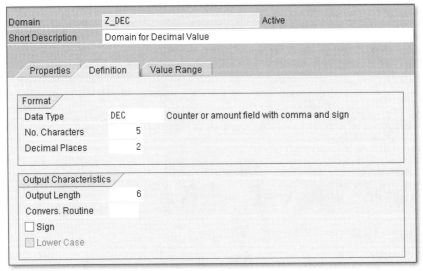

Figure 3.9 Relationship among No. Characters, Decimal Places, Output Length, and Sign Attribute (Case 1)

2. Let's consider this same scenario with the SIGN flag checked. In this case, the output length comes to 7 (Figure 3.10). For example, the number -123.45 includes 5 digit places, 1 decimal, and 1 sign place.

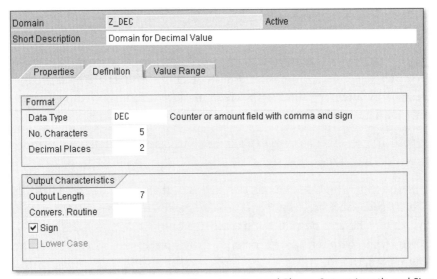

Figure 3.10 Relationship among No. Characters, Decimal Places, Output Length, and Sign (Case 2)

3. NO. CHARACTERS is 6, DECIMAL PLACE is after 2 characters, and SIGN is checked. When you press ⎡Enter⎤, the output is automatically generated. In this case, the output length is 9 (Figure 3.11). For example, the number -1234.56 includes 6 digit places—1 decimal, 1 sign, and 1 comma so the total output length is 9.

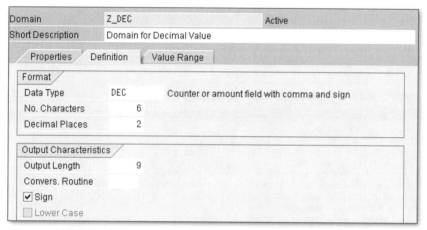

Figure 3.11 Relationship among No. Characters, Decimal Places, Output Length, and Sign (Case 3)

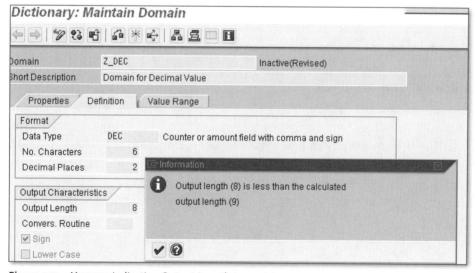

Figure 3.12 Message Indicating Output Length Inconsistency

If the output length is changed manually and inconsistency results, a message is displayed stating that "Output length is less than/greater than the calculated output length" (Figure 3.12). Also, you get a warning while activating the domain (Figure 3.13).

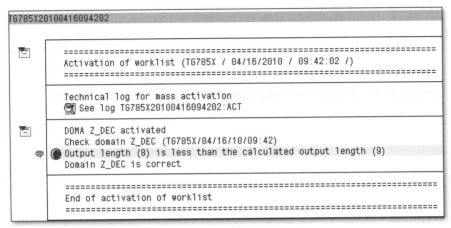

Figure 3.13 Warning Message while Activating the Domain

3.2.4 Value Range Tab

In this tab, you can define single fixed values or an interval of values for the domain. You can also define a value table for the domain.

Single Values and Intervals

You can define fixed values in this attribute. Values entered in the fixed values or intervals attributes are the only possible values that table fields or components referring to this domain can have. Fixed values for domains are defined for data types CHAR, DEC, NUMC, INT1, INT2, and INT4. Fixed values can be used during the input check in screen templates. If no other means of help (such as search help or foreign key) is defined for a field, the fixed values are offered in the input F4 help.

> **Note**
>
> If both the check table and fixed values are defined for a table field, only those values that exist in both the check table and fixed value can be entered in that table field.

In our example, we have defined the fixed values 0, 1, 8, 9, or the interval value from 15 to 20 (Figure 3.14), so any table field referring to domain Z_DEC can have a fixed value of 0, 1, 8, or 9, or an interval value from 15 to 20.

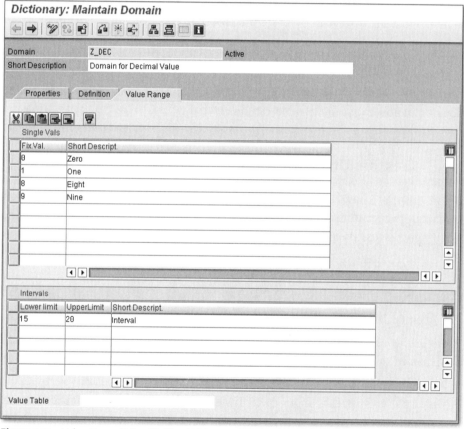

Figure 3.14 Value Range Tab with Fixed Values and Intervals

Value Table

If all the table fields referring to the domain are checked against the value of a certain table, that table is known as the *value table*. The system proposes the value table as the check table when a foreign key for the field is defined. The user can override the proposal. Entering the value table does not implement the check. The check against the value table only takes place when a foreign key is defined.

For example, assume that Table EQUI is the value table for domain EQUNR, and Table T000 is the value table for domain MANDT. Whenever a foreign key is assigned to the field referring to the domain EQUNR, the system proposes EQUI as the check table for that field. You can override the proposal, however.

3.2.5 Documentation

You can use documentation to define the use of the domain more precisely. Technical documentation about the domain can be created with GOTO • DOCUMENTATION.

3.3 Creating Domains

Before creating a new domain, check whether any existing domains have the same technical specifications required in your table field. If so, use that existing domain. We'll now discuss the procedures for creating the domain.

1. Go to Transaction SE11. Select the radio button for DOMAIN in the initial screen of the ABAP Dictionary, and enter the name of the domain. Choose the CREATE button (Figure 3.15). You can create SAP objects such as domains under the customer namespace; the name of the object always starts with "Y" or "Z."

2. Enter the explanatory short text in the SHORT TEXT field of the maintenance screen of the domain (Figure 3.16). You cannot enter any other attribute until you have entered this attribute.

3. Enter the data type, number of characters, and decimal places in the FORMAT block of the DEFINITION TAB. Press the ⌈Enter⌋ key on OUTPUT LENGTH, and it proposes and displays the output length. If you overwrite the proposed output length, you will see a warning while activating the domain. Fill in the CONVERS. ROUTINE, SIGN, and LOWER CASE fields, if required. Ordinarily, these are optional attributes (Figure 3.16).

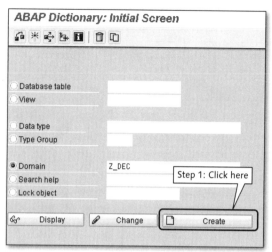

Figure 3.15 ABAP Dictionary: Initial Screen for Domain Creation

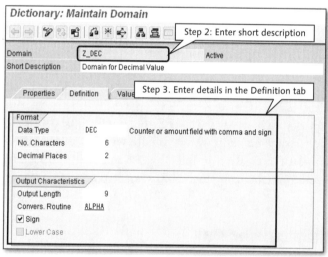

Figure 3.16 Definition Tab while Creating a Domain

4. Go to the VALUE RANGE tab. Enter the fixed values or intervals if the domain is restricted to having only fixed values. Define the value table if you want the sytem to propose this value table as a check table while defining a foreign key for the fields referring to this domain. These are optional attributes (Figure 3.17).

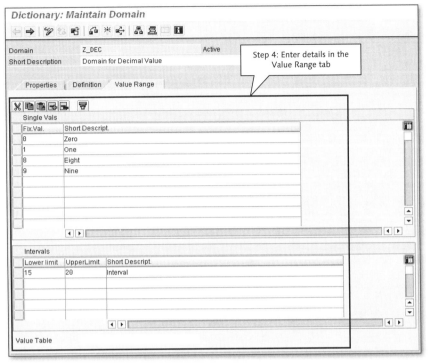

Figure 3.17 Value Range Tab while Creating a Domain

5. Save your changes. The CREATE OBJECT DIRECTORY ENTRY popup appears asking for a package. Enter the package name in which you are working. If you don't have any package, then you can create it in the Object Navigator (Transaction SE80) or you can save your domain, using the LOCAL OBJECT button, in package $tmp (Figure 3.18).

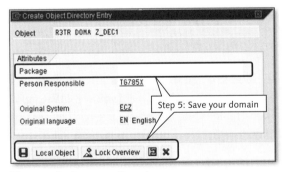

Figure 3.18 Save your Domain

6. Activate your domain. Click on the ACTIVATE icon (⁂) or press ⌈Ctrl⌉+⌈F3⌉ to activate the domain. If error messages or warnings occurred when you activated the domain, the activation log is displayed automatically. The activation log displays information about activation flow. You can also call the activation log with UTILITIES • ACTIVATION LOG.

3.4 Changing Domains

Before changing domains, please note that all the fields or components that refer to the domain are affected by changes made in the domain.

> **Note**
>
> If a domain is changed, conversion of the tables (fields refer to the domain) could be necessary. The conversion process is very time-consuming for tables containing many records. The foreign key might also become inconsistent in such tables and structures. It is always preferable to check where the domain is used by creating a where-used list before changing the domain.

Now we discuss the steps required to change the domain.

1. Goto Transaction SE11. Select the DOMAIN radio button in the initial screen of the ABAP Dictionary. Enter the name of the DOMAIN. Choose CHANGE.

2. You can change the data type, number of characters, or decimal places simply by overwriting the previous values. This change can cause all tables (fields referring to domains) to get converted. We therefore suggest creating a where-used list. To create a where-used list, click on the WHERE-USED LIST icon, select INDIRECT APPLICATION (Figure 3.19) and DATABASE TABLES (Figure 3.20) in the next dialog box, and choose the green checkmark icon (✔). All the database tables whose fields are referred to the domain are displayed.

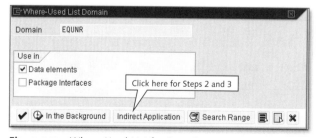

Figure 3.19 Where-Used List for Domains

3. You can also change output attributes. This change affects the dialog behavior in all the screens in which a field referring to the domain is called. Here, too, we suggest creating a where-used list, which we explained in the previous step. All the screens in which a field refers to the domain are listed.

Figure 3.20 Indirect Application List for Domains

4. The value table is used as proposal value for foreign key definition. Check if foreign keys already created need to be changed, before changing the domain. Create a where-used list to identify all the fields that refer to the domain and check them against the changed value table.

5. Save and activate the changes by clicking the ACTIVATE icon or by pressing Ctrl + F3.

3.5   Deleting Domains

You can only delete a domain if it is not used by any data element. Let's discuss the procedure to delete an existing domain.

1. Go to Transaction SE11. Select the DOMAIN radio button in the initial screen of the ABAP Dictionary. Enter the name of the domain. Choose the WHERE-USED LIST icon, and check if the domain is still being used by any of the data elements. If so, you cannot delete the domain. If you try to delete a domain that is already being used in a data element, you will get a pop-up stating that "deletion cannot be performed" (Figure 3.21).

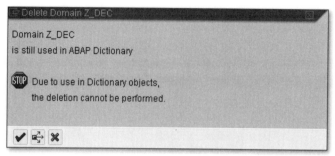

Figure 3.21 Pop-up while Deleting the Domain

2. Choose the DELETE icon (🗑) in Transaction SE11 if the domain is not used by any of the data elements. A dialog box appears for confirmation of your deletion request. Once the deletion request is confirmed, the domain is deleted.

3.6   Summary

A domain defines technical attributes such as data types, length, decimal places, and conversion routines of a table field. A domain is associated with a data element, which in turn is associated with the table field. A domain consists of attributes such as a short description, documentation, data type, number of characters, decimal places, value tables, and fixed values. Domains can be created, changed, or deleted from Transaction SE11. Before changing the domain, it is always advisable to check the data elements and table fields where that domain is used.

Data elements can be considered to be elementary or reference data types. We discuss these in Chapter 4.

Data elements are very important in the ABAP Data Dictionary because they define the semantic attributes of a table field such as domain name, documentation, field label, search help, parameter ID, etc.

4 Data Elements

In this chapter, we explain the key concepts and activities related to data elements in the ABAP Data Dictionary. We start with a general introduction to the topic. Next, we discuss attributes of data elements and how to create and change them. Finally, we conclude the chapter with an explanation of how to delete data elements.

4.1 An Introduction to Data Elements

Data elements describe the individual fields in the ABAP Data Dictionary. They are the smallest indivisible units of the complex types. They are used to define the type of the table field, structure component, or the row type of a table type. Information about the meaning of a table field or structure component and information about editing the corresponding screen field can be assigned to a data element. This information is automatically available to all the screen fields that refer to the data element. This information is displayed whenever a field is displayed in an input template using key word text, column header, and parameter IDs. The text appearing in the field help ([F1] help) in a field of an input template comes from the corresponding data element. Data elements describe either elementary types or reference types.

4.2 Attributes of Data Elements

In this section, we describe the tabs present in data elements, subscreens within those tabs, and attributes within those subscreens and details of their functionality. From Transaction SE11, you can create, change, or display the data element. From Transaction SE12, you can display the existing data element.

Once you click on any of the buttons (CREATE, CHANGE, or DISPLAY) the maintenance screen of the data element appears. Within the maintenance screen you find screen elements like DATA ELEMENT NAME and SHORT DESCRIPTION and various tabs such as the ATTRIBUTES tab, DATA TYPE tab, FURTHER CHARACTERISTICS tab, and FIELD LABEL tab, along with attributes within these tabs (see Figure 4.1).

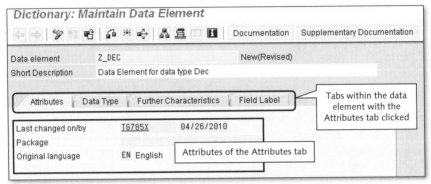

Figure 4.1 Maintenance Screen of Data Element with Attributes Tab Clicked

Now let us discuss these tabs and other attributes of data elements in more detail.

4.2.1 Short Description

When you create the data element, the first thing is to maintain the short text. This short text acts as the explanatory text when ⌴F1⌴ help is generated. Also, with the help of short text, a developer can refer to its domain at any later time.

4.2.2 Attributes Tab

The ATTRIBUTES tab (refer back to Figure 4.1) defines the general property of the domain. The attributes presented within this tab are LAST CHANGED ON/BY, PACKAGE, and ORIGINAL LANGUAGE. These attributes gets their value by the system, and you cannot change these values. They get updated automatically when the data element is activated. We discuss these in more detail below.

Last Changed On/By

This attribute displays the SAP user ID of whoever changed the domain and the date when the domain was last changed.

Package

This attribute displays the name of the package inside which the domain is saved. The package can be considered a folder: the place where different objects such as files, images, etc. of a particular business are saved. In the same way, a package is where different objects such as domains, data elements, tables, programs, and screens are saved.

Original Language

This attribute displays the language in which the domain is created. The language-specific part of an object, such as its short description, is maintained in its original language.

4.2.3   Data Type Tab

In this tab, you define whether a data element is an elementary data type or a reference data type. You can assign the data element either with the existing domain or with the predefined data types (see Figure 4.2). Let us discuss these in more detail.

Elementary Type

The elementary type has semantic attributes, such as value table, texts, and documentation, and has a data type. This type is the part of the dual-level domain concept (explained in Chapter 3, Domains) that applies to fields in the ABAP Data Dictionary. There are two situations where you should specify a data type:

▶ **When assigned with domains**
If you assign a data type with the domain, all the technical characteristics of the domain are automatically copied to the data element. The domain's technical attributes like its data type, length, decimal places, and short description are inherited by the data element (see Figure 4.2). One domain can be used by any number of data elements.

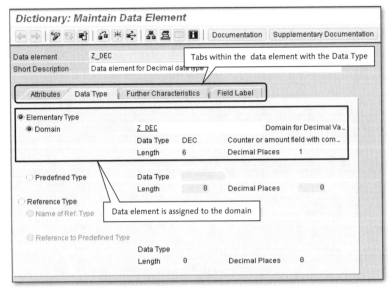

Figure 4.2 Data Type Tab with Domain Radio Button Checked

▶ **When assigned with predefined type**
If you assign the data element with the predefined type, you have to explicitly enter the values for the DATA TYPE, LENGTH, and DECIMAL PLACES attributes (see Figure 4.3).

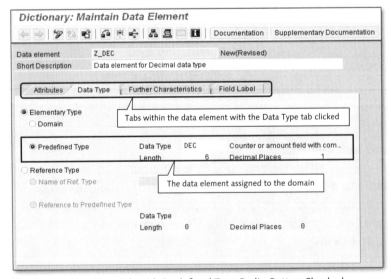

Figure 4.3 Data Type Tab with Predefined Type Radio Button Checked

Reference Type

References are used to refer to objects, and are stored in reference variables. Reference variables are treated like elementary data objects, and can occur as a component of a structure or internal table, or as an independent field. Reference types can be of the following kinds:

- Reference to a class or an interface.
- Reference to a type defined in the ABAP Data Dictionary.
- Generic references to DATA, OBJECT, and ANY.
- References to a built-in ABAP Data Dictionary type with length and decimal places specified.

Enter the name of a class, interface, or generic references like DATA, OBJECT, or ANY, in the field REFERENCED TYPE. If the reference type is a predefined ABAP Data Dictionary type, choose the REFERENCE TO THE PREDEFINED TYPE radio button. Fill the DATA TYPE, LENGTH, and DECIMAL PLACES fields in the PREDEFINED TYPE area.

4.2.4 Field Label Tab

In the FIELD LABEL tab, you can describe the field label text. This text is displayed when this data element is referred in the screen output. This text is displayed on the screen in the logon language of the user. The FIELD LABEL tab contains SHORT, MEDIUM, LONG, and HEADING attributes. You can find details on these fields in the following bullet list (also see Figure 4.4).

- SHORT
  A maximum length of 10 characters can be assigned to a data element as a field name.

- MEDIUM
  A maximum length of 20 characters can be assigned to a data element as a field name.

- LONG
  A maximum length of 40 characters can be assigned to a data element, but a maximum length of 20 characters is recommended for a data element to be assigned as a field name.

- HEADING
  A maximum length of 55 characters can be assigned for the heading. The title is

only displayed for editing list output of the corresponding column. The header is often displayed above the corresponding column when the output list is prepared. In that case, the length of the header should not exceed the length of the data element.

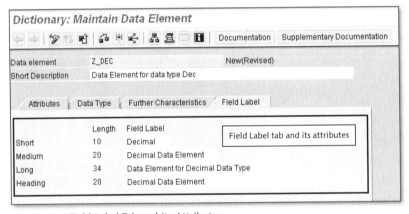

Figure 4.4 Field Label Tab and Its Attributes

4.2.5 Further Characteristics Tab

In this tab, you can define the search help, parameter ID, default component name, etc. (see Figure 4.5). Below we discuss these in detail.

Search Help

Search help is assigned to the data element. This search help is available to all the table fields that refer to the data element. You must specify the name of the search help in the NAME field and an export parameter in the PARAMETERS field (see Figure 4.5). The parameter is an export parameter, so that when the user selects the hit list in the input help, the value of the parameter can be returned to the corresponding screen field in the input help. It is not possible to return several values when the search help is attached to a data element. We explain search helps and the procedure for assigning the search help with the data element in Chapter 9, Search Helps.

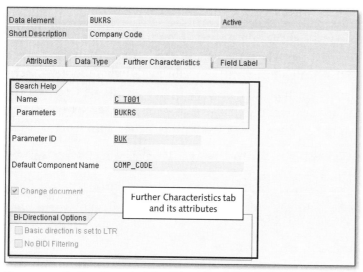

Figure 4.5 Further Characteristics Tab and Its Attributes

Parameter ID

You can fill the fields with the proposed values from SAP memory using PARAMETER ID. Parameter IDs are used only to memorize certain user-specific settings. They can be included in the user record Transaction SU03 in the PARAMETER tab. You can get the list of all the parameters and their description in Table TPARA. For example, suppose a user only has authorization for company code 0001. The system automatically fills the COMPANY CODE field with the value 0001 on all screens called by the user. However, if this company code is not predetermined using the parameter ID in the user record, the system automatically adopts the first value entered by the user for the rest of the transactions. The value has to be re-entered when the user next logs on to the system. Fields on screens are automatically filled with the parameter ID of the data element if the SET PARAMETER/GET PARAMETER attributes for the corresponding fields have been explicitly set in the screen painter for that field.

Default Component Name

In this attribute, a proposal for the name of the table field or structure components can be stored. You should use English for the default name. Always use this default name for components in BAPI (Business Application Programming Interface) structures; i.e., structures that have a fixed interface. Because of this, field and component name assignments are interconnected.

Change Document

This flag is used to create the change document for business objects. This change document contains the table in which the data of the business object is stored. Changes are logged in the change document, when the fields (whose contents were changed) refer to a data element and the CHANGE DOCUMENT flag is set (checked) for that data element. You can't use the change management checkbox for date or time fields. Now let us discuss the steps to display the change document.

1. Follow the path MENU • SAP MENU • TOOLS • ABAP WORKBENCH • DEVELOPMENT • OTHER TOOLS • CHANGE DOCUMENTS.

2. Click on the CHANGE DOCUMENTS (Figure 4.6) to go to the CHANGE DOCUMENT OBJECTS: OVERVIEW screen (Figure 4.7).

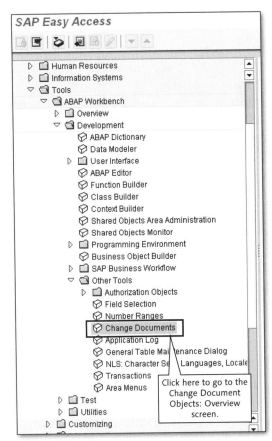

Figure 4.6 SAP Easy Access Screen to Display Change Document

3. Write the change document name in the text box or select it from the list.

4. If you have proper authorizations, you can CHANGE, CREATE, DISPLAY, GENERATE UPDATE PGM., or GENERATE INFO for the change document (Figure 4.7).

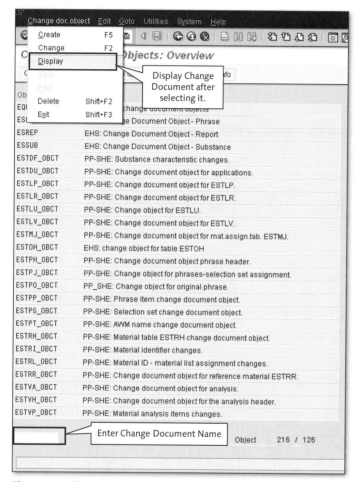

Figure 4.7 Change Document Object Overview Screen

5. Click on DISPLAY, and you get the detailed view of the change document (Figure 4.8).

Change Document Object: Change

Generation info

| Object | EQUI | Change Document object details |
| Text | Equipment change document objects | |

Tables

Name of Table	Copy as internal tab.	Doc. for individual fields at delete	Name of Ref. tab.	Name of old field string
EQKT	☐	☐		
EQUI	☐	☐		
EQUZ	☐	☐		
FLEET	☐	☐		
ILOA	☐	☐		

Figure 4.8 Change Document Object Change Details

Change document EQUI contains Tables EQKT, EQUI, EQUZ, FLEET, and ILOA (Figure 4.8). Any changes made in the fields of these tables are logged in the change document EQUI if the CHANGE DOCUMENT checkbox of the data element (which is referred by the table field) is checked.

For example: Changes are logged in the change document if changes are made in field EQUNR. This is because the CHANGE DOCUMENT checkbox is checked for the data element EQUNR (see Figure 4.9).

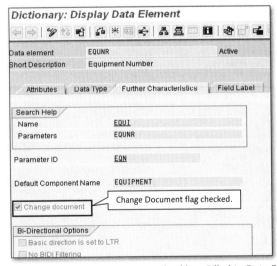

Figure 4.9 Change Document Checkbox Filled in Data Element EQUNR

Basic Direction is Set to LTR

If this checkbox is checked, the field contents are always displayed in the basic writing direction LTR (left to right), even if the writing direction of the window or writing language is RTL (right to left). Keep in mind that Hebrew and Arabic languages are right-to-left oriented. This checkbox is irrelevant if the writing direction of logon language is LTR.

No BIDI Filtering

If this checkbox is checked, no filtering of bidirectional formatting characters takes place when values are entered via scrccn templates. This parameter can be set using the report I18N_SET_DATAELEMENTS_FLAGS. These characters can be entered when they are present in the system codepage and the frontend codepage. This flag is irrelevant if the system codepage does not contain any bidirectional formatting characters.

4.2.6 Documentation

Documentation is displayed when ⌐F1⌐ help is selected for the fields that refer to the data element. If there is no documentation available, only the short text appears for the ⌐F1⌐ help (see Figure 4.10). DOCUMENTATION STATUS defines whether documentation is required and SUPPLEMENTARY DOCUMENTATION can enhance the documentation. We discuss these in detail next.

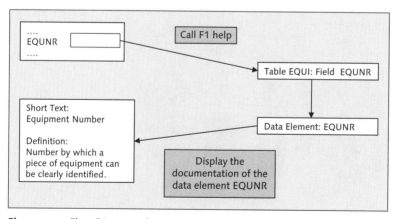

Figure 4.10 Flow Diagram when F1 Help on Screen Field is Pressed

Document Status

The document status specifies whether documentation is required for the data element and whether the documentation has already been done. To display documentation status follow the path Goto • Documentation • Status. You may see the following status entries:

▸ Object should be documented.

▸ Object is not used in any screens.

▸ Object is explained sufficiently by the short text.

▸ Documentation postponed.

Supplementary Documentation

Using supplementary documentation, you can enhance documentation with screen-specific information. These supplements must be assigned to the screen. The text of the data element supplement appears on the screen in addition to the documentation of the data element. If a data element supplement is created directly with the corresponding screen (by calling [F1] help on the screen, going to documentation maintenance with [F7] or the right mouse key, and entering the number of the data element supplement in the next dialog box), the screen and the data element supplement are automatically assigned to each other. Otherwise the link is to be maintained in Table THLPF.

The following example illustrates the concept of documentation (Listing 4.1).

```
Report ztr_data_element_example.
DATA z_dec1 TYPE z_dec.
Z_dec1 = '12345'.
WRITE z_dec1.
```

Listing 4.1 Documentation

When the program `ztr_data_element_example` is activated and executed, you get the output 12345 (see Figure 4.11). When you click on value 12,345.0 and press [F1], you get the short text and documentation of data element `Z_dec` (see Figure 4.12).

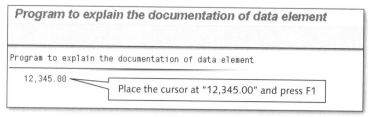

Figure 4.11 Output Screen of Program ztr_data_element_example

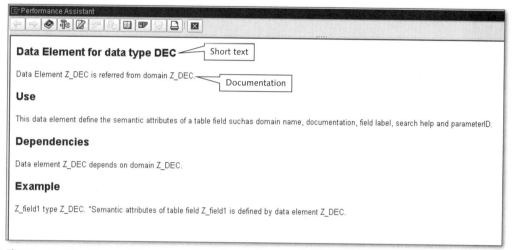

Figure 4.12 Short Text and Documentation of Data Element z_dec

4.3   Creating Data Elements

In the next two sections, we explain the steps involved in creating and deleting data elements. Before creating a new data element, check whether any existing data elements have the same semantic specifications required in your table field. If so, use that existing data element. You can assign the data element with a predefined type, domain, or reference type.

Let us discuss the procedure for creating the data element.

1. Go to Transaction SE11. Select the radio button for Data Type in the initial screen of the ABAP Data Dictionary, and enter the name of the data element. Choose the Create button (see Figure 4.13). You can create an SAP object such as a data

element under the customer namespace (the name of the object always starts with "Y" or "Z").

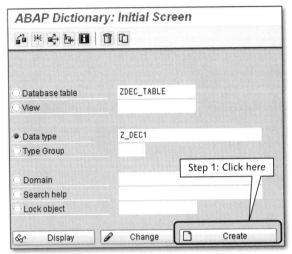

Figure 4.13 ABAP Data Dictionary: Initial Screen for Data Element Creation

2. You see a CREATE TYPE pop-up with three radio buttons. Check the DATA ELEMENT radio button (see Figure 4.14). Choose the green checkmark icon (✔). You are directed to the maintenance screen of the data element (see Figure 4.15).

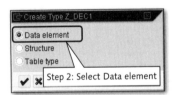

Figure 4.14 Pop-up While Creating Data Element

3. Enter the explanatory short text in the SHORT TEXT field of the maintenance screen of the data element (Figure 4.15). This is a mandatory attribute, and you cannot enter any other attribute without entering this one first.

4. Assign the data element with the type. You can create an elementary data element by checking ELEMENTARY TYPE or a reference data element by checking REFERENCE TYPE. You can assign a data element to a DOMAIN or PREDEFINED TYPE

within ELEMENTARY TYPE and with NAME OF REFERENCE TYPE or REFERENCE TO PREDEFINED TYPE within PREDEFINED TYPE (see Figure 4.15).

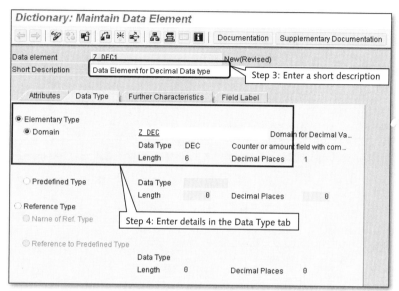

Figure 4.15 Data Type Tab of Data Element

5. Enter values for SHORT TEXT, MEDIUM TEXT, LONG TEXT, and HEADING in the FIELD LABEL tab. Press ⟨Enter⟩ and the length is automatically generated for these labels (see Figure 4.16).

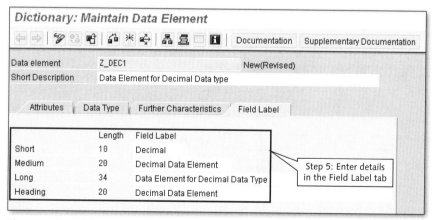

Figure 4.16 Field Label Tab of Data Element

6. Go to the FURTHER CHARACTERISTICS tab and define SEARCH HELP, PARAMETER ID, DEFAULT COMPONENT NAME, CHANGE DOCUMENT, and BASIC DIRECTION IS SET TO LTR as required. These are optional parameters (see Figure 4.17).

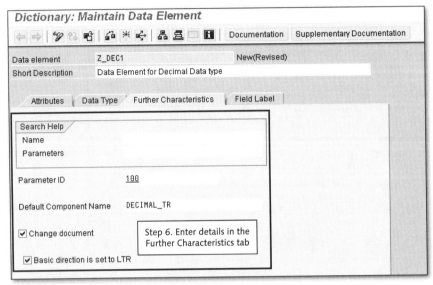

Figure 4.17 Further Characteristics Tab of Data Element

7. Save your changes. The CREATE OBJECT DIRECTORY ENTRY pop-up appears and asks for the package. Enter the name of the package in which you are working. If you don't have any package, you can create it in Object Navigator (Transaction SE80) or you can save your data element in the Local object in the *$tmp* package (see Figure 4.18).

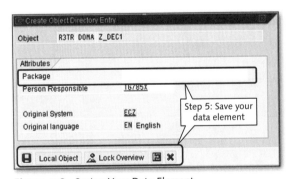

Figure 4.18 Saving Your Data Element

8. Activate your data element. To do this, click on the ACTIVATE button (✳) or press ⌈Ctrl⌉+⌈F3⌉ to activate the data element. If errors or warnings occur when you activate the data element, the activation log is displayed automatically. An activation log displays information about activation flow. You can also call the activation log via the menu path UTILITIES • ACTIVATION LOG.

4.4   Deleting Data Elements

You can only delete data elements if they are not used by any table field or component. Let us discuss the procedure for deleting an existing data element.

1. Go to Transaction SE11.

2. Select the DATA TYPE radio button in the initial screen of the ABAP Data Dictionary. Enter the name of the data element.

3. Choose the WHERE-USED LIST button, and check if the data element is still being used by any component (see Figure 4.19). If the data element is in use and you delete the data element, all the tables and programs become inconsistent. Therefore, you should never delete a data element that is still in use.

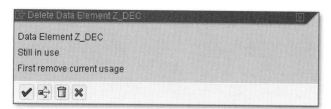

Figure 4.19   Pop-up after Performing Where-Used List for Data Element

4. Choose the DELETE icon (🗑) in Transaction SE11. A dialog box appears for confirmation of deletion request (see Figure 4.20). Once the deletion request is confirmed, the data element is deleted.

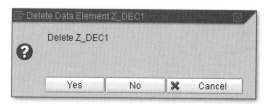

Figure 4.20   Dialog Box to Confirm Deletion Request

4.5   Summary

As you just learned in this chapter, a data element defines the semantic attribute of a table field. Data elements can be created as elementary or reference types. When created as an elementary type, they can be assigned to an existing domain or predefined type; and when created as a referenced type, they can be assigned to an existing reference type or a predefined reference type. Remember that a data element also defines the labels, search help, parameter ID, change document, and other functions we have already learned about.

Data elements can be created, changed, or deleted from Transaction SE11. Before changing the domain, we always suggest that you check the data elements and table fields where that domain is used. Never try to delete a data element that is in use. If deleted, then all the programs and tables referring to that data element become inconsistent.

Tables are one of the most important and crucial object of the ABAP Data Dictionary. We discuss tables, their attributes, and characteristics in Chapter 5.

Tables are collections of values or data about particular topics or entities. Tables are organized using a model of vertical column and horizontal rows. Table rows represent records and table columns represent table fields.

5   Tables

Tables are one of the most important features of the ABAP Data Dictionary. In this chapter, we explain the key concepts and activities related to tables. We start with a general introduction in which we categorize tables. Next, we discuss these categories in details. We also discuss the attributes of the table, such as table fields, foreign keys, technical settings, indexes, enhancements, delivery classes, and activation types. Next, we explain how to create and change a table and its attributes. We end this chapter with an explanation of how to delete a table.

5.1   An Introduction to Tables

Tables are the collection of table fields (values) that are organized using a model of vertical columns and horizontal rows. In the ABAP Data Dictionary, tables can be defined independently of the database. Table fields are defined with the help of data elements or with pre-existing data types. There are three categories of tables in the ABAP Data Dictionary.

► Transparent tables

► Pooled tables

► Cluster tables

Below we cover these categories in detail.

5.1.1   Transparent Tables

A transparent table is one that has a one-to-one relationship with the database table; that is, the structure of the transparent table is the same as that of the database table. When the table is activated, a physical definition of the table is created in the database from the table definition stored in the ABAP Data Dictionary. The database table has the same structure, name, attributes, fields, length, and data types in its fields as the table definition in the Data Dictionary (see Figure 5.1). The database table is created from the replica of the Data Dictionary table. A transparent table holds application data.

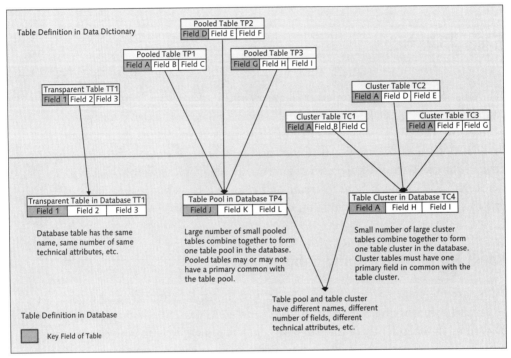

Figure 5.1 Different Categories of Tables in the ABAP Data Dictionary

Pooled Tables

A pooled table has many-to-one relationships with the database table. There are many tables in the Data Dictionary for one table in the database. Unlike a transparent table, a pooled table has a different name, different number of fields, and different names for fields in the database. The data from several different pooled tables are stored together in the table pools in the database (see Figure 5.1). Table pools are used exclusively for storing internal control information such as screen sequences, program parameters, temporary data, and documentation. Table pools are used to hold large numbers of very small tables. A table pool stores 10 to 10,000 pooled tables of 10 to 100 rows each. Hence, table pools reduce the amount of database resources needed when many small tables have to be open at the same time. Pooled tables are generally used to store customizing data. Figure 5.2 shows the maintenance screen of the table pool.

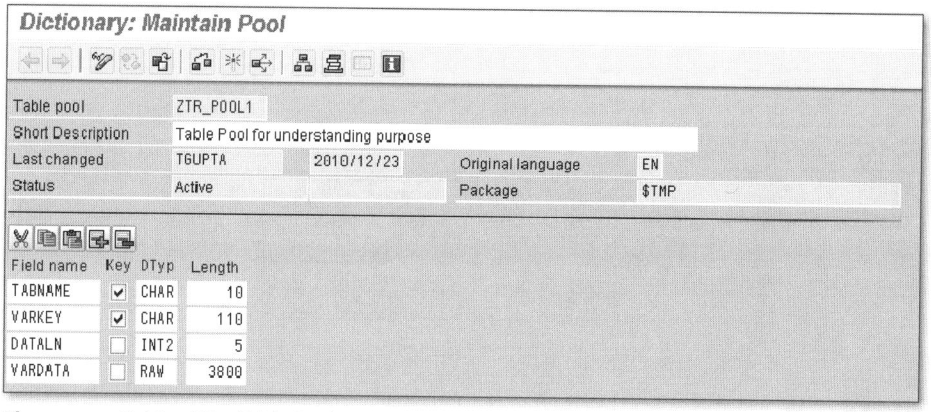

Figure 5.2 Fields of the Table Pool

Field	Data Type	Meaning
TABNAME	CHAR (10)	Name of pooled table
VARKEY	CHAR (n)	Contains the entries from all key fields of the pooled table record as a string Maximum length for n is 110
DATALN	INT2 (5)	Length of the string in Vardata
VARDATA	RAW (n)	Contains the entries from all data fields of the pooled table record as a string Maximum length for n depends on the database system used

Table 5.1 Description of Pooled Table Fields

The name of the pooled table is written in the field TABNAME. VARKEY contains the data of all the key fields and VARDATA contains the data of all the data fields of the pooled tables. Contents of VARKEY and VARDATA are written as a string. The length of the string stored in VARDATA is entered in field DATALN by the database interface.

The name of a pooled table cannot exceed 10 characters. Because VARKEY is a character field, all key fields of a pooled table must have character data types. The total length of all key fields or all data fields of a pooled table must not exceed the length of VARKEY or VARDATA respectively in the assigned table pool. Figure 5.3 shows the mapping between the pooled table of the Data Dictionary and the table pool of the database.

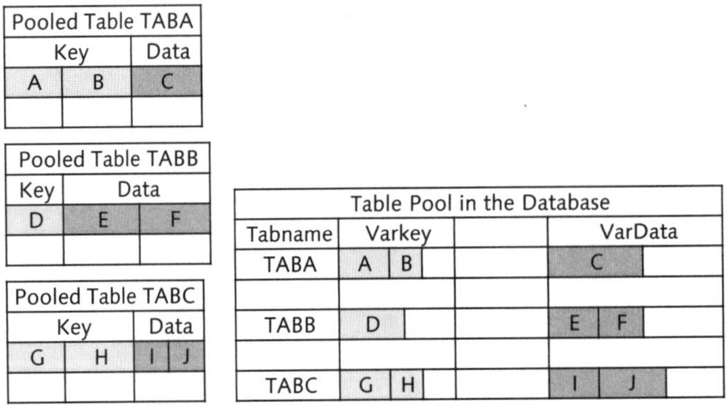

Figure 5.3 Mapping between Pooled Table and Table Pool

Cluster Tables

A cluster table is similar to a pooled table. It has many-to-one relationships with the database table. Many cluster tables of the Data Dictionary are stored in a table cluster in the database. Unlike a transparent table, a cluster table has a different name, different number of fields, and different names of fields in the database. A table cluster is similar to table pools where several logical data records from different cluster tables are stored together in one physical record in a table cluster. Table clusters are used to store data from those few cluster tables that have a very large numbers of records. They are used when the tables have a part of their primary keys in common and when these tables are accessed simultaneously.

Table clusters contain fewer tables than table pools. Rows are arranged on the basis of common primary key. Thus, when a row is read from any one of the cluster tables, all the related rows of all the cluster tables are also retrieved. Table 5.2 defines the structure of a table cluster.

Field	Data Type	Meaning
CLKEY1	*	First key field
CLKEY2	*	Second key field

Table 5.2 Structure of Cluster Tables

Field	Data Type	Meaning
CLKEY3	*	Third key field
...	...	...
CLKEYN	*	*n*th key field
PAGENO	INT2(5)	Number of the continuation records
TIMESTAMP	CHAR(14)	Time stamps
PAGELG	INT2(5)	Length of the string in Vardata
VARDATA	RAW(n)	Contains the entries from the data fields of the cluster tables as a string, max. length n depends on the database used

Table 5.2 Structure of Cluster Tables (Cont.)

A table cluster contains key fields defined by the CLKEY and PAGENO fields for distinguishing continuation records, the TIMESTAMP field to give the timestamp, and the VARDATA field to contain the data from the data field of the cluster table. The value of the key field of the cluster tables is stored in the CLKEY field of the table cluster, and the value of the data field is stored in the VARDATA field of the table cluster. If the string exceeds the maximum length of the VARDATA field, a continuation record is written with the same key values. These records are distinguished by the PAGENO field. The actual length of the string in the VARDATA field is stored in the PAGELG field by the database interface. Figure 5.4 defines the mapping between the cluster tables of the Data Dictionary with the table cluster of the database.

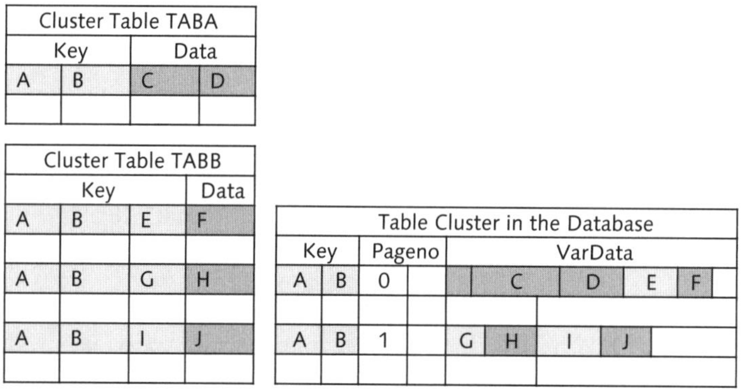

Figure 5.4 Mapping between Cluster Table and Table Cluster

Restrictions of Pooled Tables and Cluster Tables

Pooled and cluster tables are proprietary SAP constructs. Also, you need the structure information stored in the ABAP Data Dictionary to read the data correctly. Therefore, these tables are restricted as follows:

▶ You cannot create the secondary index.

▶ You cannot use the ABAP/4 constructs "`select distinct`" and "`group by`."

▶ You cannot use native SQL.

▶ You can only use "`order by`" clause with a primary key and not with any other fields.

Later in this chapter, we discuss the following:

▶ Creating table pools

▶ Creating table clusters

▶ Creating pooled tables/cluster tables

▶ Deleting table pools/table clusters

5.2   Components of a Table

This section defines all the components of a table. A table definition in the ABAP Data Dictionary contains the following components:

▶ **Table fields**
The table consists of table field. It defines the field name, data type, and length of the field contained in the table. Table fields are associated either with data elements or with built-in data types.

▶ **Includes**
Fields of another structure can be included in the tables and structures. Individual fields and structures can be combined. If the include is changed, all the tables and structures that contain this include adjust themselves automatically.

▶ **Foreign keys**
Foreign keys define the relationships among tables. Foreign keys are also used to link various tables in a view or a lock object. Foreign keys can also be used to create value checks for the input fields.

► **Search help**

Search help is an object of the ABAP Data Dictionary in which input help (F4 help) is defined. We have to define the search help name to attach a search help to the table field. This search help defines the input help flow for all the screens in which the field is used.

► **Technical settings**

Technical settings define how the table is handled when it is created in the database. The table can be buffered in technical settings. The size and data class of the table, among other things, are dealt with in the technical settings of the table.

► **Indexes**

Indexes are used to search table records faster. An index also contains a pointer to the corresponding record so that the fields not contained in the index can also be read.

► **Customizing includes**

Customizing includes are used to modify the SAP tables. This modification ensures that the customer's enhancements are automatically merged with the new version of SAP tables whenever there is a release upgrade.

► **Append structures**

Append structures are used for enhancements that are not included in the standard. An append structure is assigned to exactly one table or structure.

► **Delivery class**

The delivery class controls the transport of table data when installing or upgrading in a client copy and when transporting data between customer systems.

► **Activation type**

The activation type checks whether the table is activated directly from the ABAP Data Dictionary, or whether its runtime object is generated first with a C-language program.

► **Data Browser/Table View Maintenance**

The Data Browser/Table View Maintenance decides whether a table can be maintained and displayed in various table maintenance transactions like Transaction SE16 (Data Browser), Transaction SM30 and SM31 (Table View Maintenance), and Transaction SE11 (ABAP Dictionary initial screen).

Let us discuss these components in detail.

5.2.1 Table Fields

A table consists of number of table fields. Table fields combine to make a table. Table fields are the attributes a table can have. A table field is associated with either a data element or with a predefined type. It is defined with its attributes such as data type, length, decimal, and short description.

Let's discuss these attributes one by one.

► FIELD

The field name defines the name of the field. It may contain letters, digits, and an underscore. A field name should begin with a letter. If the entries in the field are in the form of .INCLUDE or .APPEND, this shows that the field is not a regular field but rather an include or append structure. The field name can have a maximum of 16 places.

► KEY

The KEY flag determines whether a table field belongs to a key (primary key). The key field should always be located at the beginning of the table. No non-key fields are allowed between two key fields. Otherwise, you get an error message while activating the table (see Figure 5.5).

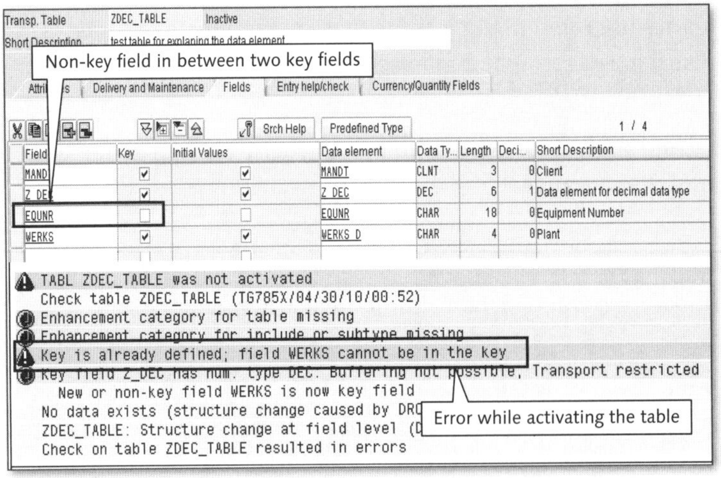

Figure 5.5 Error when Non-Key Field is between Two Key Fields

► INITIAL VALUES

This flag is set when the fields to be inserted in the database are filled with the initial values. This initial value depends on the data type of the field. Table 5.3 defines the initial values of all the data types.

Data Type	Initial Value
ACCP	' ' blank
CHAR	' ' blank
CLNT	000
CUKY	' ' blank
CURR	0
DATS	00000000
DEC	0
FLTP	0
INT1	0
INT2	0
INT4	0
LANG	' ' blank
NUMC	000000..... for field length <= 32 No initial value for field length >32
QUAN	0
RAW	No initial value provided
TIMS	000000
UNIT	' ' blank
VARC	No initial value (VARC not supported from 3.0 onwards)
LRAW	No initial value
LCHR	No initial value

Table 5.3 Initial Values of Data Types

While creating or converting a table, all the fields are set as NOT NULL and filled with initial values automatically. Newly added or inserted fields are filled with initial values if the flag is set. Key fields are automatically filled with initial values.

Restrictions on Initial Values

The initial value cannot be set for long data types (LCHR, LRAW, RAW). If the field length is greater than 32 places, the initial flag cannot be set for fields of data type NUMC. Whenever a new field is inserted with the initial flag set, the complete table is scanned on activation and an UPDATE is made to the new field. This process is very time-consuming and may result in table conversion.

If the initial flag is set for an included structure, those fields that are marked as initial in the structure definition have this attribute set in the table definition as well. This means attributes from the structure are transferred automatically.

Data type, field length, decimal places, and short text for the table field can be assigned in two different ways, with *data elements* or with *predefined types*. Let's discuss them both.

▶ **Data elements**

In this attribute, specify the data element for the table field. When the data element is assigned, data type, length, number of decimal places, and short description automatically are assigned from the corresponding domain to the table field. The semantic attributes of the data element such as field help, search help, representation of the field in input template, and column header for list output are also copied. If the field name contains the entry in the form of .INCLUDE or .APPEND, the field type contain the name of the include or append structure (see Figure 5.6).

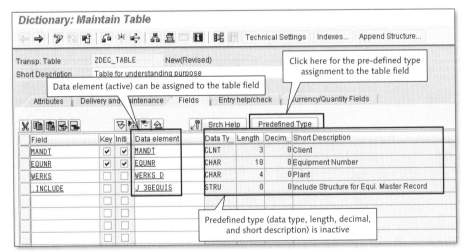

Figure 5.6 Data Element Assignment for Table Field

▶ **Predefined type**

When the PREDEFINED TYPE button is clicked, its attributes (data type, length, decimal places, and short description) become active and its data element attribute becomes inactive. Now the user can enter the values for DATA TYPE, LENGTH, DECIMAL PLACES, and SHORT DESCRIPTION. In the data type attribute, a built-in data type can be entered manually. The LENGTH field defines the length of the data type for the table field. DECIMAL PLACES defines the number of places after the point (decimal), and SHORT DESCRIPTION describes the meaning of the field. Some text is displayed when F1 help is activated and when the list is displayed (see Figure 5.7).

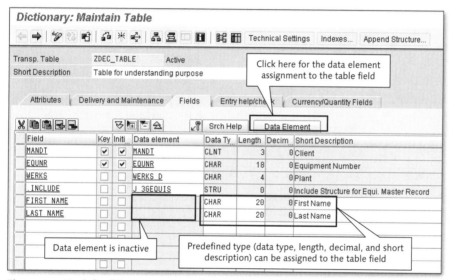

Figure 5.7 Predefined Type Assignment for Table Field

Reference Table and Reference Field

Quantity (QUAN) or currency (CURR) fields should be referred with the reference unit (UNIT) field or reference currency (CUKY) field respectively. This is needed because the user can only enter the quantity or currency value; the corresponding unit is determined at runtime. For example, suppose a user enters the value 100 in the CURR field. This value can be in rupees, dollars, euros, pounds, etc. This unit of currency is determined at runtime with the help of an assigned reference field (see Figure 5.8).

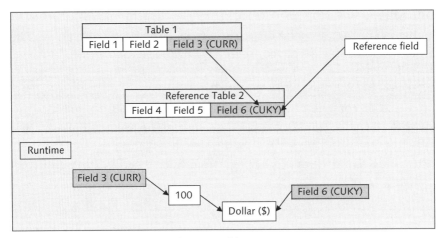

Figure 5.8 Reference Table and Reference Field

The reference table and reference field must be specified for QUAN/CURR fields. If the reference field is not specified, an error message appears while you are activating the table (see Figure 5.9). The reference field can be specified from the same table or from any other reference table (see Figure 5.10).

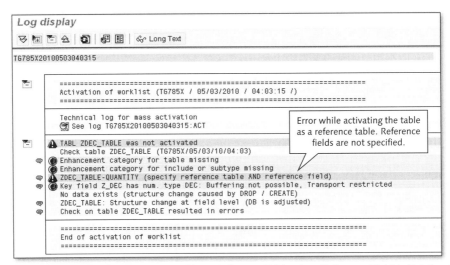

Figure 5.9 Error While Activating Table as Reference Table when Reference Field Is Not Specified

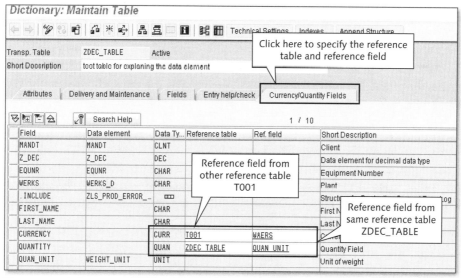

Figure 5.10   Reference Table and Reference Field are Specified

5.2.2   Includes

Fields of another structure can be included in the tables and structures. Individual fields and structures can be combined. If the include is changed, all the tables and structure that contain this include adjust automatically. For example, Structure R is included in Table T. When a new field is inserted in Structure R, table T adjusts itself automatically to the changes. This means a new field automatically gets inserted in the table.

Includes can also be nested. The maximum nesting depth is nine. Nesting means that Structure A includes Structure B, which in turn includes Structure C, and so on. The maximum length of a path of nested includes in a table or a structure is nine. The tables/structure itself is not included in this maximum.

> **Note**
>
> Only one table can lie on the path of nested includes. This means that a table can include only a structure whereas a structure can include other structures and one table. For example, Table TAB1 includes the structure STRUCT1, which in turn includes the structure STRUCT2. Table TAB1 can only include other structures and not other tables. Structure STRUCT0 can include the table TAB1, but no other table can be included. This is because only one table can lie on the path of nested includes.

Only flat structures can be included. Flat structures are those where every field either refers to a data element or is directly assigned to data type, length, and decimal places. In a table, a field name can be up to 16 places long, whereas in a structure the field name can be up to 30 places long. Therefore, a structure can be included in the table only if none of the field names of the structure are longer than 16 places.

Fields can be grouped together with the help of includes. This group of fields can be accessed in the ABAP code by the group name. In ABAP programs, fields can either be accessed directly by the menu path Table/Structure name • Field Name or with Table/structure name • Group name • Field Name. Groups can be accessed by the menu path Table/structure name • Group name.

For example, structure EMPLOYEE includes structure ADDRESS with a group name ADDR. Fields like CITY and STREET are present within the structure ADDRESS. The city field can be accessed by EMPLOYEE-CITY or with EMPLOYEE-ADDR-CITY. Structure ADDRESS can be accessed with EMPLOYEE-ADDR.

Same structures can be included more than once. In this case, the field name must be renamed and must be unique. A suffix is assigned to each group and each field, in order to make it unique. In ABAP, fields can be addressed with menu path Table/Structure name • Field Name (with suffix) or with Table/structure name • Group name • Field Name (with suffix). For example, structure EMPLOYEE includes structure ADDRESS twice. One structure represents the home address with a group name ADDR and suffix *H*. Another structure represents the office address with a group name ADDR and suffix *O*. Fields like CITY and STREET are present in both the structures. The city field for home address can be accessed by EMPLOYEE-CITYH or with EMPLOYEE-ADDRH-CITY. The structure representing the home address can be accessed with EMPLOYEE-ADDRH, and the structure representing the office address can be accessed with EMPLOYEE-ADDRO.

> **Note**
>
> While including the same structure twice, keep in mind that the fields should be unique both times. This means that group and name suffixes should be unique for both includes. The field length should not exceed 16 characters after adding the name suffix.

Otherwise, you get an error message during table activation. For example, the structure ADDRESS having suffix name HME contains a field CITY_OF_EMPLOYE (the field name is 15 places long). After adding a suffix, the field name becomes CITY_OF_EMPLOYEHME, which is longer than 16 places. In this case, you get an error message while activating the table.

Let us discuss the procedure for inserting an include into the table.

1. Follow the menu path EDIT • INCLUDE • INSERT. Click on INSERT (see Figure 5.11).

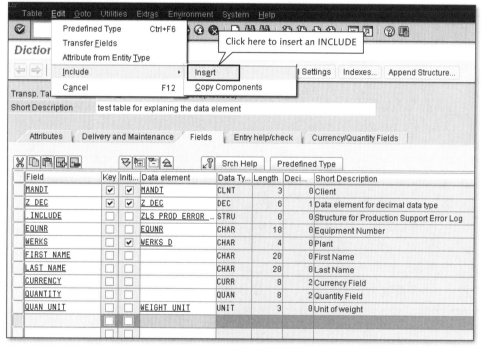

Figure 5.11 Procedure for Inserting an Include into a Table

2. Enter the structure name, group, and name suffix in the INSERT INCLUDE pop-up (see Figure 5.12). The suffix can have three places. The suffix is used to avoid the collisions between fields in include and fields already present in the table.

3. Choose the green checkmark icon(✔). A line with .INCLUDE in the FIELD field and the name of include in the DATA ELEMENT field is inserted.

If the KEY column is checked, all the fields in the include become the key fields of the table. All the key fields should be placed together at the start of the program.

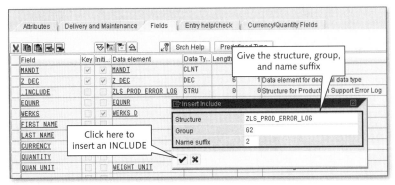

Figure 5.12 Insert Include Pop-up to Insert an Include into the Table

4. An include is inserted into the table (see Figure 5.13). Activate it by clicking the ACTIVATE button (✳) or by pressing Ctrl + F3 .

Field	Key	Initi...	Data element	Data Ty...	Length	Deci...	Short Description	Group
MANDT	✔	✔	MANDT	CLNT	3	0	Client	
Z_DEC	✔	✔	Z_DEC	DEC	6	1	Data element for decimal data type	
.INCLUDE			ZLS_PROD_ERROR_LOG	STRU	0	0	Structure for Production Support Error Log	61
EQUNR			EQUNR	CHAR	18	0	Equipment Number	
WERKS		✔	WERKS_D	CHAR	4	0	Plant	
FIRST_NAME				CHAR	20	0	First Name	
LAST_NAME				CHAR	20	0	Last Name	
CURRENCY				CURR	8	2	Currency Field	
QUANTITY				QUAN	8	2	Quantity Field	
.INCLU-2			ZLS_PROD_ERROR_LOG	STRU	0	0	Structure for Production Support Error Log	62
QUAN_UNIT			WEIGHT_UNIT	UNIT	3	0	Unit of weight	

Figure 5.13 Include is Inserted into the Table

5.2.3 Foreign Key

Foreign keys are used to define relationships between tables. Two or more tables can be joined together with the help of a foreign key. Foreign keys can also be used to link several tables in other dictionary objects such as views or lock objects. Let us consider Tables T1 and T2 that are linked together with the help of foreign keys.

Foreign keys (field F3 and field F4 of Table T1) are linked to the primary keys (field F5 and field F6 of Table T2). Table T1 is known as a foreign key table or dependent table and Table T2 is known as a check table or reference table. All the primary keys of the check table should be linked with the foreign keys of the foreign key table. Both the pairs of fields that are linked should have the same technical characteristics; i.e., the same data type and length (see Figure 5.14).

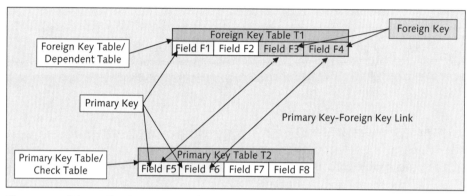

Figure 5.14   Primary Key-Foreign Key Relationship

Foreign keys are also used to create value checks for input fields. When a foreign key relationship is maintained for a particular field, that foreign key field is known as the check field. When the value is entered in the check field (foreign key field) then that value is checked in the check table. If the check table contains that value, the entry is valid; otherwise the entry is invalid. Let us understand how input check works. Whenever an entry is made in the foreign key field, a `select` statement is generated with the values of the foreign key field. This `select` statement is submitted in the background. If an entry is found in the check table with the values entered in the check field, the entry is valid. Otherwise, the entry is invalid.

Let us consider some examples for the same scenario. Field3 is linked with Field5 and Field4 is linked with Field6.

▶ **Example 1**

Field3 = 2 and Field4 = 2. This is a valid entry because a record exists in the check table T2 having value Field5 = 2 and Field6 = 2 (see Figure 5.15).

93

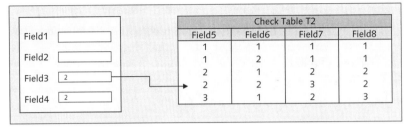

Figure 5.15 Valid Entry of Value Check

The following SELECT query is submitted in background:

```
SELECT * from T2
Where T2-Field5 = T1-Field3
And T2-Field6 = T1-Field4.
```

Listing 5.1 Select Query when Input Check is Submitted

If the check table contains a record, it is displayed as a value check. If it doesn't contain the record, an error occurs.

► **Example 2**
Field3 = 3 and Field4 = 2. This is an invalid entry because no record exists in check table T2 having value Field5 = 3 and Field6 = 2 (see Figure 5.16).

				Check Table T2			
Field1		No entry exists in the check table with Field5 = 3 and Field6 = 2.		Field5	Field6	Field7	Field8
Field2				1	1	1	1
				1	2	1	1
Field3	3			2	1	2	2
				2	2	3	2
Field4	2			3	1	2	3

Figure 5.16 Invalid Entry of Value Check

► **Example 3**
In Table EQUI, ELIEF is the foreign key associated with the check-table field LIFNR of check Table LFA1 (see Figure 5.17).

When Table EQUI is executed and F4 help is pressed, a pop-up screen appears for search help (see Figure 5.18). When Enter is pressed after writing the value at the appropriate variable, a list appears of valid records that are present in the check table (see Figure 5.19).

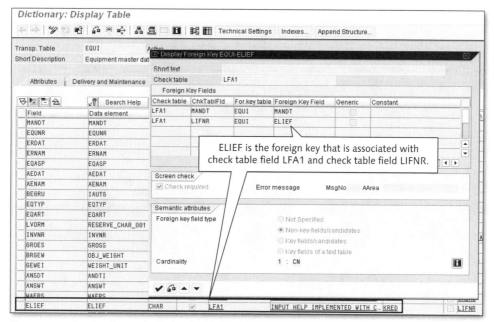

Figure 5.17 Foreign Key and Check Table Example

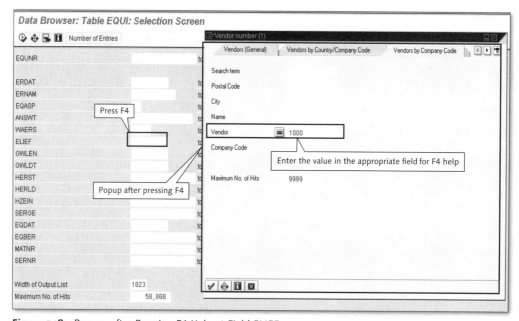

Figure 5.18 Pop-up after Pressing F4 Help at Field ELIEF

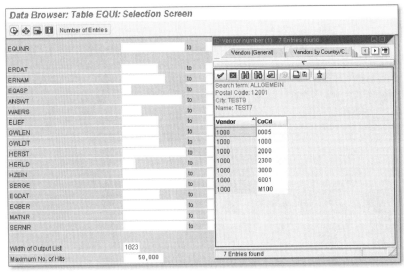

Figure 5.19 List of Entries Displayed from Check Table

The foreign key table should check all the key fields of the check table. If you don't want to check some key fields of the check table, you can define those key fields as generic foreign keys or constant foreign keys. Let us discuss these in more detail.

Generic and Constant Foreign Keys

Generic keys are used to exclude the assignment from the key fields of the check table to foreign key fields. For example, If the check table contains three key fields, these three key fields must be assigned to the foreign key field. If you don't want to assign all three key fields with the foreign keys of the table, you can assign those fields with a *generic foreign key*.

When a constant value is assigned to the key field of the check table, that key is known as a *constant foreign key*. In this case a check is also made with respect to the constant. The only valid records of the check table field are those that contain the checked constant in their record value fields. In this case, a select query is performed as shown in Listing 5.2.

```
SELECT * from T2
Where T2-Field5 = T1-Field3
And T2-Field6 = T1-Field4
And T2-Field8 = 'R'.
```

Listing 5.2 Select Query for Generic and Constant Foreign Key

This query selects a record only if the value entered in Field3 is present in check table's Field5, the value entered in Field4 is present in check table's Field6, and the value entered in Field8 is the constant R. Field7, which is one of the primary keys of the check table, can have any value because this field is generic (see Figure 5.20).

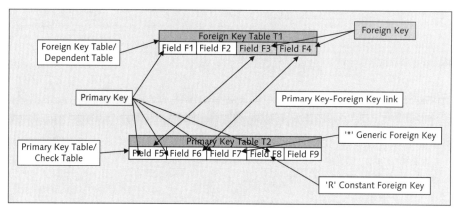

Figure 5.20 Generic and Constant Key Relationship

Let us consider some examples of using generic and constant foreign keys.

▶ **Example 1**

Field3 = 2 and Field4 = 1. This is a valid entry because a record exists in the check table T2 having value Field5 = 2, Field6 = 1, and Field8 = R (see Figure 5.21).

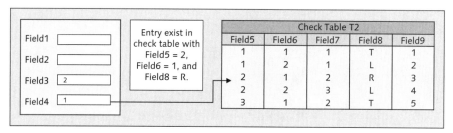

Figure 5.21 Valid Entry of Value check

▶ **Example 2**

Field3 = 3 and Field4 = 1. This is an invalid entry because no record exists in the check table T2 having value Field5 = 3, Field6 = 1, and Field8 = R (see Figure 5.22).

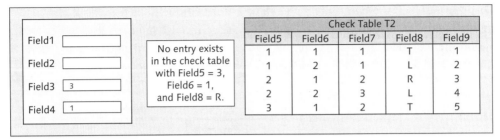

Figure 5.22 Invalid Entry of Value Check

Multi-Structured Foreign Keys

Apart from generic and constant foreign keys, you can also define *multi-structured foreign keys*. In this type of foreign key, the field of the work area or any other table field not present in the foreign key table can be assigned to the check table. This is possible for all fields except the check field.

In this case, select query is performed as shown in Listing 5.3.

```
SELECT * from T2
Where T2-Field5 = T1-Field3
And T2-Field6 = wa-F.
```

Listing 5.3 Select Query for Multi-Structured Foreign Key

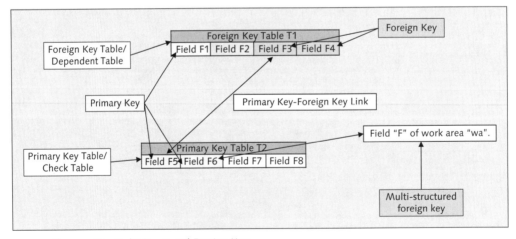

Figure 5.23 Multi-Structured Foreign Key

This query selects a record only if the value entered in Field3 is present in check table's Field5 and check table's Field6 contains the value from the work area (see Figure 5.23). If the record is found from the above select statement, the entry is valid; otherwise it is invalid. When a work area is assigned to the check table's key field, the value to this field must be assigned at the time of input check. Otherwise the check always fails and no value can be entered in the check field.

Text Tables

A *text table* is a special table that contains text in a multilingual format. Due to this requirement, text tables also contain the language field (SPRAS) as a key field. A table is said to be the text table of another table if it contains all the key fields along with the additional language key field. It can also contain explanatory short text as an optional field.

For example, Table T2 is a text table of Table T1 if Table T2 contains the same key fields that are contained by Table T1 and an additional language key field (see Figure 5.24). Text Table T2 can also contain explanatory text in several languages for each key field entry of Table T1. Text Table T2 must be linked with Table T1 using the foreign key (see Figure 5.25). In semantic attributes of foreign keys, the KEY FIELDS OF A TEXT TABLE option should be selected. Only one text table can be generated for any table. This is checked with the help of the KEY FIELDS OF A TEXT TABLE option while activating the table.

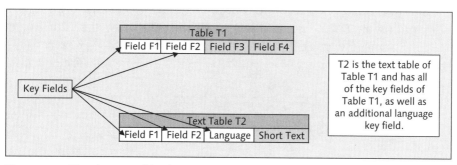

Figure 5.24   T2 is the Text Table of Parent Table T1

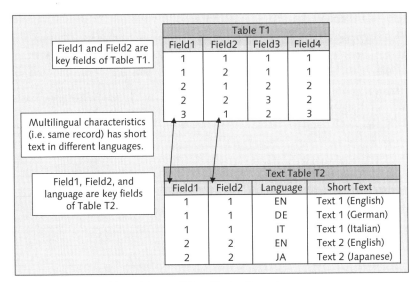

Figure 5.25 Text Table and Parent Table: Display Records

Short text is displayed in the user's SAP logon language. This short text entry is taken from the language field of the text table. For example, TSTC is an SAP transaction's code table, and TSTCT is a text table of Table TSTC. Let's execute TSTCT with Transaction SE11. You get two records: one with language key D (German) and the other with language key E (English), each having a different TTEXT (short description) (see Figure 5.26). Now when you execute Table TSTC, you get the TTEXT (short description) on the basis of logon language. If the logon language is English, you get the TTEXT entry as ABAP DICTIONARY MAINTENANCE. If the logon language is German, you get the TTEXT entry as ABAP DICTIONARY PFLEGE (see Figure 5.27).

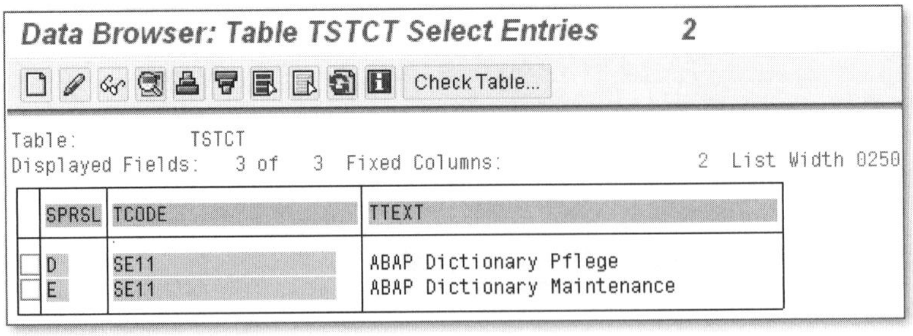

Figure 5.26 Text Table TSTCT when Transaction SE11 is Executed

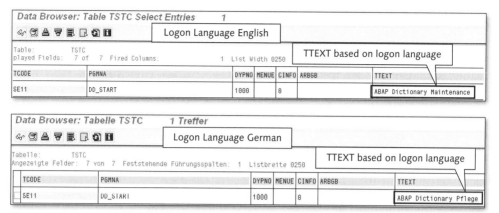

Figure 5.27 Entry in Table TSTC with Logon Languages as English and German

Semantic Attributes of Foreign Keys

A foreign key defines the relationship between two tables. With the help of semantic attributes, this relationship can be defined more accurately. The type of foreign key and cardinality can be defined within the semantic attributes of foreign keys. These attributes are optional and are primarily used only for documentation. These values are not used in the value check for the foreign key. However, these attributes should be specified if you are using the foreign key for defining maintenance views, help views, matchcodes, lock objects, or text tables.

Foreign Key Field Type

The FOREIGN KEY FIELD TYPE flag shows whether the foreign key field indentifies the foreign key table. This flag can have the following categories:

▶ NOT SPECIFIED
The semantic attributes of the foreign key relationship are optional. If you don't want to specify any semantic attribute, you have to select this option. However, if you are using your foreign key for defining maintenance views, help views, matchcodes, or lock objects, these semantic attributes must be defined.

▶ NON-KEY-FIELDS/CANDIDATES
This category applies when the foreign key is neither a primary key of the foreign key table nor the candidate key of the foreign key table; i.e., the foreign key does not uniquely identify a record of the foreign key table. In that case, you must select the NON-KEY-FIELDS/CANDIDATES option. For example, the GEWEI field is a unit field in Table EQUI (see Figure 5.28). This field does not define

any record of the table uniquely. Hence, this field belongs to the category NON-
KEY-FIELDS/CANDIDATES.

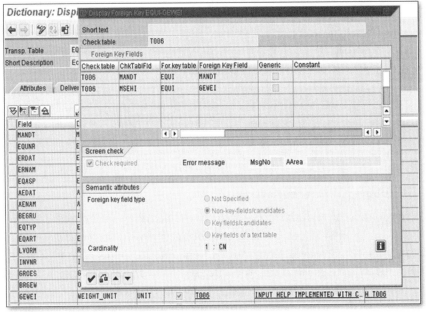

Figure 5.28 Scenario where Non-Key Fields/Candidates Option is Checked

▶ KEY FIELDS/CANDIDATES
Use this category when the foreign key is either a primary key of the foreign key
table or the candidate key of the foreign key table; i.e., the foreign key uniquely
identifies a record of the foreign key table. In that case, you must select the
KEY FIELDS/CANDIDATES option. For example, Table VBAP is an item level sales
document table. The VBELN field (sales document number) is a primary key of
the Table VBAP. This field uniquely identifies all the records of the table, so this
field belongs to the KEY FIELDS/CANDIDATES category (see Figure 5.29).

▶ KEY FIELDS OF A TEXT TABLE
The foreign key table is the text table for the check table. It means that—apart
from the additional language key fields present in the foreign key table—both
the foreign key table and the check table have the same key fields. This is the
special case of category KEY FIELDS/CANDIDATES. For example, Table TSTCT is a
text table of Table TSTC. The foreign key must have the KEY FIELDS OF A TEXT
TABLE option checked (see Figure 5.30).

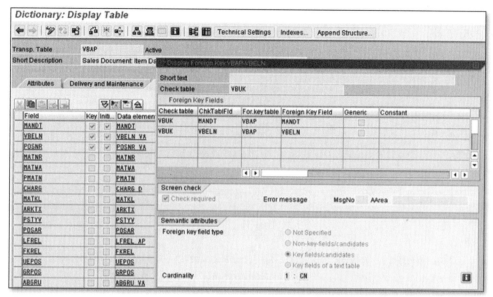

Figure 5.29 Scenario where Key Fields/Candidates Option is Checked

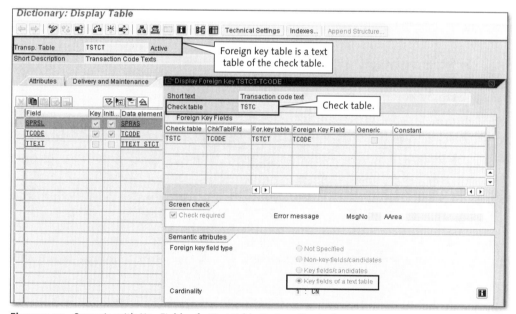

Figure 5.30 Scenario with Key Fields of a Text Table Option Checked

Cardinality

As already discussed, foreign keys are used to define the relationship between tables. Cardinality defines the number of records occurrences in either side of the relation. Cardinality (*n:m*) defines the foreign key relationship between the number of possible dependent records and the number of possible reference records. It defines the relationship between the records of the foreign key table (*n*) and the records of the check table (*m*).

The *n* side of the cardinality can be replaced by following values:

▶ **n=1**
For each record of the foreign key table, there is exactly one record assigned to the check table.

▶ **n=C**
The foreign key table may contain some records that are not assigned to any record of the check table. This is possible because foreign key fields can be empty (given that the foreign key field is not always mandatory or initial). If the foreign key field is optional, the value in the field can be blank and there is no record in the check table that corresponds to the foreign key table.

The *m* side of the cardinality can be replaced by following values:

▶ **m=1**
For each record of the check table, there is exactly one dependent foreign key table record.

▶ **m=C**
For each record of the check table, there is at most one dependent foreign key table record.

▶ **m=N**
For each record of the check table, there is at least one dependent foreign key table record.

▶ **m=CN**
For each record of the check table, there can be any number of dependent foreign key table records.

With reference to the values of *n* and *m*, there are eight possible scenarios. We describe these next.

▶ **Scenario 1: When n=1 and m=1**
In this scenario, each and every record of the foreign key table is assigned to

exactly one reference record of the check table. Also, each and every record of the check table is assigned to exactly one dependent foreign key record. There is one-to-one mapping between the foreign key records and check table records (see Figure 5.31).

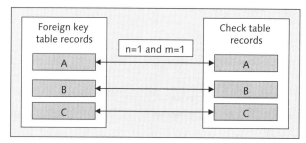

Figure 5.31 Scenario 1, n=1 and m=1

▶ **Scenario 2: When n=1 and m=C**
In this scenario, each and every record of the foreign key table is assigned to exactly one reference record of the check table. However, each and every record of the check table is assigned to at most one dependent foreign key record. This means that the check table can be assigned to either one dependent record or no dependent record of the foreign key table (see Figure 5.32).

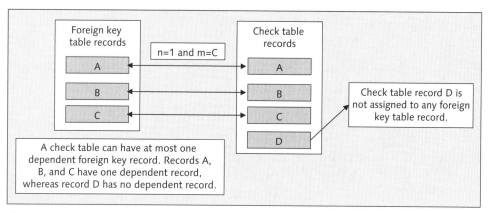

Figure 5.32 Scenario 2, n=1 and m=C

▶ **Scenario 3: When n=1 and m=N**
In this scenario, each and every record of the foreign key table is assigned to exactly one reference record of the check table. However, each and every record

of the check table is assigned to at least one dependent foreign key record. This means that the check table can be assigned to either one dependent record or more than one dependent record of the foreign key table (see Figure 5.33).

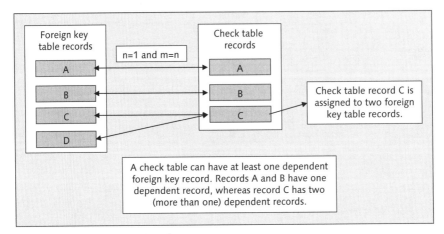

Figure 5.33 Scenario 3, n=1 and m=n

▶ **Scenario 4: When n=1 and m=CN**

In this scenario, each and every record of the foreign key table is assigned to exactly one reference record of the check table. However, each and every record of the check table is assigned to any number of dependent foreign key records (see Figure 5.34).

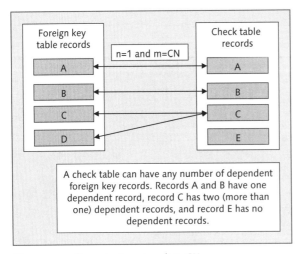

Figure 5.34 Scenario 4, n=1 and m=CN

▶ **Scenario 5: When n=C and m=1**

In this scenario, some of the records of the foreign key table are not assigned to any reference record of the check table. However, each and every record of the check table is assigned to exactly one dependent foreign key record (see Figure 5.35).

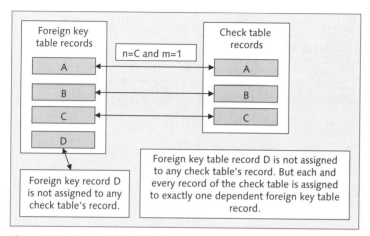

Figure 5.35 Scenario 5, n=C and m=1

▶ **Scenario 6: When n=C and m=C**

In this scenario, some of the records of the foreign key table are not assigned to any reference record of the check table. However, each and every record of the check table is assigned to at most one dependent foreign key record. This means that the check table can be assigned to either one dependent record or no dependent record of the foreign key table (see Figure 5.36).

▶ **Scenario 7: When n=C and m=N**

In this scenario, some of the records of the foreign key table are not assigned to any reference record of the check table. However, each and every record of the check table is assigned to at least one dependent foreign key record. This means that the check table can be assigned to either one dependent record or more than one dependent record of the foreign key table (see Figure 5.37).

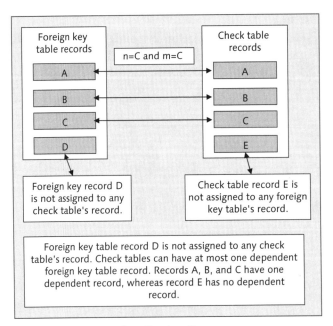

Figure 5.36 Scenario 6, n=C and m=C

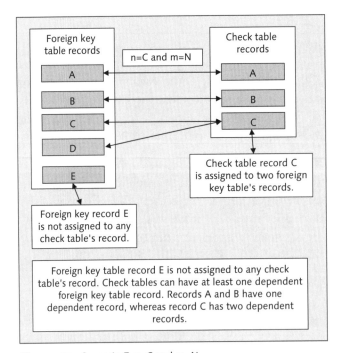

Figure 5.37 Scenario 7, n=C and m=N

▶ **Scenario 8: When n=C and m=CN**

In this scenario, some of the records of the foreign key table are not assigned to any reference record of the check table. However, each and every record of the check table is assigned to any number of dependent foreign key records (see Figure 5.38).

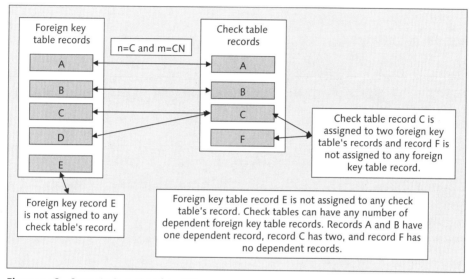

Figure 5.38 Scenario 8, n=C and m=CN

Screen Check

The CHECK REQUIRED flag defines whether an input check should be executed on the screen fields. If this flag is set, the definition will apply to all the screens on which a check field appears. This check can be switched off for certain screens by canceling the FOREIGN KEY flag in the attribute of the corresponding screen field (see Figure 5.39).

Figure 5.39 shows a screen that is a part of a module pool program. If the CHECK REQUIRED flag is set, the value entered in the foreign key field is checked in the corresponding check table. If the value is not found in the check table, an error message is displayed in the status bar. For example, the value entered in the foreign key field EQUIPMENT is checked in the check Table EQUI (see Figure 5.40). Because the value is not present in the check table, an error message is displayed. This error message is applied to all the screens in which this field is called. However, this check can be disabled in particular screens or programs by canceling the FOREIGN

KEY flag in the SPECIAL ATTRIBUTE tab of the screen in the module pool program (see Figure 5.39).

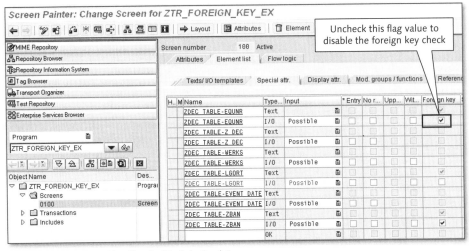

Figure 5.39 Foreign Key Flag in Module Pool Program

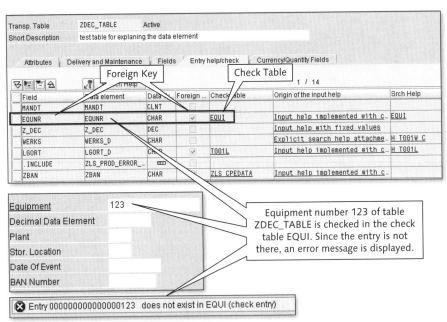

Figure 5.40 Foreign Key and Corresponding Check Table of Transparent Table ZDEC_TABLE

Error Message

A standard error message is displayed if the check fails. However, this standard message can be replaced with any message in the definition of the foreign key. You can use up to four placeholders while defining the message. The system automatically fills the placeholders with the content of the foreign key field and the name of the check table. The first three placeholders are filled with the contents of the foreign key and the fourth placeholder is filled with the name of the check table (see Figure 5.41).

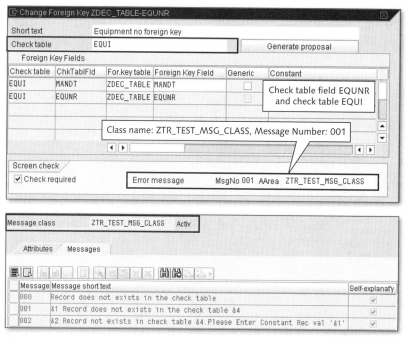

Figure 5.41 User-Defined Messages in Message Class ZTR_TEST_MSG_CLASS

In the above example, we get the standard error message "Entry 123 does not exist in EQUI (check entry)." This message is replaced by user-defined message "123 record does not exist in the check table EQUI" (see Figure 5.42).

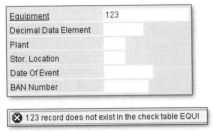

Equipment	123
Decimal Data Element	
Plant	
Stor. Location	
Date Of Event	
BAN Number	

⊗ 123 record does not exist in the check table EQUI

Figure 5.42 User-Defined Error Message when Entry Does Not Exist in Check Table

5.2.4 Technical Settings

The technical settings of the table define how the table is created in the database. Once the table is activated, it gets created in the database on the basis of technical settings. It is mandatory to define technical settings; otherwise you see an instructional message to maintain and save the technical settings (see Figure 5.43). Unless you have maintained the technical settings, you cannot activate the table. Details of all the tables and their technical settings can be found in Table DD09L.

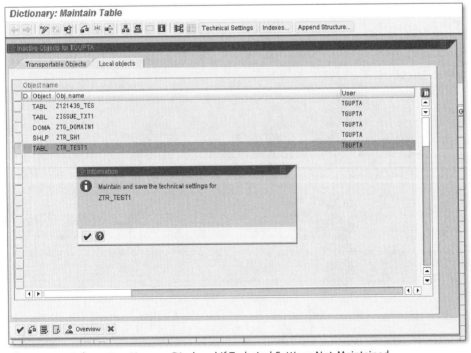

Figure 5.43 Information Message Displayed if Technical Settings Not Maintained

Technical settings have the following parameters:

▶ DATA CLASS
The data class defines the physical area of the database in which a table is logically stored when created.

▶ SIZE CATEGORY
Size category defines the size of the *extents* created for the table. An extent is a continuous area in the database that is reserved for the table. Hence, size category defines the expected space required for the table in the database.

▶ BUFFERING
Buffering specifies whether the table can be buffered. If buffering is set, the table records are buffered and loaded into the buffer area of the application server.

▶ BUFFERING TYPE
If the BUFFERING flag is set for the table, you need to specify the type of buffering. Buffering type defines how table records are loaded in the table buffer. Buffering can be of full, generic, or single-record.

▶ LOG DATA CHANGES
If this flag is checked, all the changes to a table record are logged in the log table.

▶ WRITE ACCESS ONLY WITH JAVA
If this flag is set, contents of the table can be changed only within Java. However, if the changes are made in the table through ABAP programs, they may not be read properly within Java. (This is really all you need to know about this checkbox, so we do not discuss it in more detail below.)

▶ CONVERT TO TRANSPARENT TABLE
You can convert the pooled tables into transparent tables with the help of the CONVERT TO TRANSPARENT TABLE flag. The pooled table must have an active status.

Data Class

The data class defines the physical area of the database in which a table is logically stored when created. A table is automatically assigned to that physical area (DBspace or tablespace) of the database. Tables can be assigned to one of the following data classes (see Figure 5.44):

▶ **APPL0**

Master data; transparent tables. Tables in which data is seldom changed are assigned to this data class; for example, data contained in the address file, such as name and address. Table E070, which is a table for CHANGE AND TRANSPORT SYSTEM: HEADER OF REQUESTS/TASKS, seldom changes, so it is defined in the physical area APPL0.

▶ **APPL1**

Transaction data; transparent tables. Tables in which data is frequently changed. It is generally used for transaction data such as inventory tables or warehouse tables where goods movement is frequent.

▶ **APPL2**

Organization and customizing. Tables that are defined when the system is installed. Data in this table seldom changes. Examples are Table T001, which is a table for company codes, and Table T000, which is a table for clients.

▶ **USER**

Customer data class. This data class is provided to the customer. The tables assigned in this data class are stored in a tablespace for user development.

▶ **USER1**

Customer data class. This data class is provided to the customer. The tables assigned in this data class are stored in a tablespace for user development.

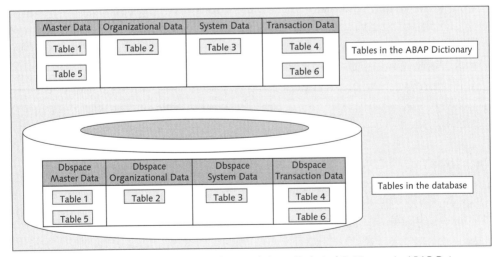

Figure 5.44 Tables Created in the Database with Same Technical Settings as in ABAP Data Dictionary

Other data classes are:

▶ DDIM: Dimension tables in BW

▶ DFACT: Facts table in BW

▶ DODS: ODS tables in BW

▶ USER2: Customer data class USER2 generated by BRSPACE

▶ SDIC: ABAP Dictionary table

▶ SDOCU: Documentation

▶ SLDEF: Repository switch tablespace 700

▶ SLEXC: Repository switch tablespace 700

▶ SLOAD: Screen and report loads

▶ SPROT: SPOOL and logs

▶ SSRC: Source for screen and reports

Size Category

The size category determines the space required by the table in the database. It defines the size of the extents created for the table. The size category can have values from 0 to 9 (see Figure 5.45).

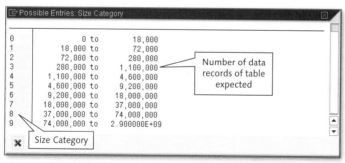

Figure 5.45 Possible Entries of Size Category

In the database, each category has a fixed storage area. When the table is created, initial space or initial extent is reserved for the table in the database. If more space is required later, additional memory is allocated to the table depending on the size category (see Figure 5.46).

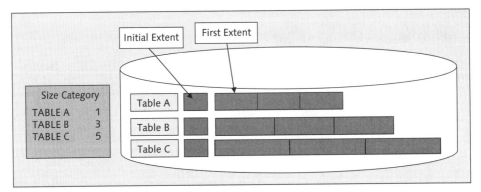

Figure 5.46 Size Category: Database View

Advantages of selecting the correct size category are:

▶ Large numbers of very small extents are not created.

▶ Extents are created on the basis of data records present in the table. Hence, very large extents are not created and space is not wasted.

Buffering

The buffering setting specifies whether a table can be buffered. If buffering is set, the table records are buffered and loaded into the buffer area of the application server. Buffering depends on the expected volume of the data in the table and on the type of access to the table (read access or write access). If the table is frequently written to, buffering should be avoided. Buffering can have one of the following values:

▶ BUFFERING NOT ALLOWED
When table buffering is not needed, you must check this flag. Buffering should be avoided when the table is frequently written to and when the application program needs the most recent data.

▶ BUFFERING ALLOWED BUT SWITCHED OFF
Buffering is allowed from the business and technical points of view. Applications that access the table execute correctly with or without buffering. Because performance depends on the number of records present in the table and the frequency of table access, it is difficult to know the volume of records present

in the production system. For this reason, buffering is switched off. Buffering can be activated at any time in the customer's production system, if it is found that buffering improves performance.

▶ BUFFERING SWITCHED ON
If buffering is needed for a table, this flag should be set. After switching on the buffering, you should specify the buffering type.

If the BUFFERING flag is set for the table, you need to specify the type of buffering. The buffering type specifies how table records are loaded in the buffer of the application server. Buffering can be of the types discussed below.

Fully Buffered

If you choose FULLY BUFFERED, all the records are loaded in the table buffer when any part of the table record is accessed. With full buffering, either the entire table is in the buffer or the table is not in the buffer at all (see Figure 5.47).

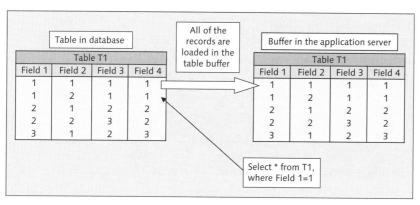

Figure 5.47 Whole Table Buffered in Full-Buffering Type

Data records are sorted in the buffer with the help of the table key. If the first key field is not defined, the system scans the whole table buffer. If secondary indexes are defined, the table is sorted on the basis of secondary indexes.

Before buffering the table, you should keep in mind the size of the table, the number of read accesses, and the number of write accesses. Tables that are small, frequently read, and rarely written to should be fully buffered.

Full buffering is recommended in the following scenarios:

▸ Size of table is up to 30 KB. Table is frequently read.

▸ Large tables where large number of records are frequently accessed. In this case, a very selective WHERE condition should be formulated using a database index.

▸ Tables in which non-existing records access are frequently submitted. In full buffering, all the records reside in buffers, so non-existing records can be easily determined from the buffer.

Generic Area Buffered

If you choose GENERIC AREA BUFFERED, records are buffered on the basis of the generic key field. When a record having a generic key is accessed, all the records having that generic key are loaded in the table buffer (see Figure 5.48). The generic key is the part of the primary key that is left-justified.

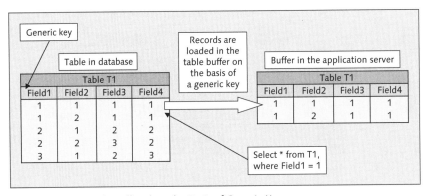

Figure 5.48 Records Buffered on the Basis of Generic Key

Generic buffering is helpful if only certain generic areas of the table are needed frequently. The client field is the generic key. Client-specific, fully buffered tables are automatically generically buffered on the basis of the client field. This is because one person cannot work on all clients at the same time. Language-specific tables are also generically buffered. This is because only records of the logon language are needed on an application server. In this case, the generic key includes all the key fields along with the language field.

Defining a generic key plays a very important role in generic buffering. If the generic key is too small, the buffer contains very large generic areas. Too much record data might be loaded in the buffer when the records are accessed. If the generic key is too large, a very small generic area is contained in the buffer. It is possible that some of the accesses bypass the buffer and directly hit the database. This is because these accesses do not fully define the generic key of the table. Only 64 bytes of the generic key are used. If the generic key is longer than 64 bytes, the part of the key exceeding the 64 bytes is not used to create the generic areas.

Single Record Buffering

If you choose SINGLE RECORD BUFFERING, only those records that are actually accessed are buffered in the table buffer (see Figure 5.49). Therefore, single-record buffering requires less storage area in the buffer than do generic or full buffering. This method requires more database accesses to load the record compared to other buffering methods. Single-record buffering should be used for large tables where only a few records are accessed with a `Select single` statement. The size of records that are accessed should fall between 100 KB and 200 KB. Several database accesses are required in the case of single-record buffering. All the accesses that are not submitted with `Select single` bypass the buffer and directly hit the database. For small tables, full buffering should be done; because only one database access is needed to load the table and data can be accessed later from the buffer.

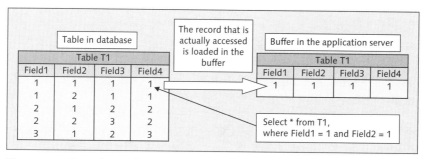

Figure 5.49 Record Actually Accessed is Buffered

Log Data Changes

You can log the changes made in the data record of the table by setting the LOG DATA CHANGES flag. If this flag is set and if the profile-containing parameter has appropriate values, each change made on the existing data record of the table by the user (with the `update`, `delete`, `modify` commands) or by the application program is recorded in the log table (DBTABPRT) in the database. To switch on logging, the SAP ECC system must be started with a profile-containing parameter (REC/CLIENT). This parameter is responsible for switching logging on or off (see Figure 5.50).

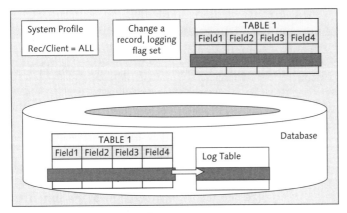

Figure 5.50 Logging in Database

Rec/client can have the values shown in Table 5.4.

Rec/Client Value	Description
ALL	Log all clients.
000, [ ], [ ]...	Log the specified clients.
OFF	Log switched off.

Table 5.4 Rec/Client Value and Descriptions

Logging is independent of the update. Existing logs can be displayed in Transaction SCU3.

> **Note**
>
> Activating logging slows down accesses that change the table. This is because records should be written in the log table for each change. Also, many users are using this log table in parallel. This can cause the lock situation even though the users are working with different application tables.

Convert to Transparent Table

You can convert the pooled tables into transparent tables with the help of CONVERT TO TRANSPARENT TABLE flag. The pooled table must have an active status. This option is used when the pooled table needs to be accessed from outside the SAP

ECC system. Let us discuss the procedure for converting the pooled table into a transparent table.

1. Go to the technical settings of the pooled table with the help of the TECHNICAL SETTINGS tab.

2. Select the CONVERT TO TRANSPARENT TABLE flag. This flag only changes the technical settings and not other table definitions (see Figure 5.51).

3. Maintain other attributes of the technical settings and activate the table.

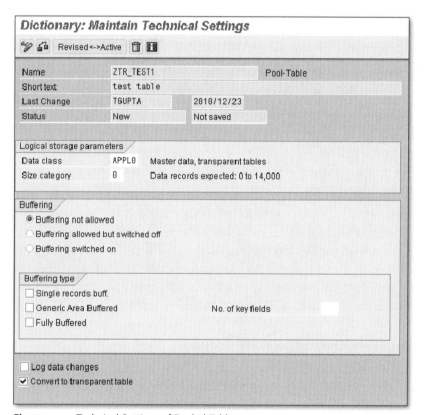

Figure 5.51 Technical Settings of Pooled Table

If there is a revised version of the pooled table, it cannot be converted into the transparent table with this flag. In this case if the flag is set, technical settings of the table cannot be activated. There are restrictions such as number of key fields, key length, and table length for a transparent table. These restrictions are not valid for a pooled table. A pooled table that satisfies all the conditions of a transparent table is converted to a transparent table with the transparent flag. If any of the restrictions are violated, technical settings will not be activated. In this case, an error can be found in the activation log.

5.2.5 Indexes

Indexes are used to search data records faster. An index can be considered a copy of a database table that has some selection criteria in it for faster selection of data records. This copy is always in sorted form, as sorting provides fast access to the data records of the table. The index also contains a pointer to the corresponding record of the actual table so that the fields not contained in the index can also be read with the help of the index. An index can be of two types:

▶ **Primary index**
   The primary index contains the key field of the table. It also contains the pointer to the non-key field of the table so that the non-key field can be read with the help of the primary index. When the table is created, the primary index is automatically created in the database.

▶ **Secondary index**
   Secondary indexes are created manually by the user. More than one secondary index can be created for the table in the database with the help of three-digit index identifiers. If the table with a very large number of data records is accessed frequently and sorting of the primary index does not speed up access of the data records, one or more secondary indexes should be created.

Points to Note before Creating Secondary Indexes

The order of the fields in the index plays an important role in accessing speed. The first field of the index should have constant values for a large number of selections. An index should have those fields that can restrict the set of results in selection criteria. An additional index can also place a load on the system because it must be adjusted each time the table content changes. Hence, tables that are frequently written should have few indexes.

The database optimizer selects the index that is to be used. Sometimes the database optimizer does not use the suitable index for a selection. An index that has already been used successfully for selection might no longer be used by the optimizer if the optimizer finds a more effective index. In short, creating an index can produce side effects on performance. For this reason, the indexes on a table should contain as few fields in common as possible. If two indexes on a table have a large number of common fields, the database optimizer may become confused about which index is most selective.

Checking Which Index is Used

Let us discuss how we can check which index is used to select the entries.

1. After creating an index, follow menu path SYSTEM • UTILITIES • PERFORMANCE TRACE (Transaction ST05).

2. Select ACTIVATE TRACE. This records all the database operations for this user (see Figure 5.52).

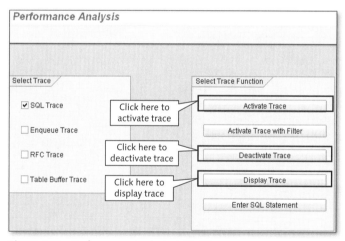

Figure 5.52 Performance Analysis, Initial Screen

3. Perform the action in which the index is used. Go to Transaction SE16N, SE16, or SE11 and display the entries (see Figure 5.53).

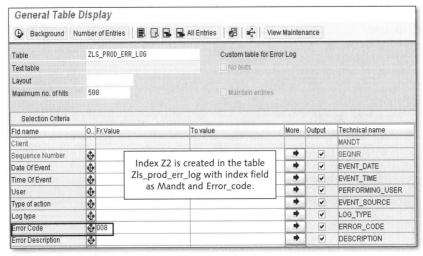

Figure 5.53 Display Entries for Checking the Index Used

Deactivate and display the trace (Figure 5.52). You see the pop-up shown in Figure 5.54. Once you click on the checkmark, the TRACE LIST icon will be displayed.

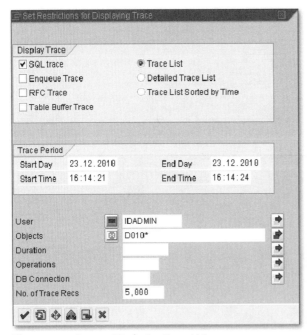

Figure 5.54 Pop-up Displaying Trace List

4. Select the appropriate value (PREPARE, OPEN, FETCH, or REOPEN).Click on the
   EXPLAIN button to get the detailed execution plan list (see Figure 5.55).

```
Trace List

  DDIC information   Explain

                                        Click here to get the detailed execution plan list

Transaction SE16N Work process no 1 Proc. Type  DIA Client  305 User      TG785X TransGUID 4BEDE6454C325932E100000096EB2E64 Date

Duration  Obj. name  Op.      Recs. RC   Statement

   1,367 DDTYPES   PREPARE         0  SELECT WHERE "TYPENAME" = :A0
      10 DDTYPES   OPEN            0  SELECT WHERE "TYPENAME" = 'ZLS_PROD_ERR_LOG'
   1,247 DDTYPES   FETCH       1   0
     384 DD02L     PREPARE         0  SELECT WHERE "TABNAME" = :A0
      10 DD02L     OPEN            0  SELECT WHERE "TABNAME" = 'ZLS_PROD_ERR_LOG'
     847 DD02L     FETCH       1 1403
      12 DD02L     REOPEN          0  SELECT WHERE "TABNAME" = 'ZLS_PROD_ERR_LOG' AND "AS4LOCAL" = 'A'
     395 DD02L     FETCH       1 1403
     295 USER_TABL... PREPARE       0  select from user_tables where table_name = :A0
       9 USER_TABL... OPEN          0  select from user_tables where table_name = 'ZLS_PROD_ERR_LOG'
   8,440           FETCH       1 1403
     362 DD02L     PREPARE         0  SELECT WHERE "TABNAME" = :A0 AND ROWNUM <= :A1
       8 DD02L     OPEN            0  SELECT WHERE "TABNAME" = 'ZLS_PROD_ERR_LOG' AND ROWNUM <= 1
     499 DD02L     FETCH       1   0
     282 DD02L     PREPARE         0  SELECT WHERE "TABNAME" = :A0 AND ROWNUM <= :A1
       8 DD02L     OPEN            0  SELECT WHERE "TABNAME" = 'ZLS_PROD_ERR_LOG' AND ROWNUM <= 1
     725 DD02L     FETCH       1   0
      12 DD08L     REOPEN          0  SELECT WHERE "CHECKTABLE" = 'ZLS_PROD_ERR_LOG' AND "FRKART" = 'TEXT' AND "AS4LOCAL" =
     291 DD08L     FETCH       0 1403
      14 DDNTT     REOPEN          0  SELECT WHERE TABNAME = ' '
   8,721 DDNTT     FETCH       0 1403
     357 ZLS_PROD... PREPARE       0  SELECT WHERE "MANDT" = :A0 AND "ERROR_CODE" = :A1 AND ROWNUM <= :A2
       9 ZLS_PROD... OPEN          0  SELECT WHERE "MANDT" = '305' AND "ERROR_CODE" = '008' AND ROWNUM <= 500
  31,133 ZLS_PROD_... FETCH     58   0
   1,221 ZLS_PROD_... FETCH     58   0
   1,058 ZLS_PROD_... FETCH     58   0
     678 ZLS_PROD_... FETCH     28 1403
```

Figure 5.55 Trace List Display

5. In the execution plan list you will see the index used in selecting the records
   (see Figure 5.56).

An index entry can refer to several data records that have the same value of index
fields. If the UNIQUE INDEX flag is set, multiple entries are not allowed. The unique-
index function identifies each record of the table uniquely. The primary index is by
default a unique index because the index is formed by the table's key field, which
will always identify the data record uniquely. If you are creating a secondary index
as a unique index, please ensure the following:

▸ The client (MANDT) field is included in the index for the client-dependent
  table.

▸ The table should not have multiple records when searched with the index key.

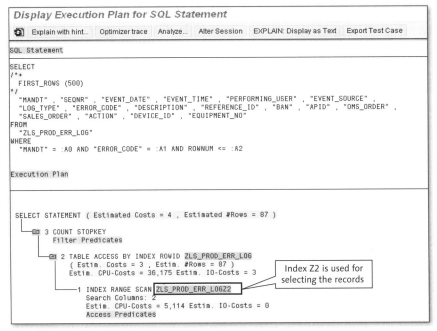

Figure 5.56 Execution Plan for SQL StatementUnique Indexes

Accessing speed does not depend on whether an index is unique. A unique index simply ensures that certain field combination present in the index can identify unique records.

Index Identifier

You can distinguish between several indexes on the same table with the help of three-place index identifiers. The index ID 0 is reserved for primary indexes. The index identifier can only contain letter and digits. The index name on the database follows the convention <TABLE NAME>~<INDEX ID>. For example, the ZLS_PROD_ERR_LOG table contains the index Z2; this index can be accessed by ZLS_PROD_ERR_LOG ~Z2.

Prior to release 3.0, indexes have eight-place names. The first seven places are reserved for the table name, and the eighth place is reserved for the index. After release 3.0, indexes have 13 place names with the first 10 places reserved for the database table name and the last three places reserved for the three-place index identifier.

5.2.6 Enhancements in Tables (Append Structures and Customizing Includes)

Tables and structures can be enhanced with the help of append structures and customizing includes. With these enhancements, special developments, country versions, and customer fields can be included in the tables and structures. The enhancements not only apply to the structure/tables themselves but also to the dependent structures that adopt an enhancement as an include or as referenced structures.

An enhancement category can have one of the following values:

- **Cannot be enhanced**
  The structure or table cannot be enhanced.

- **Can be enhanced or character type**
  Structure and tables can be enhanced, but these components and their enhancements must be of character type (C, N, D, or T). Customizing includes and append structures of the original table or structure are also subject to this limitation.

- **Can be enhanced or character type or numeric**
  The structure or table and its enhancement can contain character or numeric data types, but they cannot contain deep data types such as tables types, references, and strings.

- **Can be enhanced in any way**
  The structure or table and its enhancement can contain components whose data type can be of any type.

- **Not classified**
  This value is used if you do not want to classify the enhancement category. This category can be chosen for a transition status. However, it must not be chosen for creating structures.

Let us discuss the rules for defining the enhancement category.

1. If the object contains at least one numeric type or its substructure or component (in which the field has a structure/table/view as its type) is marked as CAN BE ENHANCED NUMERICALLY, you cannot enhance the object by character-type value. In this case, the object should be enhanced using character-type or number-type value.

2. If the object contains at least one deep structure component (strings, references, or table types) or its substructure or component is marked as CAN BE ENHANCED IN ANY TYPE, you cannot enhance the object by the CAN BE ENHANCED OR CHARACTER-TYPE OR NUMERIC value. In this case, the object should be enhanced using CAN BE ENHANCED IN ANY WAY.

3. If the object does not contain any substructure or component with value CAN BE ENHANCED, you have to select the CANNOT BE ENHANCED value. If the structure has not yet been enhanced, you can choose the category CANNOT BE ENHANCED.

Now, let us discuss both enhancement methods in detail.

Append Structures

Append structures are used to enhance tables and structures by adding dictionary components to the tables and structures that are not included in the standard. An append structure is a structure that is assigned to exactly one table and structure. More than one append structure can be assigned to a particular table or structure. With append structures, you can perform the following enhancements:

- Insert new fields in the table or structure.
- Define foreign keys for fields of the table or structure that already exist.
- Attach search helps to the fields of the table or structure that already exist.

When a table or structure is activated, all the append structures attached to the tables are searched, and all the fields of these append structures are added to the table or structure and activated with the table or structure. If the append structure is created or changed, the table or structure attached with the append structure is also adjusted in the database along with the changes made by the append structure. Foreign keys and search-help attachments added in the append structures are also added to the table when it is activated. With the help of append structures, existing foreign keys of the appending objects cannot be changed. Only further foreign key relationship can be added.

The order of the fields in the ABAP Data Dictionary can differ from the order of the fields in the database. Adding fields in append structures does not result in a table conversion. Append structures are also impervious to upgrades provided by SAP. This is because append structures are created in the customer namespace. The field name in the append structure should begin with ZZ or YY, in order to prevent any name conflicts with a field inserted in the table by SAP. The new version of the standard table is imported after an upgrade. All the fields, foreign key definitions, and search help attachments present in the append structures are also added to the updated standard table during activation (see Figure 5.57).

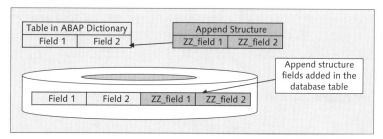

Figure 5.57 Append Structure Fields Added in the Database

Let us discuss some important points related to append structures.

▶ An append structure can be assigned to only one table or structure. If you want to add the same fields to more than one table or structure, add those fields in an include structure. Create append structures for all the tables and structures separately and attach that include to the append structure.

▶ Append structures are always added at the end of the tables or structures. If a table contains a long field (VARC, LCHR, or LRAW), append structures cannot be added to the tables. This is because long fields must always be the last field in the table. However, structures containing long fields can be enhanced with the help of append structures.

▶ If a table or structure containing an append structure is copied to another table, the fields of the append structure become the fields of the target table. Foreign key definitions and search-help attachments present in the append structure are also copied to the target table.

▶ Indexes on the append structures must be defined in the original table.

▶ If you want to insert any field that is a part of a new release, you must include that field as a repair in the customer system. If you include such a field in an append structure, it occurs twice when the new standard table is imported, and this results in an activation error.

Follow this procedure when adding an append structure to a table:

1. Go to the maintenance screen of the table in change mode where you want to add the append structure. If the table contains a long field (data type VARC, LCHR, LRAW), you cannot add an append structure to that table.

2. Click on the APPEND STRUCTURE button or follow the menu path GOTO • APPEND STRUCTURES. While creating the append structure for the first time for a particular table, you will get an informational message pop-up.

3. Click on the checkmark to create a new append structure. Write the name of the new append structure and press the checkmark (see Figure 5.58). The name must lie in the customer namespace.

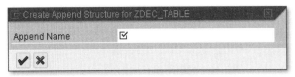

Figure 5.58 Creating Append Structures

4. Goto the maintenance screen of the Append structure. Enter the short text (see Figure 5.59).

5. Define the fields of the append structure. The field of an append structure must lie in the customer namespace; that is, the field name must begin with ZZ or YY. Like other includes and structures, append structures must be flat. This means that append structure fields either refer to a data element directly or are assigned to predefined data types, lengths, decimal places, and short texts. Field names should be shorter than 16 places while adding append structures to tables; otherwise, you get an activation error while activating the append structure (see Figure 5.60). This is because table fields can be no longer than 16 characters.

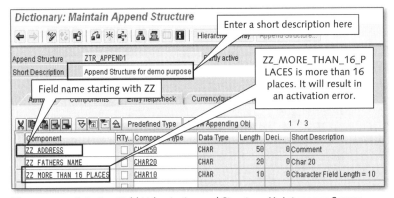

Figure 5.59 Entering Field Value in Append Structure Maintenance Screen

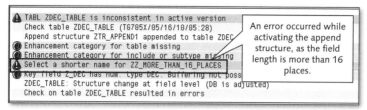

Figure 5.60 Error Occurred while Activating Append Structure

6. If the INITIAL VALUES flag is set, newly added fields (through append structures) in the table will have initial values for the existing data records that are already present in the table. If this flag is not checked, existing data records will have null values in these newly added fields and it may cause some data inconsistency while selecting the records (see Figure 5.61). You can switch on the INITIAL VALUES flag by using the path DB ATTRIBUTES • INITIALIZATION FLAG ON/OFF.

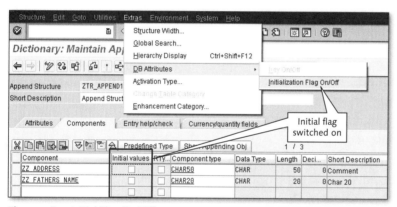

Figure 5.61 Initial Flag On/Off

7. To create foreign keys or search-help attachments for existing table fields, click on SHOW/HIDE APPENDING OBJECTS and then on ENTRY/HELP CHECK. Create the foreign key or search help. You cannot change the definition of the existing defined foreign key or search help with the append structure (Figure 5.62).

8. Click on the ACTIVATE icon and activate the append structure. The table will also be activated when the append structure is activated. The fields of the append structure are added to the table in the database. Foreign keys or search-help attachments for the fields that were defined by the append structure are also activated when the append structure is activated.

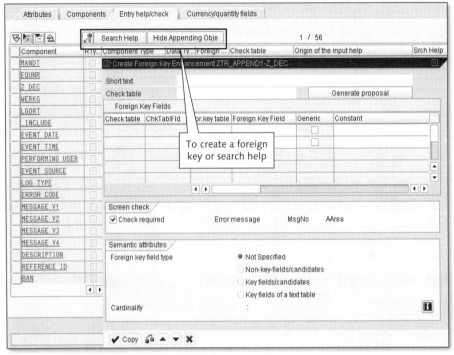

Figure 5.62 Adding Foreign Keys for Existing Table Fields

Customizing Includes

Customizing includes are structures with special naming conventions. Customizing includes are provided by SAP per business requirements, but the customer supplies the fields for the includes. A customizing include begins with CI. It is a part of a customer namespace. One customizing include can be inserted in more than one table. The customizing include is usually created in the customer system, and fields are added in it by special customizing transactions.

With the help of customizing includes, customers can enhance tables and structures without modifying the standard tables and structures. These enhancements are not lost if SAP upgrades the table. These fields are automatically inserted in the newly delivered tables and structures during an upgrade. For example, Table EQUI contains the customizing include CI_EQUI. If you add fields in customizing include CI_EQUI, fields are automatically added to Table EQUI and all other tables and structures where CI_EQUI is used.

The order of the field in the ABAP Data Dictionary can be different from the order of the fields in the database. Inserting fields in a customizing includes does not convert the table. The new fields are added to the database table.

You can add up to nine customizing includes in a custom table. Customizing includes can be considered the same as append structures provided by SAP. Customizing includes and append structures act in the same way at the database level.

5.2.7 Delivery Class

The delivery class controls the transport of table data when installing or upgrading in a client copy and when transporting between customer systems. The delivery class is also used in extended table maintenance. This means that the delivery class is responsible for transportation of data records. Delivery classes can have the following values:

- **A:** Application table (master and transaction data).
- **C:** Customer table. Data is maintained by the customer only.
- **L:** Table for storing temporary data.
- **G:** Customer table. SAP may insert new data records, but may not overwrite or delete existing data records. The customer namespace must be defined in Table TRESC.
- **E:** System table with its own namespaces for customer entries. The customer namespace must be defined in Table TRESC.
- **S:** System table. Data changes have the same status as program changes.
- **W:** System table (for example, table of the development environment). Data is transported with its own transport objects (such as R3TR PROG, or R3TR TABL).

Below we discuss the behavior of the delivery class in its different phases.

During Client Copy

Only the data of client-dependent tables is copied.

▸ **Classes C, G, E, and S**
If the client-dependent table has one of these values in the delivery class, the data records of the table are copied to the target client.

▸ **Classes W and L**
If the client-dependent table has one of these values in the delivery class, the data records of the table will not be copied to the target client.

▸ **Class A**
Data records are copied to the target client if explicitly requested with the parameter option. Normally, such data is not transported, but an entire client environment can be copied.

During Installation, Upgrade, and Language Import

The behavior of delivery classes differs for client-dependent and client-independent tables. Let us discuss both the cases.

Client-Dependent Tables
▸ **Classes A and C**
Data is only imported into client 000. Existing data records are overwritten.

▸ **Classes E, S, and W**
Data is imported into all clients. Existing data records are overwritten.

▸ **Class G**
Existing data records are overwritten in client 000. In all other clients, new data records are inserted but existing data records are not overwritten.

▸ **Class L**
No data is imported.

Client-Independent Tables
▸ **Classes A, L, and C**
No data is imported for these classes.

▸ **Classes E, S, and W**
Data is imported. Existing data records with the same key are overwritten.

▸ **Class G**
Data records that do not exist are inserted, but existing data records are not overwritten.

During Transport Between Customer Systems

▶ **Class L**
Data records of tables are not imported into the target system.

▶ **Class A, C, E, G, S, and W**
Data records of tables of delivery classes A, C, E, G, S, and W are imported into the target system. This is done for the target client specified in the transport for client-dependent tables.

Use of Delivery Class in Extended Table Maintenance

The delivery class is also analyzed in extended table maintenance (Transaction SM30). The maintenance interface generated for a table makes the following checks:

▶ For delivery class W and L, you cannot transport the data that is entered by the transport link of the generated maintenance interface.

▶ When the data is entered, the namespace of the table is checked with the namespace defined in Table TRESC. The input is rejected if the data violates the namespace.

5.2.8   Activation Types

The activation type checks whether the table is activated directly from the ABAP Data Dictionary or whether its runtime object is generated first with a C-language program. The activation type is optional and only important for tables of the runtime environment. The activation type can have one of the following values:

▶ **00**
Tables with activation type value as 00 can be activated directly from the ABAP Data Dictionary. This is the default setting for the activation type.

▶ **01**
Tables with activation type value 01 cannot be activated directly from the ABAP Data Dictionary. The runtime object first must be generated using a C program, and then the table can only be activated from the ABAP Data Dictionary. This activation type ensures that important system tables cannot be changed and activated directly.

▶ **02**
  Tables with activation type value 02 are also used in C programs. When the table is changed, the data structure must be adjusted manually. The activation log for such a table contains relevant comments.

▶ **10**
  Tables with activation type value 10 are needed before R3TRANS runs. Such tables must exist before all other tables when upgrading. R3TRANS is a SAP transport program used to transport data between SAP systems and for data migration between different SAP releases. However, R3TRANS is usually called from other programs, generally from TP (transport control program) and R3UP (upgrade control program).

5.2.9 Data Browser/Table View Maintenance

A table can be displayed or maintained in MAINTENANCE TOOLS DATA BROWSER (Transaction SE16), in TABLE VIEW MAINTENANCE (Transaction SM30 and SM31), and in ABAP DICTIONARY INITIAL SCREEN (Transaction SE11). This indicator specifies whether a table can be displayed and maintained in these transactions. This indicator can be set for tables, database views, projection views, maintenance views, and maintenance view variants using Transaction SE11. This indicator is not available for help views because help views are used for search functions and are not relevant to Transaction SE54. The indicator can have one of the following values:

▶ DISPLAY/MAINTENANCE NOT ALLOWED (N)
  Maintenance of a dictionary object is not allowed with standard table maintenance tools. Transaction SE16 does not allow maintenance and display of the dictionary object. Transaction SE54 does not allow generation of the maintenance dialog for the dictionary objects. This means that Transactions SM30 and SM34 cannot be called for the dictionary object.

▶ DISPLAY/MAINTENANCE ALLOWED WITH RESTRICTIONS
  Maintenance of a dictionary object is allowed with standard table maintenance tools to a limited extent. Transaction SE16 allows the display function, but restricts the maintenance function for the dictionary objects. Transaction SE54 allows generation of the maintenance dialog for the dictionary objects. Transaction SM30 does not allow maintenance and display functions for the dictionary objects.

▶ DISPLAY/MAINTENANCE ALLOWED (X)
  Maintenance of a dictionary object is allowed with standard table maintenance

tools. Transaction SE16 enables use of the display and maintenance function for the dictionary objects. Transaction SE54 allows the generation of the maintenance dialog for the dictionary objects. Transaction SM30 allows the maintenance and display function for the dictionary objects.

The message DISPLAY/MAINTENANCE NOT ALLOWED (N) does not apply for maintenance views and maintenance view variants. This is because the maintenance views and maintenance view variants are used exclusively to generate user interfaces.

The generated dialog can also be included in the view cluster (Transaction SM34, View Cluster Maintenance) or can be called through the function module View_Maintenance_Call in the same way as it is called in Transaction SM30.

5.3   Creating Tables

In our previous sections, we have discussed the components of tables in detail. It's now time to discuss how these components fit in the table definition and how we can create a transparent table. Let us discuss the procedure for creating a table.

1. In the initial screen of ABAP Data Dictionary, select the radio button DATABASE TABLE. Enter the name of the table you want to create. The name of the database table should start with Z or Y. Press the CREATE button (see Figure 5.63).

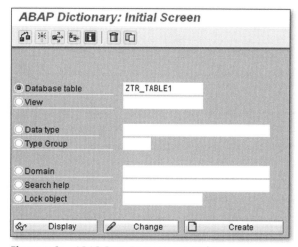

Figure 5.63   ABAP Data Dictionary: Initial Screen

2. Enter the short description in the maintenance screen of the table. This short text acts as the explanatory text when F1 help or list is generated. This is a mandatory attribute, and you cannot enter any other attribute without entering this one.

3. In the DELIVERY AND MAINTENANCE tab, enter the DELIVERY CLASS of the table. If you use F4 help on the DELIVERY CLASS field, you will get the list of delivery class values. Enter the appropriate value in the DATA BROWER/TABLE VIEW MAINTENANCE field. If you click on this field, a dropdown list will appear (see Figure 5.64).

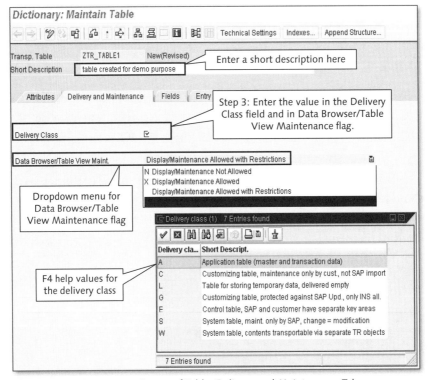

Figure 5.64 Maintenance Screen of Table: Delivery and Maintenance Tab

4. On the FIELDS tab, enter the table fields. Enter the name of the field in the column FIELDS. The field name may only contain letters, digits, and underscores, and must start with a letter. The field name in a table can be up to 16 places long.

5. Select the KEY column and INITIAL VALUE column if the field is a key field for a table and you want the field filled with initial values when left blank. All the

key fields must be placed together at the beginning of the table. Otherwise, you get an error during activation.

6. Enter the name of the data element in the DATA ELEMENT field. DATA TYPE, LENGTH, NO OF DECIMAL PLACES, and SHORT DESCRIPTION will automatically be populated when Enter is pressed after entering field type (see Figure 5.65). If you double-click on the data element, you will be directed to the DATA ELEMENT: MAINTENANCE SCREEN. If the data element entered by you in the table field does not exist, you can create the data element by double-clicking on the data element. If you click on the PREDEFINED TYPE button, your table field will not be assigned to the data element. In this case, you have to enter the DATA TYPE, LENGTH, DECIMAL PLACES, and SHORT DESCRIPTION manually. However, no foreign keys, fixed values, or F1 help are available for such manually defined fields.You can also include the fields of the existing structure in the table. The field name in the structure should not be longer than 16 places.

7. Define the reference field and reference table for currency (CURR) or quantity (QUAN) fields in the CURRENCY/QUANTITY FIELDS tab.

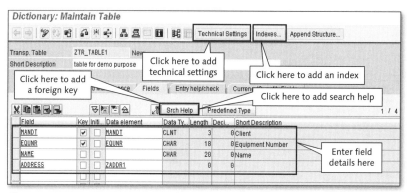

Figure 5.65 Maintenance Screen of Table: Fields Tab

8. Maintain the technical settings for the table. You can maintain the technical settings either by clicking on the TECHNICAL SETTINGS button or by following the menu path GOTO • TECHNICAL SETTING. Technical settings are used as a separate object. Settings can be activated and transported separately from the table. We discuss maintaining technical settings in an upcoming section.

9. Create the foreign key if required with the FOREIGN KEY (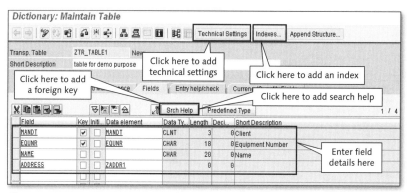) icon. The foreign key will define the relationship between the tables. We discuss creating foreign keys in detail in an upcoming section.

10. Create the search help for the fields if required with the SEARCH HELP button. Further on, we discuss creating search help and assigning search help with table and table fields.
11. Create a secondary index for the table. Click on the INDEXES button or follow the path GOTO • INDEXES to create the secondary indexes. We discuss creating secondary indexes in detail in an upcoming section.
12. Save the table. A dialog box will appear asking for the development class.
13. Activate the table by choosing the ACTIVATE icon. During activation, the table and all the indexes on the table will automatically be created in the database.

5.3.1 Options when Creating Tables

When creating tables, many other options are also available, including runtime objects, database objects, activation logs, documentation, and more. Let us discuss these options one by one.

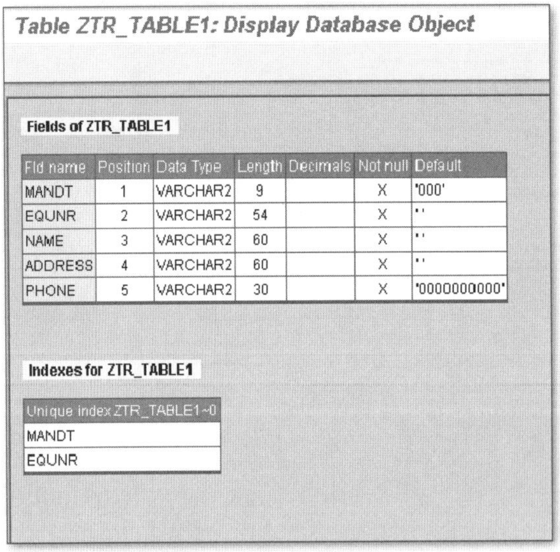

Table ZTR_TABLE1: Display Database Object

Fields of ZTR_TABLE1

Fld name	Position	Data Type	Length	Decimals	Not null	Default
MANDT	1	VARCHAR2	9		X	'000'
EQUNR	2	VARCHAR2	54		X	' '
NAME	3	VARCHAR2	60		X	' '
ADDRESS	4	VARCHAR2	60		X	' '
PHONE	5	VARCHAR2	30		X	'0000000000'

Indexes for ZTR_TABLE1

Unique index ZTR_TABLE1~0
MANDT
EQUNR

Figure 5.66 Display: Database Object

Database Objects

You can display the definition of views created in the database by following the menu path UTILITIES • DATABASE OBJECT • DISPLAY (see Figure 5.66). By following menu path UTILITIES • DATABASE OBJECT • CHECK you can check whether the definitions of views in the database are consistent with the active versions of the views.

Runtime Objects

During activation, the runtime object for the table is also created. You can display the runtime object by following menu path UTILITIES • RUNTIME OBJECT • DISPLAY (see Figure 5.67). With UTILITIES • RUNTIME OBJECT • CHECK, you can check whether the definition of views in the ABAP Data Dictionary maintenance screen is consistent with the specifications of the runtime objects of the views.

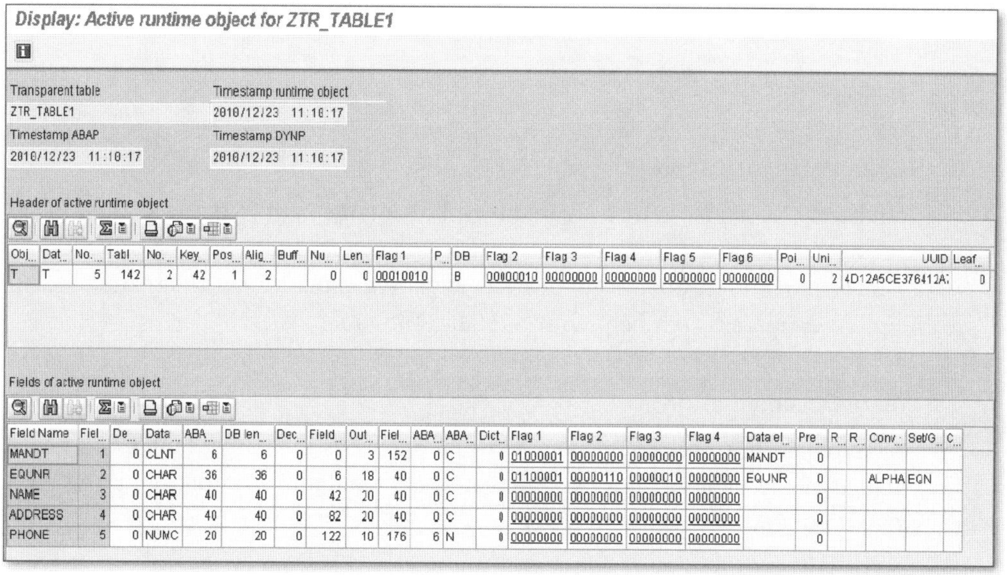

Figure 5.67 Display: Runtime Object

Activation Log

The activation log will give you the activation flow information. All the warning and error messages will be displayed in the activation log. The activation log will be automatically displayed if errors occur during activation. The activation log can be found at UTILITIES • ACTIVATION LOG (see Figure 5.68).

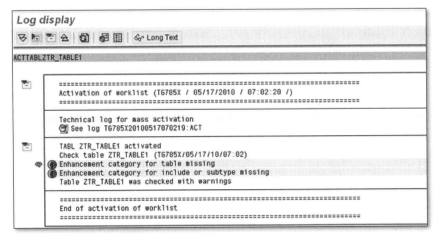

Figure 5.68 Activation Log

Search Helps for a Table

Search help for a table can be created by following the path Extras • Search helps for table. This search help can be used for all the screen fields that are checked against the table. In Chapter 9, Search Helps, we explain how to create a search help and assign a search help with the table and table fields.

Create Documentation

Documentation is used to create a text that describes the use of tables and maintenance of the table data. You can create documentation by following the path Goto • Documentation.

Assign Activation Type

Activation type can be assigned to the table by following the path Extras • Activation type. This option is relevant for the tables in the runtime environment.

Enter or Display Data

If the Table Maintenance field has the value Table maintenance allowed, you can maintain and create new entries to the table by following the path Utilities • Table contents • Create entries. You can also display the table entries with Utilities • Table contents • Display.

Points to Remember

▸ All the key fields of the table must be stored together at the beginning of the table. A non-key field should not come between the key fields.

▸ A maximum of 16 key fields for a table is permitted. A field name cannot exceed 16 places. The length of key fields cannot exceed 255 places.

▸ The key can have a maximum length of 120 places in a transport. If the key is larger than 120 places, table entries should be transported generically.

▸ A table can have a maximum of 249 fields. The sum of the length of the field cannot exceed 1,962 places. However, this does not include fields with data types LRAW and LCHR.

▸ Long fields such as LRAW and LCHR must be present at the end of the table. Long fields should be preceded by fields of data type INT2. Only one long field is allowed per table.

5.3.2 Maintaining Technical Settings

The technical settings of a table define how the table will be created in the database. As discussed, technical settings defines the data class, size category, buffering, log changes, etc. Let us discuss the procedure for maintaining technical settings.

1. Click on the TECHNICAL SETTINGS button in the maintenance screen of the table. The maintenance screen of the technical settings will appear.

2. Select the DATA CLASS and SIZE CATEGORY of the table. You can choose input help for both data class and size category (see Figure 5.69). Enter the appropriate value.

3. In the BUFFERING block, define whether you want to buffer the table in the application server buffer. If you switched on the buffering, define the buffering type (SINGLE RECORD, GENERIC, or FULL).

4. Select the LOG DATA CHANGES flag if you want to maintain the log history of the data records whenever data records are changed. If you want to log the changes, the profile parameter value (REC/CLIENT) must be switched on for that client. This is because log data flag does not log the changes on its own.

5. Select the WRITE ACCESS ONLY TO JAVA flag if you want that table content to be changed only within JAVA.

6. The CONVERT TO TRANSPARENT TABLE flag will appear for pooled tables and for the tables already converted to the transparent table with this flag. You can convert the pooled table to the transparent table with this flag.

7. Save and activate the technical settings with the ACTIVATE icon.

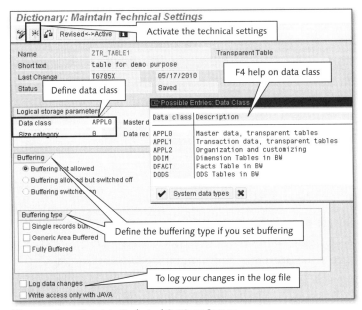

Figure 5.69 Maintain Technical Settings Screen

Points to Remember

▸ If the key length of the table is larger than 64, the table cannot be buffered generically.

▸ If the key length of the table is larger than 120, the table cannot be buffered.

▸ If the key length of the table is larger than 86 places or data stored in the table is larger than 500 places, you cannot log the table.

5.3.3 Creating Foreign Keys

As discussed, foreign keys describe the relationship between the tables in the ABAP Data Dictionary. Foreign keys can also be used to create value checks for the input fields. Let us discuss the creation of foreign keys.

1. In the maintenance screen of the table, click on the check field (the field for which you want a foreign key relation), and then click on the FOREIGN KEY icon (see Figure 5.70). If the domain of the check field has a value table assigned to it, the system generates a proposal and assigns a value table as a check table. A proposal is made for field assignment in the foreign key.

2. If the domain does not contain any value table or if you reject the proposal, you have to write the check table and save the entry. The check table must have a key field to which the check table of the field is assigned.

3. After giving the check table name, the system generates the proposal for assigning a foreign key with the check table key field. This assignment takes place if the domains of the check table key field and foreign key field are the same. If you don't want the proposal, the key fields of the check table are listed and you must assign them to a suitable field of the foreign key table.

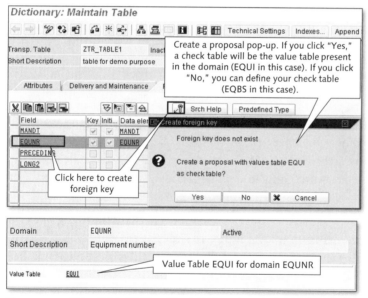

Figure 5.70 Value Table EQUI as Check Table in Proposal Pop-up

4. Enter the explanatory short text for the foreign key in the SHORT TEXT field. This short text will provide documentation for the meaning of the foreign key (see Figure 5.71).

5. You can also remove the key fields of the check table from assignment (with an exception of check field). Sometimes the check table contains more than one

key field. You do not have to assign all the key fields of the check table to any key field of the foreign key table. You can make those check table fields generic or constant foreign key fields. In both the cases, you must remove the entries in the FOREIGN KEY TABLE field and FOREIGN KEY FIELD field.

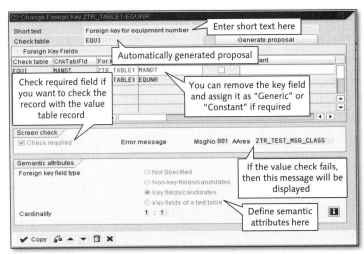

Figure 5.71 Steps for Creating Foreign Key (EQUI is Proposed Check Table)

6. You can activate or deactivate the CHECK REQUIRED flag. If you don't want the foreign key used for value checking, uncheck the flag value. This check is significant for all the screens in which the field appears. We advise deactivating this check if the field is used only to define maintenance views, help views, or lock objects.

7. You can assign a user-defined message. If the value check by the foreign key on the screen field results in an invalid input, this message is displayed. This can be done by defining the message class in the AAREA field and message number in the MSGNO field.

8. You can assign the semantic attributes to the foreign key. In semantic attributes, you can define the foreign key type and cardinality. This is for documentation purposes.

9. Click on the COPY button. The foreign key is saved and you are returned to the maintenance screen for the table.

5.3.4 Creating Secondary Indexes

Let us discuss the procedure for creating secondary indexes.

1. In the maintenance screen of the table, choose INDEXES or follow the path GOTO • INDEXES. You get a pop-up. Click on the CREATE (⬜🗏) button to create an index. You can either create a secondary index or extended secondary index (see Figure 5.72).

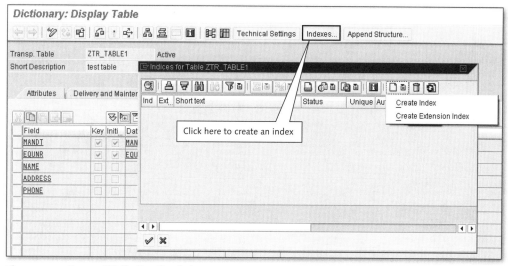

Figure 5.72 Pop-up While Creating Index

2. In the next pop-up, enter the index name. Click on the checkmark (see Figure 5.73). The maintenance screen of the index appears.

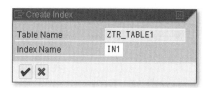

Figure 5.73 Dialog Box for Entering Index ID

3. Enter explanatory text in the SHORT DESCRIPTION field. You can identify your index and its function later by referring to the short text (see Figure 5.74).

4. Enter the field name in the FIELD NAME area for which you want to create the index. If you click on the TABLE FIELD button, all the fields present in the table appears. You can select the fields for the index.

5. If the index uniquely identifies the record, you can select the UNIQUE INDEX radio button. If your index is a unique index, the index field cannot have a duplicate value.

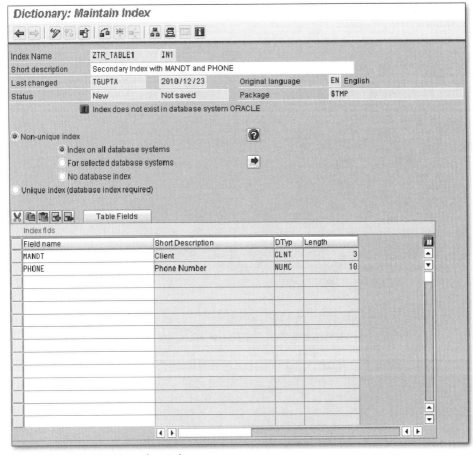

Figure 5.74 Creating Secondary Index

6. If the index is a non-unique index, select the database for which you want to create your index. If you click on FOR SELECTED DATABASE SYSTEMS, you need to define the databases. This can be done by clicking on the arrow (➡) icon to the right of the radio button. Once you click it, you see a dialog box in which you

can define the database systems (see Figure 5.75). Select SELECTION LIST if the index should be created on the given database systems. Select EXCLUSION LIST if the index should not be created on the given database. Choose the checkmark icon.

7. Activate the index by clicking on the ACTIVATE icon.

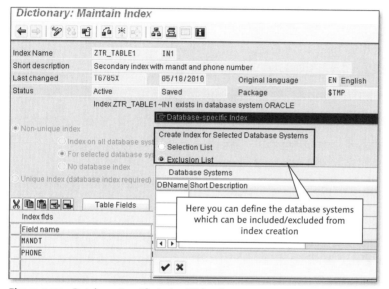

Figure 5.75 Database-Specific Index Dialog Box

Extended Index

Extended indexes are similar to normal secondary indexes. The only difference is that when an extended index is created, the relevant table remains unchanged. Extended indexes are automatically copied over extensions and upgrades. No modifications are required with the extended index. We suggest creating an extended index for the standard tables so that they are not lost during any SAP upgrade.

5.4 Changing Tables

Let us discuss the procedure for changing tables.

1. Enter the name of the table in the initial screen of the ABAP Data Dictionary, Transaction SE11, and click on the CHANGE button. You will be directed to the

maintenance screen of the table. You can perform the following changes in the database table.

▶ Adding append structures: We have already explained how to add append structures (see Section 5.2.6).

▶ Adding includes: We have already discussed how to add includes (see Section 5.2.2).

▶ Inserting new fields: We discuss this in an upcoming section.

▶ Deleting existing fields: We discuss this below.

▶ Changing existing fields: We discuss this below.

▶ Changing table categories: We discuss this below.

▶ Moving fields: We discuss this below.

▶ Copying fields from another table: We discuss this below.

5.4.1 Inserting New Fields

Let us discuss the procedure for inserting new fields in a table.

1. In the maintenance screen of the table, place the cursor on the field where you want to insert a new field. Click on the INSERT ROW (🖼) button to insert a new row (see Figure 5.76).

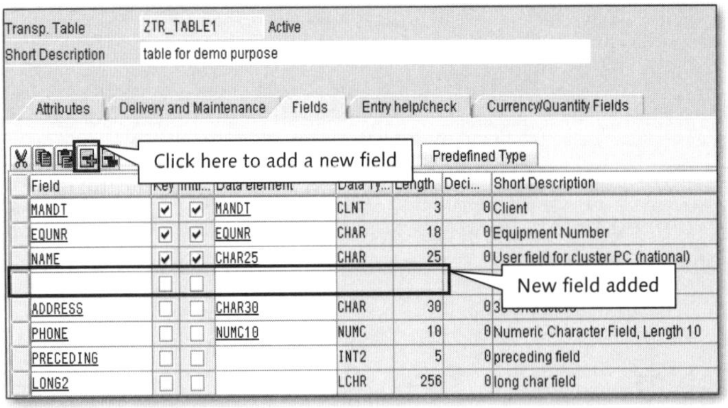

Figure 5.76 Inserting New Fields

2. An empty line appears, where you enter the values for FIELD, KEY, INITIAL FLAG, and DATA ELEMENT for the newly-added field. If you click on the KEY flag then that field is placed just after the other key field of the table. If you check the INITIAL

flag, the new field is created in the database as NOT NULL. The entire table is scanned during activation and the new field will be filled with the initial values. This is very time-consuming process for tables that have many data entries.

3. Activate the table by clicking on the ACTIVATE icon.

Points to Remember

▶ The order of the fields in the ABAP Data Dictionary can differ from the order of the fields in the database.

▶ If new key field is added to the check table, the concerned foreign key will be automatically defined as a generic key with regard to the new key field. The foreign key changed in this way is listed in the activation log. For example, Table ZTR_TABLE1 is a check table for foreign key field EQUNR of Table ZTR_TABLE2. If a key field name is added to the check Table ZTR_TABLE1, the name field will automatically become a generic key in the foreign key relationship for field EQUNR in Table Ztr_table2 (see Figure 5.77).

▶ If a client field is inserted, a table is converted. An entry is added in client Table T000. If the table is a check table of a foreign key, you cannot insert the client field. In this case you must delete the existing foreign key.

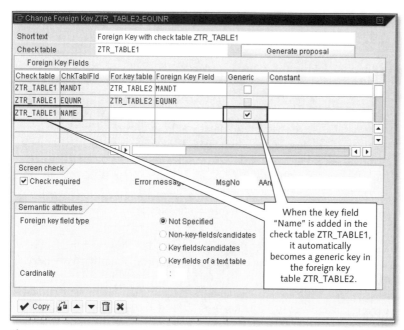

Figure 5.77 Foreign Key Automatically Changes with Insertion of Key Field in Check Table

5.4.2 Deleting Existing Fields

Let us discuss how to delete fields from the table.

1. In the maintenance screen of the table, place the cursor on the field that you want to delete. Click on the DELETE ROW (⊟) button to delete a row (see Figure 5.78).

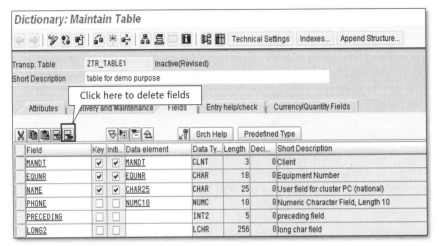

Figure 5.78 Deleting Existing Fields

2. Activate the table by clicking the ACTIVATE icon.

Points to Remember

▸ If the table in the database already contains data, you have to convert the table after deleting existing table fields from Transaction SE14. If you delete any field, your data may be lost. If the table contains data records that differ in only the deleted key field, only one of the data records can be restored.

▸ You cannot delete a field that is used as a reference field in another table. You have to remove the reference field from the referred table; only then can you can delete that field.

▸ If the table is a check table, you cannot delete the key field of the table. In this case, you first have to delete the corresponding foreign key. You can identify all the tables that are using a particular table as a check table or reference table with the help of the WHERE-USED LIST(⬚) icon. For example, as discussed in the above example, ZTR_TABLE1 is a check table for ZTR_TABLE2. If the key field NAME is deleted from the check table, you get an error message in the activation log stating that the primary key change is not permitted for the value Table ZTR_TABLE1 (see Figure 5.79).

To activate Table ZTR_TABLE1, you have to delete the foreign key relationship in foreign key Table ZTR_TABLE2.

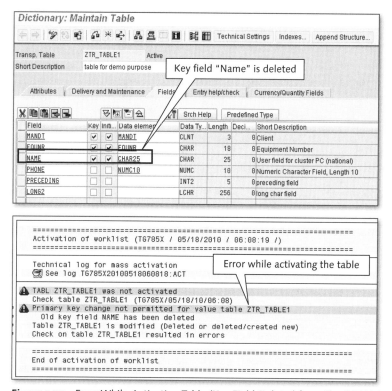

Figure 5.79 Error While Activating Table (Key Field Deleted from Check Table)

5.4.3 Changing Existing Fields

Let us discuss the procedure for changing fields that are assigned to data elements. If the field is assigned to the data element, you must change the technical settings of the field by changing the corresponding domain.

1. Double-click on the data element of the field you want to change.

2. Double-click on the corresponding domain of the data element.

3. Change the domain by clicking CHANGE/DISPLAY or pressing $\boxed{\text{Ctrl}}$+$\boxed{\text{F1}}$.

4. Activate the table by clicking on the ACTIVATE icon.

> **Note**
>
> If the domain is changed, you may need to convert the tables (fields refer to the domain). The conversion process is very time-consuming for tables containing many records. The foreign key might also become inconsistent in such tables and structures. It is always preferable to check where the domain is used by performing a where-used list. Do this by clicking on the WHERE-USED LIST icon before changing the domain.

Let us discuss the procedure for changing the fields that are assigned to a predefined type.

1. Click on the PREDEFINED TYPE button.

2. Change the entries of the predefined type field. You can change the DATA TYPE, LENGTH, NO OF DECIMAL PLACES, and SHORT TEXT fields.

3. Activate the table by clicking on the ACTIVATE icon.

Changing the attributes of the existing field may result in table conversion.

5.4.4 Changing Table Category

Transparent tables can be changed to one of the following objects:

▶ **Transparent to structure**
The table is deleted from the table at activation. All the data records are deleted. Technical settings are lost.

▶ **Transparent to pooled/cluster**
A table pool or table cluster must be assigned for storing the data after the conversion.

▶ **Pooled/cluster to transparent**
Because technical settings do not apply to the pooled/cluster table, you must maintain the technical settings after converting the pooled table to the transparent table and before activating the transparent table.

Let us discuss the procedure for changing table categories.

1. In the maintenance field of the table, follow the menu path EXTRAS • CHANGE TABLE CATEGORY. A dialog box appears in which the current category is checked (see Figure 5.80).

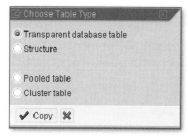

Figure 5.80 Pop-up to Change Table Category

2. Choose the table type category and click on the COPY button.

3. Activate the table by clicking on the ACTIVATE icon.

Changing the pooled/cluster table to a transparent table and vice versa always results in a table conversion.

5.4.5 Moving Fields

Let us discuss the procedure for moving fields.

1. Place the cursor on the field that you want to move.

2. Click on the CUT (✂) button. The selected field is deleted and copied to the clipboard. For example, you might place the cursor on the CURRENCY field and click on the CUT button (see Figure 5.81).

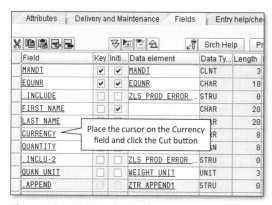

Figure 5.81 Cutting the Field

3. Place the cursor on the field where you want to move the field from the clipboard. Click on the PASTE (📋) button. The selected field is pasted to the new

position. For example, the CURRENCY field is pasted to the new position (above the QUAN_UNIT field) (see Figure 5.82).

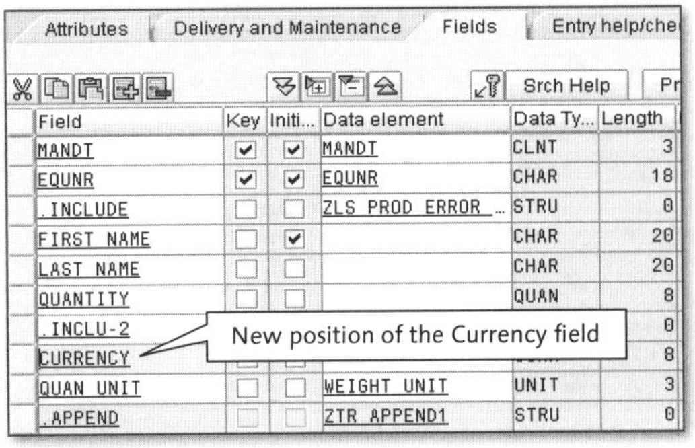

Figure 5.82 Pasting the Field

The order of the fields in the ABAP Data Dictionary can differ from the order of the fields in the database. Thus, changing the order of fields does not result in the conversion of the database table. You cannot change the order of the key fields for the check table. In this case, first delete the corresponding foreign key.

5.4.6 Copying Fields from Another Table

Let us discuss the process for copying fields from another table.

1. Go to the menu path EDIT • TRANSFER FIELDS from the FIELDS tab of the maintenance screen of the table (see Figure 5.83).

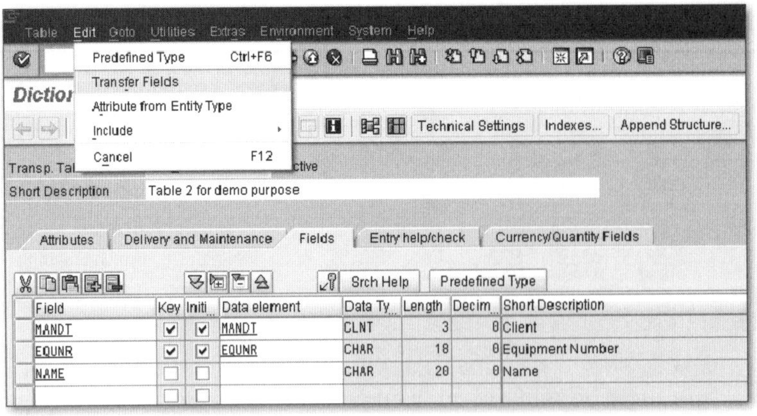

Figure 5.83 Path to Copy Field of Existing Table/Structure

2. Enter the name of structure or table from which you want to copy the field. If you want to copy all the fields, click on the COPY ALL button. If you want to copy only selected fields, click on the SELECTION button (see Figure 5.84).

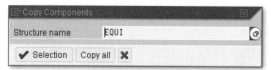

Figure 5.84 Structure/Table Name from Which Fields are Copied

3. Select the fields you want to copy by checking the checkbox. Press the COPY button after selecting the fields. All the selected fields are copied to the clipboard (see Figure 5.85).

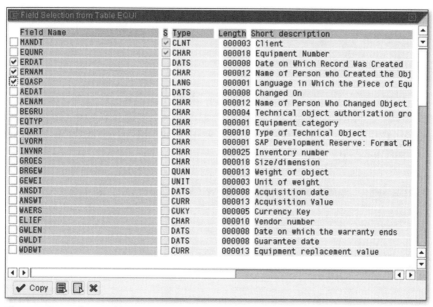

Figure 5.85 Select Fields to be Copied

4. Place the cursor on the field where you want to place the fields from the clipboard. Click on the PASTE button. The selected field is pasted to the new position. For example, selected fields ERDAT, ERNAM, and EQASP are copied to the new position (see Figure 5.86).

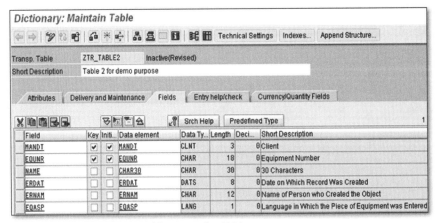

Figure 5.86 Fields are Copied from Another Table

5. Activate the table by clicking on the ACTIVATE icon.

5.5 Deleting Tables

A table can only be deleted if it is not used by objects such as programs or views. Before deleting the table, first check the where-used list by clicking on the WHERE-USED LIST icon. If the table is already in use, you get a pop-up telling you that the table is still in use (see Figure 5.87).

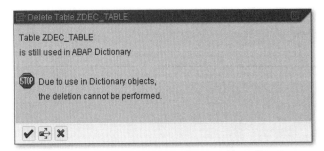

Figure 5.87 Error Message while Deleting Table Still in Use

Let us discuss the procedure for deleting the table.

1. In the initial screen of the ABAP Data Dictionary, Transaction SE11, select the DATABASE TABLES radio button and enter the name of the table. Check if the table is still in use by clicking on the WHERE-USED LIST icon.

2. If the table is not used by any other objects, click on the DELETE icon (🗑). A dialog box appears that asks for confirmation. If you press YES, your table is deleted, provided it is not used by any other objects (see Figure 5.88).

Figure 5.88 Dialog Box for Confirmation of Table Deletion Request

5.6 Creating Other Dictionary Objects

As discussed in Section 5.1, tables can be divided into three categories: transparent tables, pooled tables, and cluster tables. Transparent tables define one to one relationships with the database table. Pooled or cluster tables define many to one relationships with the database table. Data from several pool or cluster tables are grouped together and stored in one table pool or table cluster, respectively. We have already discussed creating transparent tables in Section 5.6; in this section we will discuss how to create table pools, table clusters, pool tables, and cluster tables.

5.6.1 Creating Table Pools

Data from several pool tables are grouped together into one table pool, which is then created in the database. Table pools and table clusters are used to store internal control information such as screen sequences, documentation, temporary data, and program parameters. Let us discuss the procedure for creating table pools.

1. In the initial screen of the ABAP Data Dictionary (Transaction SE11), follow the path UTILITIES • OTHER DICTIONARY OBJECTS (see Figure 5.89).

Figure 5.89 Creating Other Dictionary Objects

2. Select the table pool/cluster in the pop-up. Enter the name of the table pool. Press the CREATE button (see Figure 5.90).

Figure 5.90 Pop-up for Table Pool/Cluster

3. A dialog box appears in which you have to specify the table pool object (see Figure 5.91).

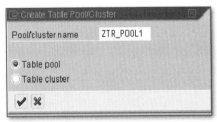

Figure 5.91 Pop-up for Selecting Object from Table Pool or Table Cluster

4. The maintenance screen for the table pool appears. Because table pools have a fixed structure, necessary entries are automatically displayed for the table pool. Try not to change these standard settings (see Figure 5.92).

5. Enter the explanatory text under the SHORT DESCRIPTION field.

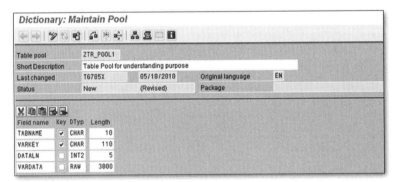

Figure 5.92 Maintenance Screen of Table Pool

6. Select the activation type of the table pool from the path UTILITIES • ACTIVATION TYPE (see Figure 5.93).

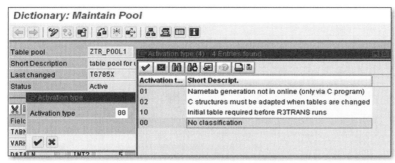

Figure 5.93 Activation Type Value for Table Pool

7. Maintain the technical settings of the table pool from the path GOTO • TECHNICAL SETTINGS. In the technical settings of the table pool you can only define the SIZE CATEGORY of the table pool. All other technical settings are predefined (see Figure 5.94).

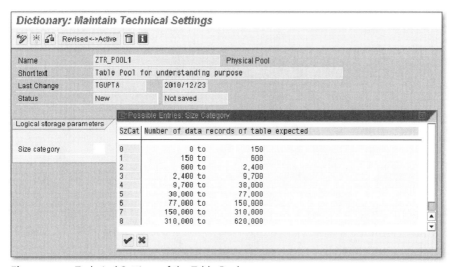

Figure 5.94 Technical Settings of the Table Pool

8. You can also create the documentation of the table pool with the path GOTO • DOCUMENTATION. This document is printed when the table pool is printed.

9. Activate the table pool by clicking on the ACTIVATE icon. Once the table pool is activated in the ABAP Data Dictionary, check if it is also created in the database. If not, you need to create it in the database. To do this, follow the path UTILI-TIES • DATABASE OBJECT • DATABASE UTILITY or go to Transaction SE14 (ABAP Dictionary: Database Utility).

5.6.2 Creating Table Clusters

Table clusters are similar to table pools, but have different structures. Data from several cluster tables are grouped together into one table cluster, and this table cluster is then created in the database. Table pools and table clusters are used to store internal control information like screen sequences, documentation, temporary data, and program parameters. Let us discuss the procedure for creating table clusters.

In the initial screen of ABAP Data Dictionary (Transaction SE11), follow the path UTILITIES • OTHER DICTIONARY OBJECTS (see Figure 5.89 earlier in this chapter).

1. Select the TABLE POOL/CLUSTER in the pop-up. Enter the name of the TABLE CLUSTER. Press the CREATE button (see Figure 5.90).

2. A dialog box appears in which you have to specify the TABLE CLUSTER object (see Figure 5.95).

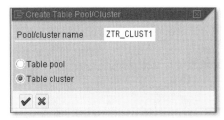

Figure 5.95 Pop-up for Selecting Objects from Table Pools or Table Clusters

3. The maintenance screen for the table cluster appears. Because table clusters have fixed structures, necessary entries are automatically proposed for the table cluster. You can adjust this proposal according to your requirements. You can add KEY fields to the table cluster. The total length of key fields should not exceed 120 places. However, make sure that you don't change the necessary structure of the table cluster (see Figure 5.96).

4. Enter the explanatory text under the SHORT DESCRIPTION field.

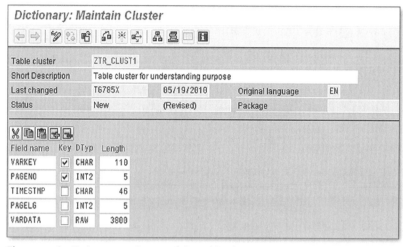

Figure 5.96 Maintenance Screen of the Table Cluster

5. Select the activation type of the table cluster from the path UTILITIES • ACTIVA-TION TYPE.

6. Maintain the technical settings of the table cluster from the path GOTO • TECHNICAL SETTINGS. In the technical settings of the table cluster, you can only define the size category of the table cluster. All other technical settings are predefined (see Figure 5.97).

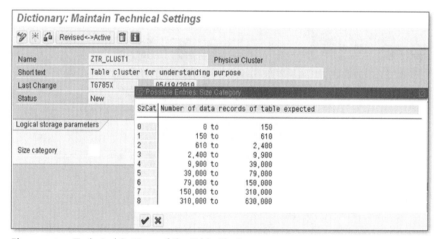

Figure 5.97 Technical Settings of the Table Cluster

7. You can also create the documentation of the table cluster with the path GOTO •
DOCUMENTATION. This document is printed when the table cluster is printed.

8. Activate the table cluster by clicking the ACTIVATE icon. Once it is activated in
the ABAP Data Dictionary, check if it is created in the database. If not, you need
to create it in the database. Do this by following the path UTILITIES • DATABASE
OBJECT • DATABASE UTILITY or go to Transaction SE14 (ABAP Dictionary: Database
Utility).

5.6.3 Creating Pooled Tables/Cluster Tables

Let us discuss the procedure for creating pooled/cluster tables.

To create a pooled or cluster table, follow the initial steps required to create a
transparent table (Section 5.6). In the initial screen of the ABAP Data Dictionary
(Transaction SE11), select the DATABASE TABLE radio button. Enter the name of the
table you want to create. Press the CREATE button.

1. Enter the SHORT DESCRIPTION on the maintenance screen of the table. This short
text acts as the explanatory text when F1 help or list is generated (see Figure
5.98).

2. Enter the values in the DELIVERY CLASS and DATA BROWSER/TABLE VIEW MAIN-
TENANCE fields.

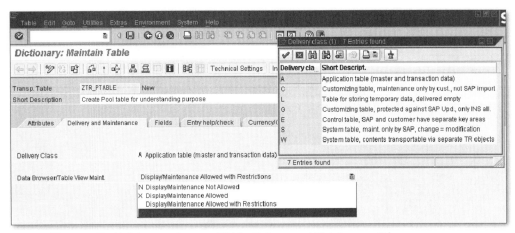

Figure 5.98 Maintenance Screen of Table: Delivery and Maintenance Tab

3. Go to EXTRA • CHANGE TABLE CATEGORY. Check the POOLED TABLE or CLUSTER TABLE value in the dialog box (see Figure 5.99). Choose the COPY button. You are returned to the table maintenance screen.

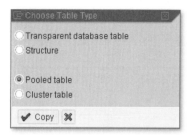

Figure 5.99 Dialog Box for Change Category

4. The new field TABLE POOL/CLUSTER is added to the DELIVERY AND MAINTENANCE tab. Enter the value of the table pool or table cluster to which you want to assign your pooled table or cluster table (see Figure 5.100). The total key length of a pooled table must not exceed the total key length of the associated table pool. The key of the cluster table must correspond to the key of the associated table cluster.

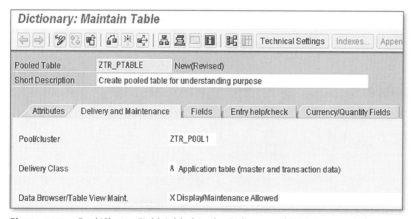

Figure 5.100 Pool/Cluster Field Added to the Delivery and Maintenance Tab

5. Proceed in the same way as when you created the transparent table. You cannot create the index for the pooled table or cluster table. This is because these tables are not directly created in the database. However, data from several pooled tables is stored in the table pool, which in turn is created in the database.

Points to Remember

The new field added to the pooled/cluster table will be automatically defined as NOT NULL. Hence, when the pooled/cluster table is activated, the complete table is scanned and the new fields are filled with the initial values. This can take time for tables having many data records. Unlike working with a transparent table, inserting new fields or making changes to the field sequence of the pooled/cluster table always results in a conversion of table. If the table pool or table cluster of the pooled/cluster table is changed, this also results in the table conversion. Pooled and cluster tables with more than 250 fields cannot be converted. New fields should always be added at the end of the table.

5.7   Deleting Other Dictionary Objects

In this section, we explain how to delete table pools and table clusters. You can delete the table pool or table cluster if it does not contain any pooled table or cluster table. We recommend performing a where-used list for a table pool or table cluster before deleting it.

1. In the initial screen of the ABAP Data Dictionary, follow the path UTILITIES • OTHER DICTIONARY OBJECTS (see Figure 5.89 earlier in this chapter).

2. Select the TABLE POOL/CLUSTER in the pop-up. Enter the name of the table pool/ cluster. Check whether it is used by any pooled/cluster table by clicking on the WHERE-USED LIST icon (see Figure 5.101).

Figure 5.101   Pop-up for Table Pool/Cluster

3. If it is not used by any pooled/cluster table, click on the DELETE icon. You get a pop-up. Confirm it by pressing YES (Figure 5.102).

Figure 5.102 Pop-up for Deletion Confirmation

Your table pool or cluster has been deleted from the database.

5.8 Summary

In this chapter, you learned that tables are collections of values or data about a particular topic or entity. Tables are organized using a model of vertical column and horizontal rows. Tables can be divided into three categories as transparent tables, pooled tables, and cluster tables. A transparent table has a one-to-one relationship with the database table. The structure of the transparent table is the same as that of a database table. When the table is activated, a physical definition of the table is created in the database from the table definition stored in the ABAP Data Dictionary. On the other hand, pooled tables and cluster tables have a many-to-one relationship with the database table. Several pooled tables and cluster tables are combined and stored together in one table pool or table cluster, respectively. This table pool or table cluster is then created in the database.

A table consists of table fields. It defines the field names, data types, and lengths of the field contained in the table. Table fields are associated either with data elements or with predefined data types. You can also include fields of another structure in the tables. Relationships between the tables can be defined with foreign keys. F4 help can be defined for the table fields by creating a search help for the field. Technical settings define how the table will be created and handled when it is created in the database. The table can be buffered in technical settings. Issues such as size and data class of the table are dealt with under the technical settings of the table. Enhancements such as customizing includes and append structures are also available in the table.

Data of one application object is often distributed to several tables. A view combines several tables and required fields from these tables according to the business requirements. We learn more about views in our next chapter.

Data from one application object is often distributed to several tables. All the required data from different tables is collected in one Data Dictionary object, called a view.

6   Views

In this chapter, we explain the key concepts and activities related to views in the ABAP Data Dictionary. We start out with a general introduction to the topic, and then discuss attributes of views. We also introduce you to different types of views and how they are created. We conclude the chapter with an explanation on how to delete views.

6.1   An Introduction to Views

Data from one application object is often distributed throughout several tables. For example, Table EQUI is the equipment master table, Table EQBS is the serial number stock segment table for equipment, Table EQKT is equipment's stock text table, and Table EQUZ is an equipment time-segment table. Similarly, there are many other tables related to equipment. Any business dealing with equipment needs details about equipment from several tables. Similarly, data of one application object is often distributed to several tables. A view combines several tables and required fields from these tables according to the business requirements (see Figure 6.1). Data of a view is derived from combining one or more tables. Views are not stored physically in the database, except for database views, which are created in the underlying database.

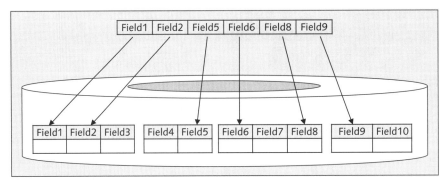

Figure 6.1 Views in ABAP Data Dictionary and Mapping with Database

6.2 Attributes of Views

All types of views share some common attributes, including joins, selections, projections, and maintenance status. Below we describe these attributes in detail.

6.2.1 Join

Base tables in the view are linked together with a relational join condition. Database views are implemented on inner joins, whereas other view types are implemented on outer joins. The join conditions for the database views are formulated using equality relationships between any base fields, whereas join conditions for the other view types are obtained from existing foreign keys of the base fields. Thus, tables in projection, help, or maintenance views can be combined only if they are linked to one another with foreign keys. Now, let us discuss different types of joins in detail and the relationships of joins to foreign keys.

Cross Join

A *cross join* or *Cartesian product join* returns tables in which each and every row of the first table is combined with each and every row of the second table. Thus, the number of rows in the result table is the product of the number of rows in both tables. For example, if TableA contains four records and TableB contains three records, then TableR—their cross-product table—contains 4*3 = 12 records (see Figure 6.2).

TableA			TableB	
Field1	Field2	Field3	Field4	Field5
1	A	Text1	1	E
2	B	Text2	5	F
3	C	Text3	6	G
4	D	Text4		

TableR				
Field1	Field2	Field3	Field4	Field5
1	A	Text1	1	E
2	B	Text2	1	E
3	C	Text3	1	E
4	D	Text4	1	E
1	A	Text1	5	F
2	B	Text2	5	F
3	C	Text3	5	F
4	D	Text4	5	F
1	A	Text1	6	G
2	B	Text2	6	G
3	C	Text3	6	G
4	D	Text4	6	G

Figure 6.2 Cross Product or Cartesian Product

The cross product results in an unnecessary selection of data. Thus, the selection criteria must be restricted by other join options such as *inner join and outer join* conditions. We will explain these next.

Inner Join

Inner join is the most commonly used join. Inner joins select common records from the tables that satisfy the joining condition in both tables. The query compares each row of TableA with each row of TableB and selects only those records that satisfy the joining condition. Let us take the above example, where TableA contains four records and TableB contains three records. Field1 of TableA is joined with Field4 of TableB; i.e., TableA-Field1 = TableB-Field4. This join condition removes all the records in which the entry in Field 1 is not equal to the entry in Field4 from the cross product (see Figure 6.3), given that Field1 and Field4 have the same entries. The redundant column Field4 will be removed automatically. The inner join can be considered a subset of the Cartesian product.

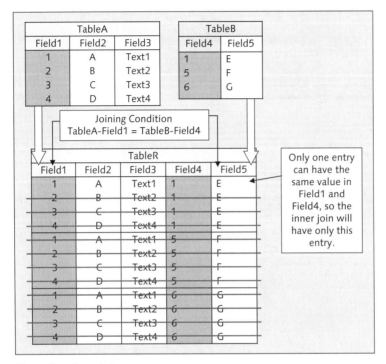

Figure 6.3 Inner Join

With inner joins, you only get the records of the cross-product for which there is an entry in all the base tables used in the view. For this reason, the database view implements inner joins. The database provides only those records for which there are entries in all the tables used in a view.

Outer Join

An outer join does not require the joining table to have matching records in the joined table. Each record of the joining table is retained, even if there are no matching records in the joining table (see Figure 6.4). Outer joins are also known as *left outer joins*. The number of hits determined by an inner join is the subset of the number of hits determined by the outer join. The help and maintenance views implement outer joins.

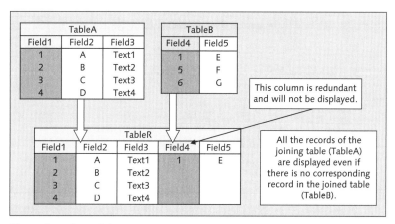

Figure 6.4 Outer Join

6.2.2 Relationship between Foreign Keys and Join Conditions

If any foreign key exists between two tables, this foreign key can act as a join condition to link both the tables. For example, TableA is the primary table and TableB is the secondary table of the view. TableA is the check table for TableB. Field4 of TableB is assigned to Field1 of TableA. The query to generate the view from the foreign key is:

```
CREATE VIEW….. AS SELECT…….
WHERE TABLEB-FIELD4 = TABLEA-FIELD1.
```

Join conditions also work for generic and constant foreign keys. If a constant is assigned to a field in a foreign key, it is also assigned to the field in the join condition. However, there are no join conditions for the generic foreign key. Suppose there are three key fields (Field1, Field2, and Field3) present in a check table TableA where Field1 is assigned to Field4 of TableB, Field2 is generic, and Field3 is assigned to a constant C. In this case, the query to generate the view from the foreign key is:

```
CREATE VIEW….. AS SELECT…….
WHERE TABLEA-FIELD1 = TABLEB-FIELD4
  AND TABLEA-FIELD3 = 'C'.
```

6.2.3 Projection

It may be that some of the fields of a view are not required for display. These fields may or may not be used in a data selection process and are not required while displaying the data. These fields can be hidden with the help of *projection*.

For example, Field3 of TableA is not required for display and can be made hidden (see Figure 6.5).

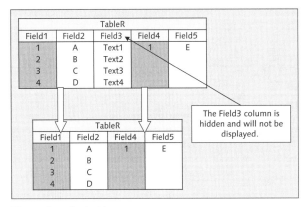

Figure 6.5 Projection

6.2.4 Selection

Selection conditions are used to filter data records of the view. Restrictions can be defined for the contents of the view fields. Only data records that satisfy these restrictions are displayed. The contents of the view fields are compared with a constant. Several selection conditions can be linked together with logical AND and OR operators. A selection condition can be formulated with the fields that are not present in the output fields of a view. For example, if we want only those records that have values A or C in Field2, the selection condition would be Table1-Field2 = 'A' or Table1-Field2 = 'C' (see Figure 6.6).

	TableR		
Field1	Field2	Field4	Field5
1	A	1	E
2	B		
3	C		
4	D		

Records that satisfy the selection condition (Table1-Field2 = A or Table1-Field2 = C) are displayed.

	TableR		
Field1	Field2	Field4	Field5
1	A	1	E
2	B		
3	C		
4	D		

Figure 6.6 Selection

6.2.5 Maintenance Status

The maintenance status of a view specifies whether data records can be changed or inserted in the table contained in a view. The maintenance status can have the following values:

▶ READ ONLY
Data can only be read in the view. You cannot change or insert the data record of the tables present in the view.

▶ READ, CHANGE, DELETE AND ADD
Data records of the table can be changed, deleted, and inserted from the view.

With database views, read only access is permitted if several tables are present in a view. However, if the database view contains only one table, data can be inserted in the table with the view. The following options are available for the fields that are not present in the database view:

▶ If the field is defined as NOT NULL with initial value in the database, the field is filled with the corresponding initial value.

▶ If the field is defined as NOT NULL without an initial value in the database, this results in a database error and values in the field cannot be inserted with the view.

▶ If the field is not defined as NOT NULL in the database, NULL values are filled for that field.

We recommend that you only insert the data record into the table from the database view if all the fields not contained in the view are marked as initial.

When data is inserted in the table with a maintenance or projection view, all the table fields not contained in the view are assigned with the default values of those table fields. It does not depend on whether the table field is defined as NOT NULL in the database. Maintenance views can have the following value for maintenance status:

▶ READ AND CHANGE
Existing data entries can be read and changed. However, records cannot be deleted or inserted.

▶ READ AND CHANGE (TIME-DEPENDENT VIEWS)
Only those entries can be inserted whose non-time dependent key is the same

as that of the existing entries. Apart from this, existing entries can be read and changed.

Let us discuss what is meant by *time dependent key* and *non-time dependent key.* Key fields of a view can be divided on the basis of time-dependency. If the key field is a date or time field—that is, if the key field depends on time—that field is time dependent. All the other fields are non-time dependent fields. For example, let us consider a stock-market view in which companies are listed by company codes. The prices of shares change on a daily basis. A view contains the COMPANY CODE, DATE, and PRICE fields where COMPANY CODE and DATE are the key fields of the view. Here, the COMPANY CODE field is a non-time dependent component of the key field whereas the DATE field is a time-dependent component of the key field. If the maintenance status has the value READ AND CHANGE (TIME-DEPENDENT VIEWS), only those data records whose company codes are already registered can be inserted in a view. New companies cannot be inserted (see Figure 6.7).

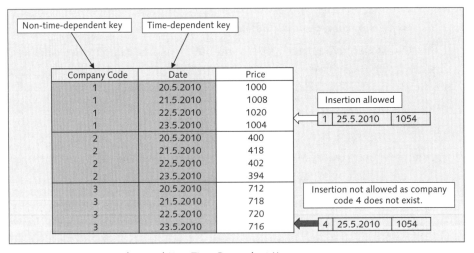

Figure 6.7 Time-Dependent and Non-Time Dependent Keys

6.3   Types of Views

Four different types of views are supported in SAP: database, projection, help, and maintenance. In this section, we discuss the functionalities of all the types of views, as well as why and in which scenarios these views should be used.

6.3.1   Database Views

Database views are defined in the ABAP Data Dictionary. Like transparent tables, database views are created in the underlying database when they are activated (see Figure 6.8). Data is selected in the database with join operations. A join operation is executed in the database to minimize the number of database accesses. You should create a database view if you want to retrieve logically connected data from different tables simultaneously. Selection of data with the database view is faster than selecting the data from individual tables. Before selecting the data from the view, you should ensure that suitable indexes are present in the table contained in the view. A database view can contain only transparent tables.

An ABAP program accesses data present in database views with the help of a database interface. A database view can be used to insert the data in the table present in the view if the database view contains only one table. However, you can only read the records if more than one table is linked in the view. Because the database view implements inner joins, you can read only those records common to all the tables present in the view, based on the join condition. The technical settings of a database view control the buffering of the view data.

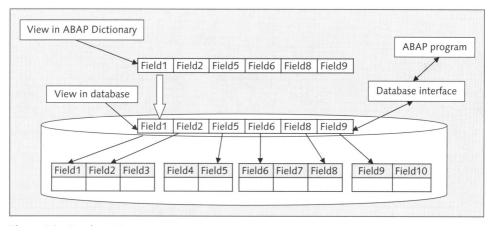

Figure 6.8   Database View

An entire table can be included in a database view. All the fields present in the table are included and become fields of the view (see Figure 6.9). However, you can explicitly exclude some of the unnecessary fields as required. If the included table is changed—that is, if new fields are added to the table or existing fields are deleted from the table—the view automatically adjusts itself to the changes by adding a new field or deleting an existing field.

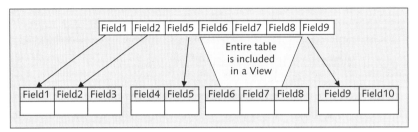

Figure 6.9 Table Included in a Database View

To include the entire table in the view, enter an asterisk (*) in the VIEW FIELD column, enter the name of the table that you want to include in the TABLE column, and enter another asterisk (*) in the FIELD column (see Figure 6.10).

To exclude any of the fields of the included table, enter a hyphen (-) in the VIEW FIELD column, enter the name of the table whose field you want to exclude in the TABLE column, and enter the name of the field that you want to exclude in the FIELD column.

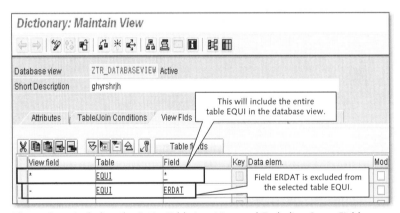

Figure 6.10 Including the Entire Table in a View and Excluding Some Fields

As with technical settings of a table, you can buffer data in the technical settings of a database view. If you switch on the buffering, you need to specify the type of buffering (single record, generic area, or full buffering). However, if the data in any of the base tables changes, the buffered view data is automatically invalidated.

6.3.2 Projection Views

Projection views are used to suppress or mask some of the unnecessary fields of a table. With the help of a projection view, only the required data of the required field is accessed from the database. This minimizes interfaces. Unlike a database view, a projection view is not physically created in the underlying database. Exactly one table is associated with a projection view.

You cannot define selection conditions for projection views. With the help of a projection view, you can also access pooled tables and cluster tables. Because projection views are not created in the database, you cannot specify their technical settings. The maintenance status of a projection view controls access to the data (see Figure 6.11).

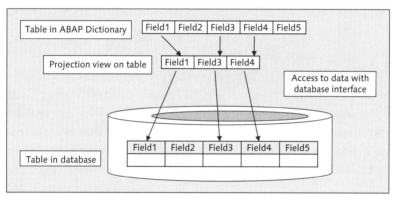

Figure 6.11 Projection View

6.3.3 Append Views

Enhancements of a database view or projection view can be done with the help of append views. Append views are special types of views used to enhance new fields in the existing database views or projection views. Append view enhancements include special development, customer modifications, and country-specific enhancements. Append views are analogous to append structures. As with append structures, one append view is assigned to exactly one database view. However, more than one append view can be created for one database view.

Whenever a database view is activated, all the append views associated with that database view are also activated and all the fields of the append view are appended to the database view. When an append view is created or changed, the assigned database view automatically adjusts to the changes.

The append view can be used only for database views. With an append view, you can only add new fields from the base tables contained in the view (see Figure 6.12). However, you cannot insert new tables into the view. Neither can you modify the existing join conditions or selection conditions of the view.

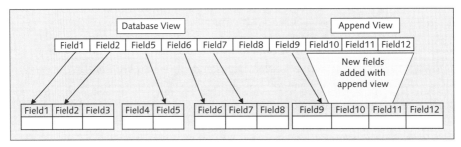

Figure 6.12 Append View

6.3.4 Help Views

A search help's selection method is based on either a table or a view. If you want your search help to select data from several tables, you can use a database view as your selection method. However, database views always implement inner joins. If you want an outer-join selection criterion for your search help, you should use HELP VIEW as your selection method (see Figure 6.13).

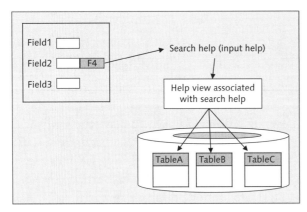

Figure 6.13 Help View

All the tables included in a help view should be linked to foreign keys. However, foreign keys need to follow some restriction criteria to be used in a help view. The first table that is inserted in the help view is known as the *primary table* of the help view. Other tables that are added to the primary table with the help of foreign keys are known as *secondary tables*.

Help views are based on outer joins in the sense that all the contents of the primary table are displayed in the search help that uses the help view. We don't recommend formulating a selection condition on the fields of the secondary table. Because of this selection condition, the records of the secondary table may get filtered. However, you do get the data record of the primary table (because of outer joins) and initial values in the corresponding fields of secondary table.

6.3.5   Maintenance Views

Maintenance views are used to maintain complex application objects. Data about one application object is often distributed throughout several tables. If you want to create, modify, or insert new data for the application object, you have to go to each and every table that is associated with an application object. This is a very tedious and confusing process. Maintenance views are used in such scenarios. They permit you to consolidate the data of an application object. If you create, modify, insert, or delete the data records through a maintenance view, your data record is created, modified, inserted, or deleted automatically in the corresponding underlying tables (see Figure 6.14).

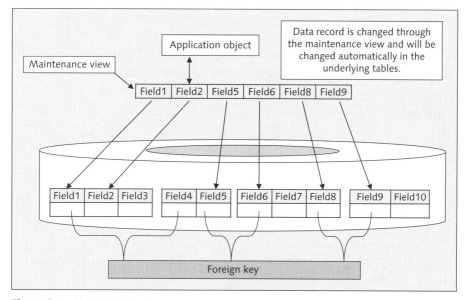

Figure 6.14   Maintenance View

The maintenance status determines which accesses to the data records of the underlying table are possible with the maintenance view. Transaction SE54 (Generate Table Maintenance Dialog), is used to create the maintenance mechanism from the view. Transaction SM30 (Maintain Table View), is used to maintain the data from the base table of a maintenance view. We discuss maintenance mechanisms in Chapter 7, Table Maintenance Dialog.

There are some restrictions to observe while creating a secondary table of a maintenance view or help view. Secondary tables should have N:1 dependencies with the primary tables or the secondary tables that precede the secondary table you are creating (see Figure 6.15). This means there should be at most one dependent record in the secondary table for each record present in the primary table.

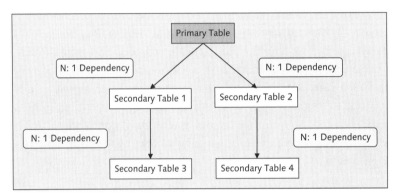

Figure 6.15 N:1 Dependency Relationship between Secondary Table and Primary Table

N:1 dependency exists if the secondary table is a check table for the foreign key used. If the secondary table is a foreign key table, the foreign key field must be the key field of the secondary table or the foreign key field must have the cardinality of N:1 or N:C with the check table.

6.4 Creating and Deleting Views

The process for creating a view depends on the type of the view. In general, you have to follow the below steps to create a view.

1. Select the base tables of the view.
2. Link the base tables with join conditions. Join conditions can also be used from a foreign key defined between the tables.

3. Select the fields from the base table to be used in the view.

4. Define the selection conditions that can restrict the records in the view.

One application object consists of many tables, and its data is often distributed into these tables. When a user wants to collect information from different tables, he creates views. Database views are created in the database, whereas other views collect the data from different tables, but don't store it physically. Projection views are used to hide some fields of a particular table. Help views are used in the search help implementation. Maintenance views are used to maintain the data distributed in different tables for one application object in one go. Below we discuss this process in more detail for each of the views. We then explain how to delete a view.

6.4.1 Creating Database Views

Follow these steps to create a database view:

1. Go to Transaction SE11. Select the radio button for VIEWS in the initial screen of the ABAP Data Dictionary and enter the name of the VIEW. Choose the CREATE button. You can create SAP objects like views under the customer namespace, which means that the name of the object always starts with "Y" or "Z".

2. A popup appears where you have to specify the VIEW TYPE (see Figure 6.16). Once you select the COPY button, you are directed to the maintenance screen of that view.

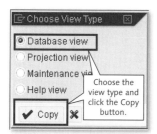

Figure 6.16 Specifying View Type in Dialog Box

3. Enter the explanatory short text in the SHORT DESCRIPTION field of the maintenance screen of the data element (see Figure 6.17).

4. Under the TABLES/JOIN CONDITIONS tab, enter the name of the table that you want to include in your view in the TABLES field. In database views, only transparent tables are allowed. You cannot include pooled or cluster tables.

5. Link your table with the join conditions. You can copy the join condition from the foreign key provided that a foreign key relationship is assigned between the tables. To get the foreign key for a particular table, place the cursor on that table name and press the RELATIONSHIP button. You get a pop-up. Select the foreign key relationship you want and press the COPY button. The join condition is derived from the definition in the foreign key. If you want to know the foreign key relationship between two particular tables, select both the tables and press the RELATIONSHIP button.

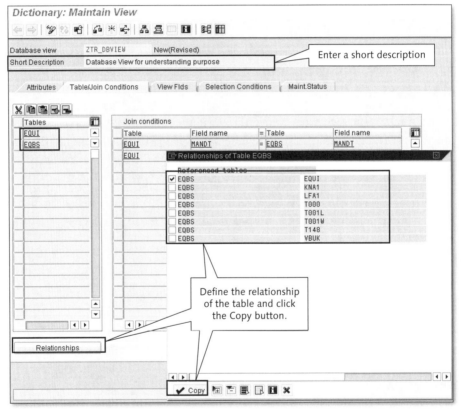

Figure 6.17 Table/Join Conditions Tab of Database View

6. On the VIEW FIELD tab, select the fields of the table that you want in the view. If you choose TABLE FIELD, you get the pop-up to select the table if you have more than one table in a view. Once you select the table and press CHOOSE, you

get the list of fields present in that table. Choose table fields and press the COPY button (see Figure 6.18). You can also include the entire table in a view.

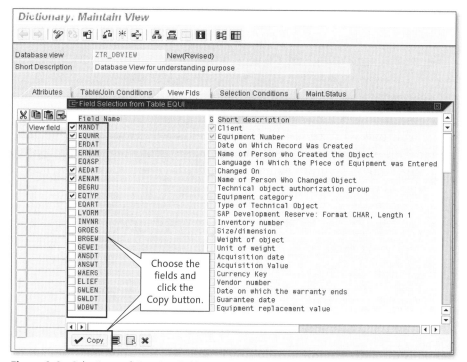

Figure 6.18 Selecting and Copying Fields

7. On the SELECTION CONDITIONS tab, you can define the selection criterion so that only useful and necessary data records are displayed (see Figure 6.19). Selection conditions can be formulated for all the table fields of the table contained in the view and also for the table fields that are not included in the view. The following fields need to be filled:

 ▶ TABLE
   Name of the base table from which the field (on which the selection condition is formulated) is taken.

 ▶ FIELD NAME
   Name of the field on which the selection condition is formulated.

▶ OPERATOR

Operator for comparing the field contents with the comparing value. You can see the valid operator by selecting [F4] help.

▶ COMPARISON VALUE

A constant value with which the field value is compared. Text literals (which must be enclosed with apostrophes) and numbers are permitted as comparison values. Comparison values depend on the data type of the field.

▶ AND/OR

Logical operators used to join two selection conditions. OR operations are possible only with the selection condition of the same field. The OR operator takes priority over the AND operator. The condition "<COND1> AND <COND2> OR <COND3>" is interpreted as "<COND1> AND (<COND2> OR <COND3>)".

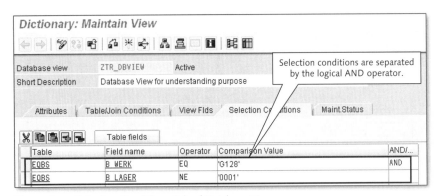

Figure 6.19 Selection Conditions Tab of Database View

8. On the MAINT. STATUS tab, select the maintenance status of the database view. However, if more than one table is used in the database view, the maintenance status has a READ ONLY value and cannot be altered (see Figure 6.20).

9. Maintain the technical settings of the database view by following the path GOTO • TECHNICAL SETTINGS. As with technical settings of tables, you can define whether database views should be buffered and how they should be buffered. Technical settings can be maintained only for database views.

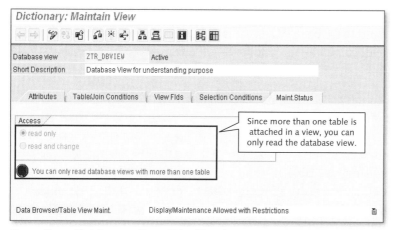

Figure 6.20 Maintenance Status Tab of Database View

10. Save your database view. Assign the development class to the view. You can change the development class from the path GOTO • OBJECT DIRECTORY ENTRY.

11. Activate the database view. Click on the ACTIVATE button (✳) or press `Ctrl`+`F3` to activate the view.

Other options while creating database views include activation logs, documentation, database objects, and runtime objects. Let us discuss these options one by one.

▶ **Database objects**
You can display the definition of a view created in the database by following the path UTILITIES • DATABASE OBJECT • DISPLAY. With UTILITIES • DATABASE OBJECT • CHECK, you can check whether the definition of a view in the database is consistent with the active version of the view.

▶ **Runtime objects**
During activation, the runtime object for the table is also created. You can display the runtime object by following the path UTILITIES • RUNTIME OBJECT • DISPLAY. With UTILITIES • RUNTIME OBJECT • CHECK, you can check whether the definition of a view in the ABAP Data Dictionary maintenance screen is consistent with the specifications of the runtime object of the view.

▶ **Activation log**
The activation log gives you the activation flow information. All the warning and error messages are displayed in the activation log. The activation log is automatically displayed if errors occur during activation. The activation log can be found at UTILITIES • ACTIVATION LOG.

▶ **Create documentation**

Documentation is used to create a text that describes the use of a database view. You can create documentation by following the path GOTO • DOCUMENTATION.

▶ **Display data**

You can display the data of the view with UTILITIES • CONTENTS.

▶ **Change data element of a view field**

In the VIEW FIELDS tab, if you select the MOD flag, you can enter the new data element. The new data element entered by you and the old data element that was already assigned with the table field should refer to the same domain. If you want to use the data element assigned to the table field, de-select the MOD flag.

▶ **Display create statement**

You can display the create statement by which the view was created in the database from the path EXTRAS • CREATE. This statement was executed when the database view was created in the database during activation (see Figure 6.21).

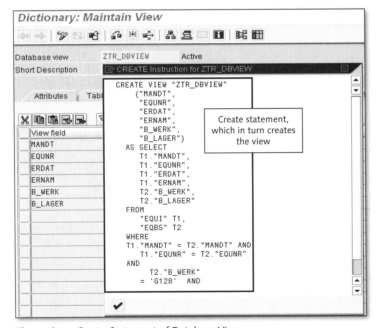

Figure 6.21 Create Statement of Database View

▶ **Append view**

By following the menu path GOTO • APPEND VIEW, you can create an append view for the database view. Append views are used to enhance new fields in the existing database or projection views. Append view enhancement includes special development, customer modifications, and country-specific enhancements.

6.4.2 Creating Projection Views

Let us discuss the procedure for creating projection views.

1. Go to Transaction SE11. Select the radio button for Views in the initial screen of the ABAP Data Dictionary, and enter the name of the view. Choose the Create button. You can create SAP objects like views under the customer namespace; the name of the object always starts with "Y" or "Z."

2. A pop-up appears where you have to specify the view type (Figure 6.16). Once you select the Copy button, you are directed to the maintenance screen of that view.

3. Enter the explanatory short text in the Short Description field of the maintenance screen of the data element (see Figure 6.22).

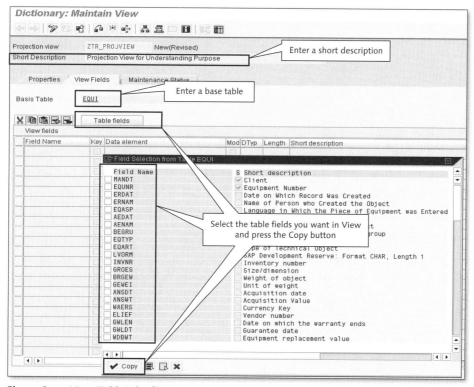

Figure 6.22 View Fields Tab of Projection View

4. Under the VIEW FIELDS tab, enter the base table in the BASE TABLE field. In a projection view, you can only include one table.

5. Select the fields that you want to include in the view. If you choose TABLE FIELDS, entire table fields are displayed in the pop-up. Select the fields that you want to copy and press the COPY button.

6. On the MAINT. STATUS tab, select the maintenance status of the projection view. ACCESS defines how the view can be accessed from ABAP programs. The DATA BROWSER/TABLE VIEW MAINTENANCE flag determines whether an entry can be created in Transaction SE16 (see Figure 6.23).

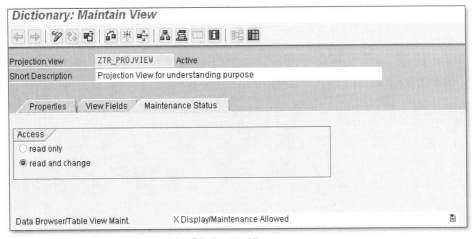

Figure 6.23 Maintenance Status Tab of Projection View

7. Save your database view. Assign the development class to the view. You can change the development class from the path GOTO • OBJECT DIRECTORY ENTRY.

8. Activate the database view. Click the ACTIVATE button or press `Ctrl`+`F3` to activate the view.

Other options such as activation logs, documentation, and runtime objects are also available while creating database views. Let us discuss these options one by one.

▶ **Runtime objects**

During activation, the runtime object for the table is also created. You can display the runtime object via UTILITIES • RUNTIME OBJECT • DISPLAY. With UTILITIES • RUNTIME OBJECT • CHECK you can check whether the definition of view in the ABAP Data Dictionary maintenance screen is consistent with the specifications of the runtime object of the view.

▶ **Activation log**

The activation log gives you the activation flow information. All the warning and error messages are displayed in the activation log. The activation log is automatically displayed if errors occur during activation. The activation log can be found via the path UTILITIES • ACTIVATION LOG.

▶ **Create documentation**

Documentation is used to create a text that describes the use of database view. You can create documentation by following the path GOTO • DOCUMENTATION.

▶ **Display data**

You can display the data of the view by following the path UTILITIES • CONTENTS.

▶ **Change data element of a view field**

In the VIEW FIELDS tab, if you select the MOD flag, you can enter the new data element. The new data element entered by you and the old data element that was already assigned with the table field should refer to the same domain. If you want to use the data element assigned to the table field, de-select the MOD flag.

▶ **Append view**

With GOTO • APPEND VIEW, you can create an append view for the projection view. Append views are used to enhance new fields in the existing database or projection views. Append-view enhancement includes special development, customer modifications, and country-specific enhancements.

Let us discuss how to create an append view in detail.

6.4.3 Creating Append Views

1. To create an append view, follow the path GOTO • APPEND VIEW from the maintenance screen of the database view or projection view (see Figure 6.24).

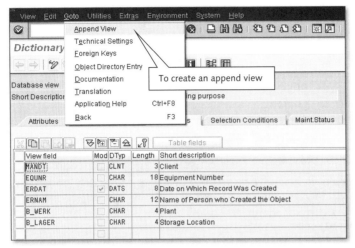

Figure 6.24 Creating Append View

2. If you are creating the append view for the first time, you get an information message: "No append defined for view XXX." Click on the green checkmark icon (✔) (Figure 6.25).

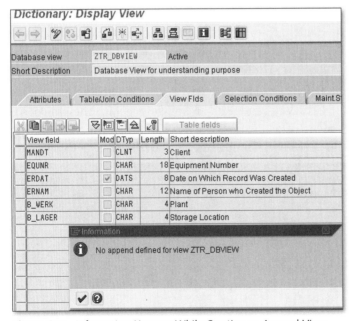

Figure 6.25 Information Message While Creating an Append View

3. You get a dialog box for creating an append view. Write the name of the append view you want to create in the APPEND NAME field. Click on the green checkmark icon (✔) (see Figure 6.26).

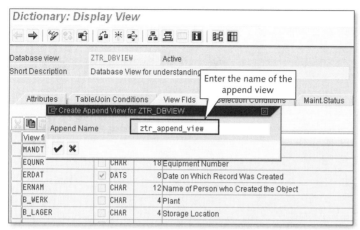

Figure 6.26 Dialog Box for Entering the Name of the Append View

4. You are directed to the maintenance screen of the append view. The tables contained in the view are displayed in the left side of the screen under the TABLES area of the VIEW FIELD tab (see Figure 6.27). With an append view, you can add more fields of the included tables. However, you cannot add more tables to the view with the help of an append view.

5. Enter the explanatory short text in the SHORT DESCRIPTION field of the maintenance screen of the data element. This text describes the role of the enhancement of the underlying database/projection view.

6. Place the cursor on the name of the table from which you want to add fields. If you choose TABLE FIELDS, entire table fields are displayed in the pop-up. Select the fields that you want to copy and press the COPY button. The selected fields are displayed in the VIEW FIELDS area.

7. Save and activate the append view by clicking on the ACTIVATE button or pressing [Ctrl]+[F3]. When the append view is activated, the underlying view (database or projection) is also activated. New fields are automatically added to the parent view.

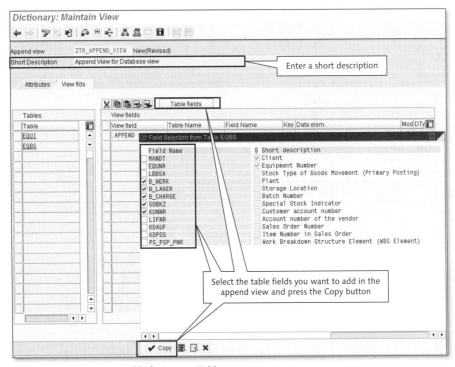

Figure 6.27 Selecting Fields from Base Table

6.4.4 Creating Help Views

Let us discuss the procedure for creating a help view.

1. Go to Transaction SE11. Select the radio button for VIEWS in the initial screen of the ABAP Data Dictionary, and enter the name of the view. Choose the CREATE button. You can create SAP objects like views under the customer namespace; the name of the object always starts with "Y" or "Z".

2. A pop-up appears where you have to specify the VIEW TYPE (refer back to Figure 6.16). Once you select the COPY button, you are directed to the maintenance screen of that view.

3. Enter the explanatory short text in the SHORT DESCRIPTION field of the maintenance screen of the data element (see Figure 6.28).

4. Under the TABLES/JOIN CONDITION tab, enter the primary table name that you want to include in your view in the TABLES area. Other secondary tables can be included only with the help of a foreign key by clicking on the RELATIONSHIP button.

5. When you click on the RELATIONSHIP button, you get a pop-up. Select the secondary table that you want to include and press the COPY button. You can also include tables that are linked to a foreign key of the secondary table that is already included. To do this, place the cursor on the secondary table and click on the RELATIONSHIP button. You get a similar pop-up as described above. Proceed as describe above.

For maintenance and help views, the secondary table should be N:1 dependent with the primary table or the preceding secondary table. Tables in which this condition is not satisfied are displayed under the header RELATIONSHIPS WITH UNSUITABLE CARDINALITY. You cannot include these tables as secondary tables.

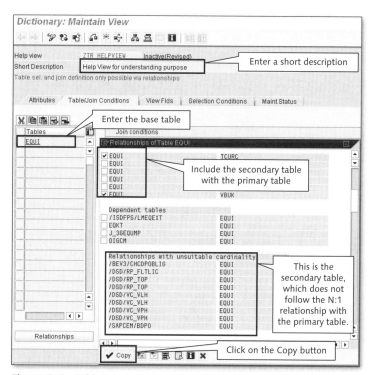

Figure 6.28 Table/Join Conditions Tab of Help View

6. On the VIEW FIELD tab, select the fields of the table that you want in the view. The key fields of the primary table automatically get copied as a proposal. If you choose TABLE FIELD, you get the dialog box where all the tables present in the view are listed (see Figure 6.29).

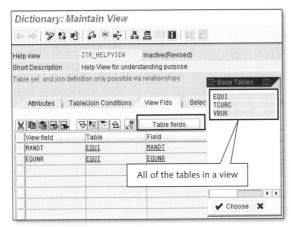

Figure 6.29 View Field Tab of Help View

7. Once you select the table and click CHOOSE, you get the list of fields present in that table. Choose the table fields and press the COPY button (see Figure 6.30).

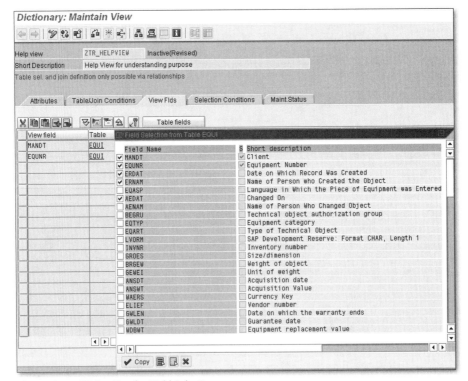

Figure 6.30 Dialog Box for Field Selection

8. On the SELECTION CONDITIONS tab, you can define the selection criterion so that only useful and necessary data records are displayed (see Figure 6.31). The selection conditions can be formulated for all the table fields of the table contained in the view and also for the table fields that are not included in the view.

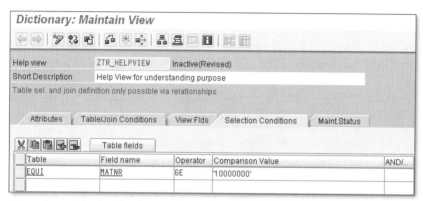

Figure 6.31   Selection Conditions Tab of Help View

9. On the MAINT. STATUS tab, select the maintenance status of the database view (see Figure 6.32).

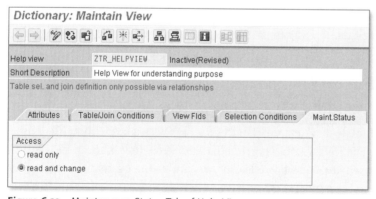

Figure 6.32   Maintenance Status Tab of Help View

10. Save your help view. Assign the development class to the view. You can change the development class from the path GOTO • OBJECT DIRECTORY ENTRY.

11. Activate the database view. Click on the ACTIVATE button or press $\boxed{\text{Ctrl}}$+$\boxed{\text{F3}}$ to activate the view.

Options including activation logs, documentation, and runtime objects are also available while creating database views. Let us discuss these options one by one.

▶ **Runtime objects**
During activation, the runtime object for the table is also created. You can display the runtime object from the path UTILITIES • RUNTIME OBJECT • DISPLAY. With UTILITIES • RUNTIME OBJECT • CHECK you can check whether the definition of the view in the ABAP Data Dictionary maintenance screen is consistent with the specifications of the runtime object of the view.

▶ **Activation log**
The activation log gives you the activation flow information. All the warning and error messages are displayed in the activation log. The activation log is automatically displayed if errors occur during activation. The activation log can be found by following the path UTILITIES • ACTIVATION LOG.

▶ **Create documentation**
Documentation is used to create a text that describes the use of the database view. You can create documentation by following the path GOTO • DOCUMENTATION.

▶ **Change data element of a view field**
In the VIEW FIELDS tab, if you select the MOD flag, you can enter the new data element. The new data element entered by you and the old data element that was already assigned with the table field should refer to the same domain. If you want to use the data element assigned to the table field, de-select the MOD flag.

6.4.5 Creating Maintenance Views

Let us discuss the procedure for creating a maintenance view.

1. Go to Transaction SE11. Select the radio button for VIEWS in the initial screen of the ABAP Data Dictionary, and enter the name of the view. Choose the CREATE button. You can create SAP objects like views under the customer namespace; the name of the object always starts with "Y" or "Z".

2. A pop-up appears where you have to specify the view type (refer back to Figure 6.16). Once you select the COPY button, you are directed to the maintenance screen of that view.

3. Enter the explanatory short text in the SHORT DESCRIPTION field of the maintenance screen of the data element (see Figure 6.33).

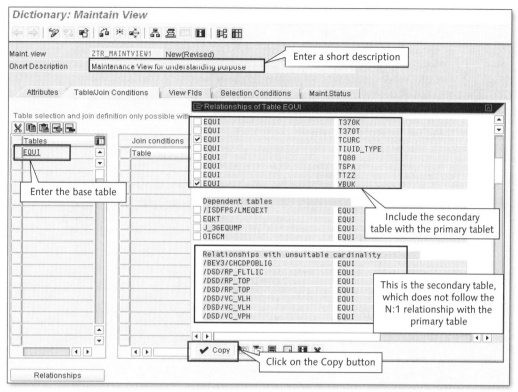

Figure 6.33 Table/Join Conditions Tab of Maintenance View

4. Under the TABLES/JOIN CONDITION tab, enter the primary table name that you want to include in your view in the TABLES area. Other secondary tables can only be included with the help of foreign keys, by clicking on the RELATIONSHIP button.

5. When you click on the RELATIONSHIP button, you get a pop-up. Select the secondary table that you want to include and press the COPY button.

   You can also include tables that are linked to a foreign key of the secondary table that is already included.

6. To do this, place the cursor on the secondary table and click on the RELATION-SHIP button. You get a pop-up similar to the one described above. Proceed as described above. For maintenance and help views, the secondary table should be N:1 dependent with the primary table or its preceding secondary table.

Tables in which this condition is not satisfied are displayed under the header RELATIONSHIPS WITH UNSUITABLE CARDINALITY. You cannot include these tables as secondary tables.

7. On the VIEW FIELD tab, select the fields of the table that you want in the view. The key fields of the primary table automatically get copied as a proposal. If you choose TABLE FIELD, you get the dialog box where all the tables present in the view are listed (see Figure 6.34).

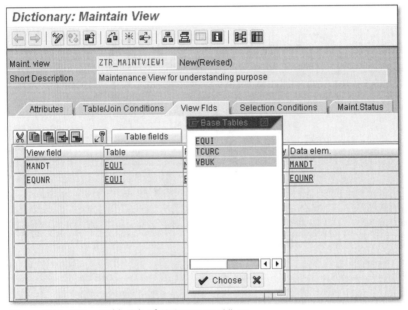

Figure 6.34 View Fields Tab of Maintenance View

8. Once you select the table and press CHOOSE, you get the list of fields present in that table. Choose the table fields and press the COPY button (see Figure 6.35). The key fields of the primary table automatically get copied as a proposal. Apart from this, all the key fields of the secondary table that are not involved in the foreign key—that is, key fields that are not linked with the join condition to key fields already present in the view—must be included in the view. This ensures that data records from the maintenance view are written correctly in the corresponding tables in the maintenance view.

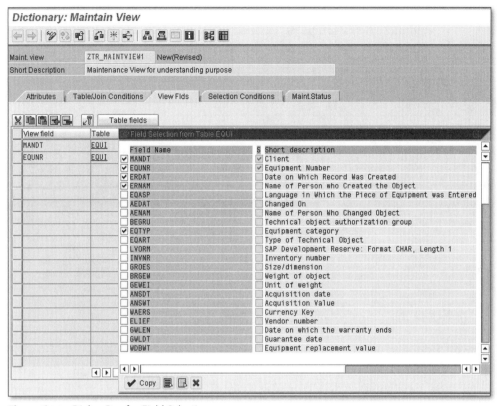

Figure 6.35 Dialog Box for Field Selection

9. Define the MAINTENANCE ATTRIBUTE OF THE VIEW FIELD in column P (see Figure 6.36). This attribute defines how to access a field of a maintenance view with the maintenance attribute. This attribute can have the following values:

   ▶ **R:** Fields with value R have read access only. These fields can only be read and cannot be maintained in Transaction SM30.

   ▶ **S:** Fields with value S are used to create subsets while maintaining the view data. Only the subset of the data is displayed in Transaction SM30.

   ▶ **H:** Fields with value H are hidden from the user in the maintenance dialog. These fields do not appear in the maintenance screen in Transaction SM30. Because these fields are hidden, they must contain correct data. By default, they are left empty.

▶ **[Space]:** Fields with a space do not have any restrictions for maintenance, and these fields can be maintained without any restrictions in Transaction SM30.

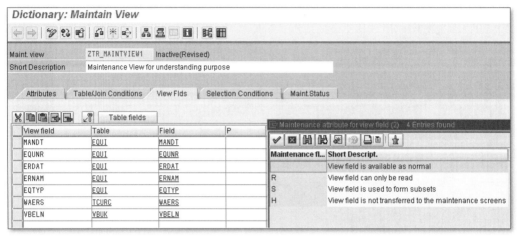

Figure 6.36 Maintenance Attribute of a View Field

10. On the SELECTION CONDITIONS tab, you can define the selection criterion so that only useful and necessary data records are displayed. Selection conditions can be formulated for all the table fields of the table contained in the view and also for the table fields that are not included in the view.

11. On the MAINT. STATUS tab, define the ACCESS of the view. Access defines how view data can be accessed by standard maintenance Transaction SM30. Define the DELIVERY CLASS of the maintenance view. The delivery class is used in the extended table maintenance by Transaction SM30. Define the value for the DATA BROWSER/TABLE VIEW MAINTENANCE field (see Figure 6.37). This indicator specifies whether the table can be displayed and maintained in Transactions SE16, SM30, and SE11.

12. Save your maintenance view. Assign the development class to the view. You can change the development class from the path GOTO • OBJECT DIRECTORY ENTRY.

13. Activate the database view. Click on the ACTIVATE button or press [Ctrl]+[F3] to activate the view.

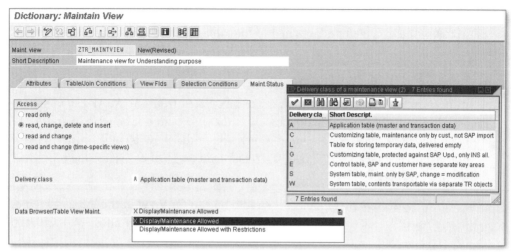

Figure 6.37 Maintenance Status Tab of Maintenance View

Options including runtime objects, activation logs, creating documentation, and changing the data element of a view field are also available while creating database views. Let us discuss these options one by one.

▸ **Runtime objects**
  During activation, the runtime object for the table is also created. You can display the runtime object by following the path UTILITIES • RUNTIME OBJECT • DISPLAY. With UTILITIES • RUNTIME OBJECT • CHECK, you can check whether the definition of a view in the ABAP Data Dictionary maintenance screen is consistent with the specifications of the runtime object of the view.

▸ **Activation log**
  The activation log gives you the activation flow information. All the warning and error messages are displayed in the activation log. The activation log is automatically displayed if errors occur during activation. The activation log can be found at UTILITIES • ACTIVATION LOG.

▸ **Create documentation**
  Documentation is used to create a text that describes the use of a database view. You can create documentation by following the path GOTO • DOCUMENTATION.

▸ **Change data element of a view field**
  In the VIEW FIELDS tab, if you select the MOD flag, you can enter the new data element. The new data element entered by you and the old data element that was

already assigned with the table field should refer to the same domain. If you want to use the data element assigned to the table field, de-select the MOD flag.

6.4.6 Deleting Views

If the view is no longer required, it can be deleted from the ABAP Data Dictionary. The prerequisite to deleting a view is that it should not be used in any ABAP programs. Before deleting a view, check where the view is still in use by other objects by clicking on the WHERE-USED LIST icon (🔁). Let us discuss the procedure for deleting views.

1. Goto Transaction SE11. Select the radio button for VIEW in the initial screen of the ABAP Data Dictionary. Enter the name of the view. Choose WHERE-USED LIST, and check if the view is still being used by any of the programs. If so, you cannot delete the view.

2. Choose the DELETE icon (🗑) in Transaction SE11 if the view is not being used by any of the data elements. A dialog box appears for confirmation of the deletion request. Once the deletion request is confirmed, the view is deleted.

6.5 Summary

In this chapter, we discussed how the data of one application object is often distributed to several tables. A view combines several tables and required fields from these tables according to business requirements. Primary tables are linked with secondary tables with a relational join condition. Database views are defined in the ABAP Data Dictionary. Tables in database views are joined by an inner join condition. Database views are automatically created in the database when activated. Projection views are used to suppress or mask some of the unnecessary table fields. With the help of a projection view, only the required data of the required field is accessed from the database. Help views are used in the search help selection method. Maintenance views are used to maintain complex application objects. Data records that are created or modified with a maintenance view automatically get created in the corresponding underlying tables.

In our next chapter, we discuss the Table Maintenance Dialog. We explain how tables and views can be created through Transaction SE54 and maintained through Transaction SM30. We also discuss in detail the functionality of view variants and view clusters.

The Table Maintenance Dialog is a special tool provided by SAP to create user interfaces for tables and views, and to customize and maintain the tables and views. Transaction SE54 is devoted to the Table Maintenance Dialog, and allows you to create the Table Maintenance Generator, view clusters, view variants, and function groups.

7 Table Maintenance Dialog

In this chapter we discuss the concepts behind the Table Maintenance Dialog. We start with a general introduction to the Table Maintenance Dialog, and then describe the Table Maintenance Generator and its components, creation, and modification. We also discuss function groups, view variants, and view clusters in detail. Transaction SE54 is the transaction for the Table Maintenance Dialog. When you give the table name, select the ABAP DICTIONARY radio button and click on CHANGE/ CREATE OR DISPLAY; you will be directed to ABAP Data Dictionary Transaction SE11. Similarly, if you select the GENERATED OBJECTS radio button and click on CHANGE/ CREATE OR DISPLAY, you will be directed to the Table Maintenance Generator.

The Table Maintenance Dialog is a special tool provided by SAP to create user interfaces for tables and views. It is used for customizing and maintaining customer tables and view contents. This involves modifying tables and views according to the business requirements. As tables and views have limited functionality, the Table Maintenance Dialog, with the help of the Table Maintenance Generator, is used to enhance it. The Table Maintenance Generator, function groups, view clusters, view variants, and authorization groups combine together to form the Table Maintenance Dialog initial screen that is Transaction SE54. For example, with the standard functionality of tables and views, all authorized users can insert, update, and delete the data records in the table or view.

Now let us consider business-specific functionality that may be needed:

▶ Users can insert or change the data records but cannot delete them.

▶ Some fields of a table are read-only and cannot be changed, while others can be changed.

- Some fields have pre-defined values that will automatically get populated while creating new entries.

- Validations of the field values are required before saving the record.

These types of customer specific functionalities can be achieved with the help of the Table Maintenance Generator, which creates standardized Table Maintenance Dialogs for tables and views and is used to maintain table and view contents. These dialogs can be created via the path GENERATE TABLE MAINTENANCE DIALOG: INITIAL SCREEN, Transaction SE54. The Table Maintenance Dialog also contains other functionalities for creating and editing authorization groups, function groups, view clusters, and view variants. Now, we will discuss these in detail.

7.1 Table Maintenance Dialog: Initial Screen (Transaction: SE54)

The initial screen of Transaction SE54 is used to create a Table Maintenance Dialog. It also contains functions for managing the objects required to generate the maintenance dialog. Four push-buttons are present in the initial screen of maintenance dialog:

- EDIT TABLE/VIEW
  Under this section, tables or views can be created, changed, or displayed (as with Transaction SE11). Dialog definitions can be generated and maintained, new authorization groups can be created, and assignments of authorization groups with tables or views can be changed. Entire tables, views, and generated objects can also be deleted (see Figure 7.1).

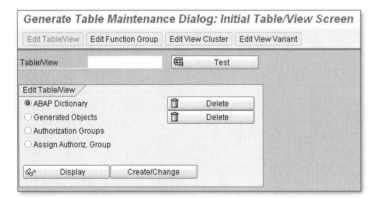

Figure 7.1 Generate Table Maintenance Dialog: Initial Table/View Screen

▶ EDIT FUNCTION GROUP

Function groups or source texts can be changed. The following group specific subprograms can be regenerated (see Figure 7.2).

- ▶ Structure-specific PAI modules
- ▶ Structure-specific data declarations
- ▶ Structure-specific form routines
- ▶ General data declarations
- ▶ Function group main program

However, dialog changes may be lost if general data declarations or the function group main program is regenerated.

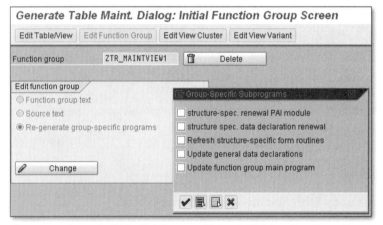

Figure 7.2 Generate Table Maintenance Dialog: Initial Function Group Screen

▶ EDIT VIEW CLUSTER

In this section, view clusters can be created, changed, or displayed (see Figure 7.3).

Figure 7.3 Generate Table Maintenance Dialog: View Cluster Initial Screen

▶ EDIT VIEW VARIANT

In this section, view variants can be created, changed, or displayed (see Figure 7.4).

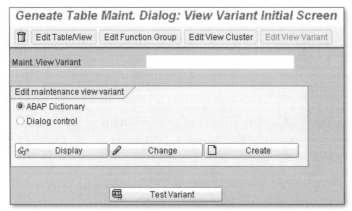

Figure 7.4 Generate Table Maintenance Dialog: View Variant Initial Screen

7.2   Table Maintenance Generator

Before describing how to maintain a table or view, let us discuss various components used in the Table Maintenance Generator.

7.2.1   Components of Table Maintenance Generator

The Table Maintenance Generator consists of the following components (see Figure 7.5).

▶ Authorization object

▶ Authorization group

▶ Function group

▶ Package

▶ Maintenance screen

▶ Recording routine

▶ Compare flag

Let us discuss these components in detail.

Generate Table Maintenance Dialog: Generation Environment

Table/View	ZTR_MAINTVIEW

Technical Dialog Details

Authorization Group	&NC&	w/o auth. group
Authorization object	S_TABU_D..	
Function group	ZTR MAINTVIEW	Fn.Gr.Text
Package	$TMP	Temporary Objects (never transported!)

Maintenance Screens

Maintenance type	⦿ one step	
	○ two step	
Maint. Screen No.	Overview screen	1
	Single screen	

Dialog Data Transport Details

Recording routine	○ Standard recording routine
	⦿ no, or user, recording routine
Compare Flag	Automatically Adjustable [i] Note

Figure 7.5 Components of Table Maintenance Generator

Authorization

Authorization is a vast topic that is dealt with under SAP Basis. Before discussing authorization groups and authorization objects, you need to know what authorization is. So, let us discuss the basic concepts and terminologies used in authorization.

Authorization in SAP is used to assign authorization checks to users. To illustrate this, consider a company where decisions are taken by high-level management and sensitive information is handled and accessed by them. Lower-level employees are not authorized to access such sensitive and confidential information. Similarly, in SAP, some users have limited access to certain data. This is where the concept of authorization comes into the picture. Here are the key terms used in authorization:

- **Authorization class**

  An authorization class can be considered to be a logical grouping of authorization objects. It contains authorization objects of one component.

▶ **Authorization object**
One or more authorization objects are grouped under an authorization class. Authorization objects contain authorization fields. One authorization object can have a maximum of 10 authorization fields.

▶ **Authorization field**
This is the smallest unit against which an authorization check executes. It contains various activities. Change, display, lock, delete, and archive are among the activities present in the authorization field ACTVT.

Now, let us try to map the authorization concept with our Table Maintenance Generator dialog. Authorization class BC_A (Basis: Administration) contains the entire Basis administration's authorization objects. S_TABU_DIS (table maintenance via standard tools such as SM30) is one of the authorization objects within this class (see Figure 7.6). Whenever you maintain a table or create a Table Maintenance Dialog, this object will be automatically displayed in the authorization object attribute of the Table Maintenance Generator. This authorization object contains authorization fields DICBERCLS and ACTVT. You will see these authorization fields when you double-click on the authorization object. If you click on the PERMITTED ACTIVITIES button, you will get the list of activities that an authorized user can perform under this authorization object (see Figure 7.7).

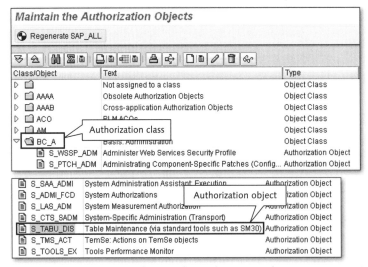

Figure 7.6 Authorization Object under Authorization Class in Transaction SU21

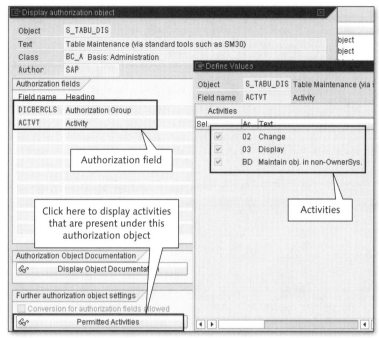

Figure 7.7 Authorization Field of Object S_TABU_DIS

DICBERCLS is also known as an authorization group. You have to assign an authorization group to your table or view. All the users with access to that particular group can access that table or view. An authorization group can have a maximum length of four characters. Entries can be maintained and new authorization groups can be created in Transaction SE54. If no authorization group (&nc&) is assigned to the table, every user with authorization to access the S_TABU_DIS object can access the table.

The ACTVT field contains the options to CHANGE, DISPLAY, and MAINTAIN-OBJECT IN NON-OWNER SYSTEM. Let us discuss some important tables used in authorization (see Figure 7.8).

▶ **TACT**
  You can get the list of activities that can be assigned to an authorization field in this Data Dictionary table.

▶ **TACTZ**

You can get the activities that are assigned to a particular object in this database table.

▶ **TDDAT**

The table name along with its authorization class and authorization group can be found in this table.

▶ **TBRG**

The authorization object with its corresponding authorization group can be found in this table.

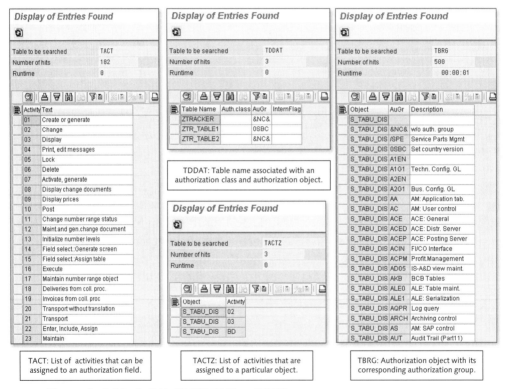

Figure 7.8 Entries in Table TACTZ, TACT, and TBRG

Function Group

Function groups are containers for function modules. When you execute the function modules, the function group is loaded by the system into the internal session of the calling program. However, you cannot execute a function group. The name of a function group can be up to 26 characters long. You have to assign the function group to your Table Maintenance Generator. The function group name can be the same as the name of the table or can have a different name. The generated mainte nance module of the table will belong to this function group. When you assign the function group, the main program and its include are generated automatically.

The automatically generated programs have the following naming conventions (see Figure 7.9):

▶ SAPL<fgrp>

The main program generated has the naming convention of SAPL<fgrp>. This program will only contain INCLUDE statements such as L<fgrp>TOP, L<fgrp>UXX, and L<fgrp>F00 in the program.

▶ L<fgrp>TOP

This include will contain the FUNCTION-POOL statement. It will also contain global data declarations for the entire function group. This is a system-generated include.

▶ L<fgrp>UXX

This contains further INCLUDE statements for the include programs L<fgrp>U01, L<fgrp>U02, and so on. These includes contain the actual function modules. This include is a system-generated include.

▶ L<fgrp>FOX

These include programs contain the coding of subroutines that can be called with internal subroutine calls from all function modules of the group. L<fgrp>F00 is a view-related include file, and L<fgrp>F01 is a user-defined sub-routine include file.

▶ L<fgrp>IOX

These include programs contains the coding of the PAI module. L<fgrp>I00 is a view-related include file, and L<fgrp>I01 is a user-defined sub-routine include file.

▶ L<fgrp>OOX

These include programs contain the coding of PBO module. L<fgrp>O01 is a user-defined sub-routine include file.

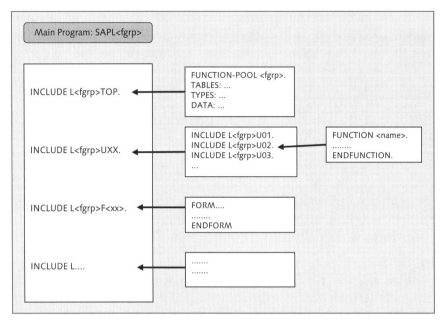

Figure 7.9 Includes Program in Main Program SAPL<fgrp>

For example, if you create a Table Maintenance Generator for your maintenance view ZTR_MAINTVIEW, the main program name is SAPLZTR_MAINTVIEW. This program contains the following includes (see Figure 7.10):

▶ LZTR_MAINTVIEWTOP, which is a TOP include and contains global data.

▶ LZTR_MAINTVIEWUXX, which contains the function module details.

▶ LZTR_MAINTVIEWF00, which contains the sub-routines. It is a view-related include file.

▶ LZTR_MAINTVIEWI00, which contains the PAI module. It is a view-related include file.

▶ LSVIMFXX is a general routine file for sub-routines.

▶ LSVIMOXX is a general routine file for PBO module.

▶ LSVIMIXX is a general routine file for PAI module.

▶ LZTR_MAINTVIEWFXX is a user-defined include file that contains the user defined sub-routines.

▶ LZTR_MAINTVIEWOXX is a user-defined include file that contains the user-defined PBO modules.

▶ `LZTR_MAINTVIEWIXX` is a user-defined include file that contains the user-defined PAI modules.

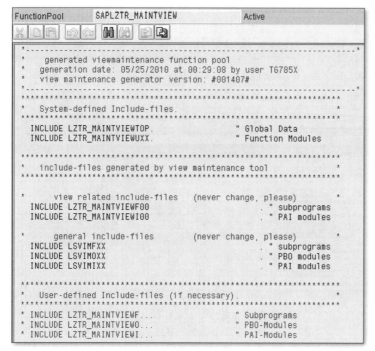

```
FunctionPool        $APLZTR_MAINTVIEW              Active

[toolbar icons]

*--------------------------------------------------------------*
 *    generated viewmaintenance function pool
 *    generation date: 05/25/2010 at 00:29:08 by user TG785X
 *    view maintenance generator version: #001407#
 *--------------------------------------------------------------*
*************************************************************
 *   System-defined Include-files.                        *
*************************************************************
   INCLUDE LZTR_MAINTVIEWTOP.           " Global Data
   INCLUDE LZTR_MAINTVIEWUXX.           " Function Modules

*************************************************************
 *   include-files generated by view maintenance tool     *
*************************************************************

 *     view related include-files  (never change, please)  *
   INCLUDE LZTR_MAINTVIEWF00           . " subprograms
   INCLUDE LZTR_MAINTVIEWI00           . " PAI modules

 *     general include-files        (never change, please)  *
   INCLUDE LSVIMFXX                    . " subprograms
   INCLUDE LSVIMOXX                    . " PBO modules
   INCLUDE LSVIMIXX                    . " PAI modules

*************************************************************
 *   User-defined Include-files (if necessary).           *
*************************************************************
 * INCLUDE LZTR_MAINTVIEWF...          " Subprograms
 * INCLUDE LZTR_MAINTVIEWO...          " PBO-Modules
 * INCLUDE LZTR_MAINTVIEWI...          " PAI-Modules
```

Figure 7.10 Function Pool and Its Includes

Package

A package can be thought of as a folder under which your functional group is created. This package is same as the package of the table. When you create a maintenance dialog, this field will automatically be populated with the package of your table.

Maintenance Screen

While creating the Table Maintenance Generator, the maintenance screen is also generated. In this maintenance screen, table entries are maintained (created, changed, or displayed) in Transaction SM30. One or two maintenance screens are created depending on the maintenance type. Maintenance type can be established in a one-step or two-step process.

In a one-step maintenance type, only one maintenance screen is created. This screen is known titled OVERVIEW SCREEN. Entries are displayed in this screen in the form of lists. Entries are displayed in one line of the screen.

In a two-step maintenance type, two maintenance screens are created: OVERVIEW SCREEN and SINGLE SCREEN. A list of entries is generated in the overview screen and a single entry is displayed on the single screen. For every entry, a single screen is called from the overview screen by a function key (see Figure 7.11).

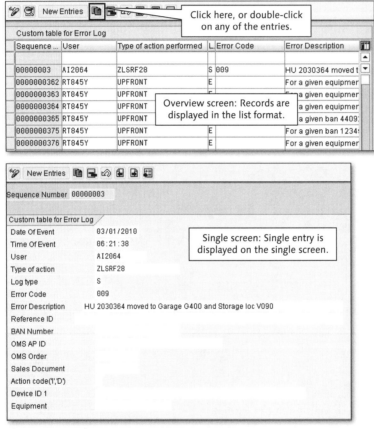

Figure 7.11 Single Screen

You have to give the screen number to the maintenance screen (overview screen in one-step and overview, and single screen in two-step). You can give any number to this field or generate the screen number by clicking on the FIND SCREEN NUMBER button. However, if you are assigning the screen number manually, you cannot assign screen number 0 because it is already assigned by SAP. Similarly, screen numbers 1,000 to 1,010 are reserved for selection screens, so you cannot provide these screen numbers.

Recording Routine

Changes to the contents of the table can be recorded. This recording can be done either automatically or manually depending on the client settings. Recording routines can be standard or individual (manual). The standard recording routine can be further enhanced with individual routines. Individual recording routines are defined by events. Events can be accessed from the path ENVIRONMENT • EVENTS. There are a number of events that can be defined, and we will discuss these later in this chapter. The following client settings are possible for recording:

▶ **Changes without automatic recording**
Changes are not automatically recorded. Recording can be done and changes can be recorded manually.

▶ **Automatic recoding of changes**
All the changes are recorded automatically.

▶ **No changes allowed**
Changes cannot be made. However, table contents can be recorded manually for transport.

▶ **No transport allowed**
Changes can be made, but these changes can neither be automatically nor manually recorded for the transport.

Compare Flag

This flag indicates whether the maintenance transaction allows the activation and adjustment of Business Configuration sets (BC sets). The BC set is a management tool that helps users to record, save, and share customized settings. Customers can either use BC sets provided by SAP (for select industries) or they can create their own BC sets. The COMPARE flag is responsible for activating BC sets. This flag can have the following settings:

▶ No Information

The system does not know whether the maintenance transaction allows BC set activation and adjustment. As with the setting Not Adjustable (discussed next), the content of the BC sets is written to the customizing tables without being checked.

▶ Not Adjustable

In this case, BC sets cannot be activated and checked. The maintenance transaction does not support the adjustment. The content of the BC sets is written to the customizing tables without being checked. Views and tables cannot be adjusted, but they can be compared with another client or system. All the modifications that arise from adjustment must be made manually.

▶ Adjustable in Dialog

As with the setting Not Adjustable, the content of the BC sets is written to the customizing tables without being checked. Views and tables cannot be adjusted, but they can be compared with another client or system, and differences (either all of them or a selected one) can be adjusted with the dialog-adjustment function.

▶ Automatically Adjustable

BC sets are activated with all fields checked. The object can be adjusted automatically against another client as part of a customizing import. This means that the data with differences can be imported from the comparison client. With this automatic-adjustment option, the maintenance transaction also offers dialog adjustment.

7.2.2   Creating the Table Maintenance Generator

Let us discuss the procedure for creating the Table Maintenance Generator.

1. In Transaction SE54 (Generate Table Maintenance Dialog: Initial Table/ View Screen), select the radio button Generated Objects and click on Create/ Change button (see Figure 7.12). You can also create a Table Maintenance Generator by following the path Utilities • Table Maintenance Generator from the maintenance table or view screen of Transaction SE11.

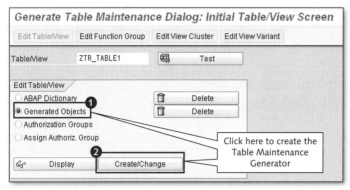

Figure 7.12 Transaction SE54 to Generate Table Maintenance Dialog

2. Enter the value in AUTHORIZATION GROUP. If you select the [F4] help on the authorization group, you will get the list of authorization groups present in the authorization object. Authorization object S_TABU_DIS will automatically get populated and cannot be changed (see Figure 7.13).

3. Enter the value in the FUNCTION GROUP. This function group will contain all the modules of the Table Maintenance Generator.

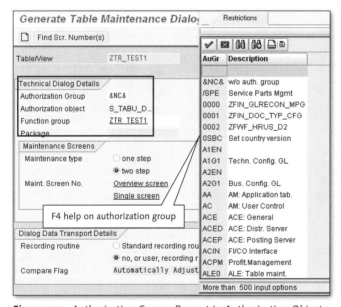

Figure 7.13 Authorization Groups Present in Authorization Object

4. In the MAINTENANCE SCREEN area, enter the value of MAINTENANCE TYPE. It can be ONE STEP or TWO STEPS. Enter the screen number for maintenance screen in the MAINTENANCE SCREEN NO. field. You can also find the screen number automatically by clicking on the FIND SCREEN NUMBER button. If you click on this button, you will get a dialog box. In this dialog box, you can propose a screen number for your maintenance screen, display a number range that can be allocated to the screen number, and call up a list of screen numbers that are reserved. To propose the screen number by the system, click on the radio button PROPOSE SCREEN NUMBER and click on the checkmark (✔) icon (see Figure 7.14).

5. Enter the value in RECORDING ROUTINE. It can have values of STANDARD RECORDING ROUTINE or NO OR USER, RECORDING ROUTINE.

6. Enter the value in COMPARE FLAG.

7. Click the CREATE (⬜) icon to generate the Table Maintenance Generator (see Figure 7.14).

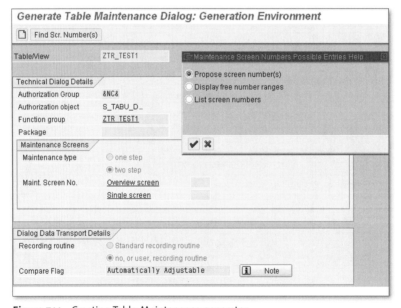

Figure 7.14 Creating Table Maintenance generator

8. Save your changes. The CREATE OBJECT DIRECTORY ENTRY popup will appear asking for a package. Enter the name of the package in which you are working. If you don't have a package, then you can create it in the Object Navigator (Transaction SE80), or you can save your domain in the LOCAL OBJECT in package *$tmp*.

When the Table Maintenance Dialog is generated successfully you will get the success message in the status bar.

7.2.3   Modifying the Table Maintenance Generator

After creating the Table Maintenance Generator, you can modify the screens and program according to the business requirements. You can also change the user interface and add events. You can also view and change the source code of the Table Maintenance Generator. You can do the modifications from the path ENVIRONMENT • MODIFICATIONS. Let us discuss the various options when modifying the Table Maintenance Generator.

Maintenance Screen

Under this, you can change the maintenance screen of the Table Maintenance Dialog. If one step maintenance type is selected, modifications can be done in the OVERVIEW screen. If two-step maintenance type is selected, modifications can be done in the OVERVIEW and SINGLE screens. Follow the path ENVIRONMENT • MODIFICATIONS • MAINTENANCE SCREEN (see Figure 7.15).

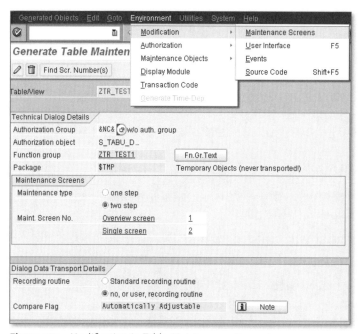

Figure 7.15   Modification in Table Maintenance Generator

You will get the dialog box where you have to select the screen you want to modify. Click on the checkmark icon after selecting the screen (see Figure 7.16). You will be directed to the Screen Painter of that screen. Among the changes possible with the maintenance screen, a field can be made non-editable, and a default value can be displayed in the field. Make the changes in the screen as required.

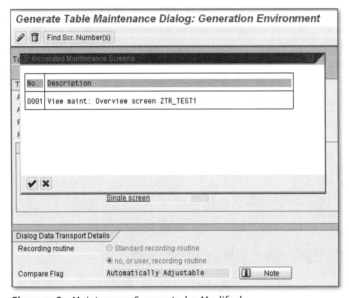

Figure 7.16 Maintenance Screens to be Modified

For example, assume Table ZTR_TEST1 contains the following fields (see Figure 7.17).

▸ MANDT: Client

▸ EQUNR: Equipment number

▸ PLANT: Plant

▸ SLOC: Storage Location

▸ CHANGED_BY: User name who changed the record

▸ CHANGED_ON: Last change date

▸ CHANGED_AT: Last changed time

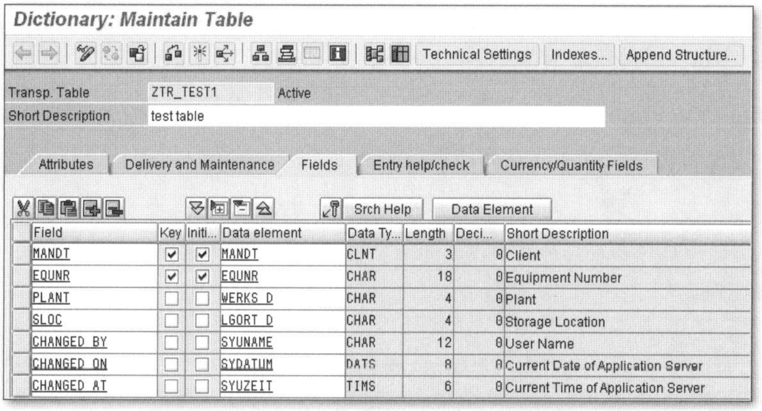

Dictionary: Maintain Table

Technical Settings | Indexes... | Append Structure...

| Transp. Table | ZTR_TEST1 | Active |
| Short Description | test table | |

Attributes | Delivery and Maintenance | Fields | Entry help/check | Currency/Quantity Fields

Srch Help | Data Element

Field	Key	Initi...	Data element	Data Ty...	Length	Deci...	Short Description
MANDT	✓	✓	MANDT	CLNT	3	0	Client
EQUNR	✓	✓	EQUNR	CHAR	18	0	Equipment Number
PLANT	☐	☐	WERKS_D	CHAR	4	0	Plant
SLOC	☐	☐	LGORT_D	CHAR	4	0	Storage Location
CHANGED_BY	☐	☐	SYUNAME	CHAR	12	0	User Name
CHANGED_ON	☐	☐	SYDATUM	DATS	8	0	Current Date of Application Server
CHANGED_AT	☐	☐	SYUZEIT	TIMS	6	0	Current Time of Application Server

Figure 7.17 Field List in Table ZTR_TEST1

Now let us suppose that the business wants CHANGED_BY, CHANGED_ON, CHANGED_AT to be non-editable fields. Data in these fields should be populated automatically. Now these fields can be maintained as display and non-editable fields with the help of the maintenance screen. To do this, follow the path ENVIRONMENT • MODIFICATIONS • MAINTENANCE SCREEN and go to maintenance screen 0001 by double-clicking it. You will be directed to the maintenance screen. There are two possible ways to make the fields non-editable:

1. Under the ELEMENT LIST tab, uncheck the INPUT flag of the fields that are required to be non-editable fields (see Figure 7.18).

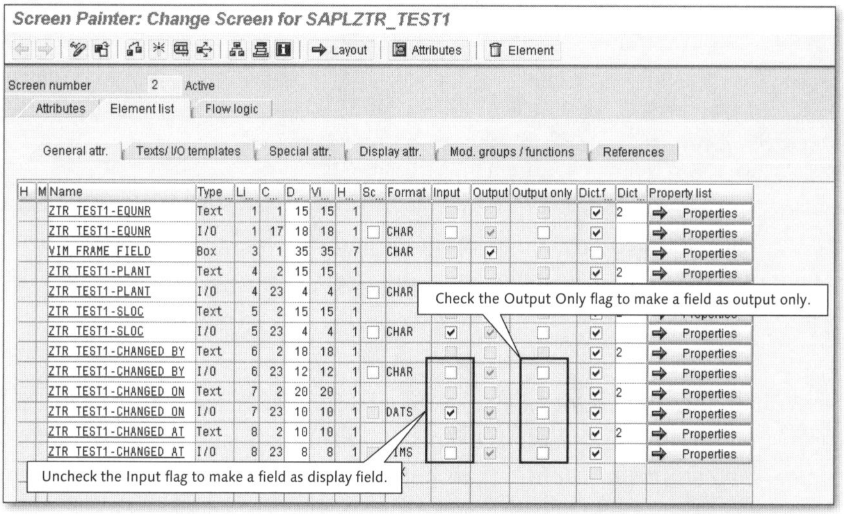

Screen Painter: Change Screen for SAPLZTR_TEST1

➡ Layout | 🖼 Attributes | 🗑 Element

| Screen number | 2 | Active |

Attributes | Element list | Flow logic

General attr. | Texts/ I/O templates | Special attr. | Display attr. | Mod. groups / functions | References

H	M	Name	Type	Li	C	D	Vi	H	Sc	Format	Input	Output	Output only	Dict.f	Dict	Property list
		ZTR_TEST1-EQUNR	Text	1	1	15	15	1						✓	2	➡ Properties
		ZTR_TEST1-EQUNR	I/O	1	17	18	18	1		CHAR	☐	☐	☐	✓		➡ Properties
		VIM_FRAME_FIELD	Box	3	1	35	35	7		CHAR		✓		☐		➡ Properties
		ZTR_TEST1-PLANT	Text	4	2	15	15	1						✓	2	➡ Properties
		ZTR_TEST1-PLANT	I/O	4	23	4	4	1	☐	CHAR				✓		➡ Properties
		ZTR_TEST1-SLOC	Text	5	2	15	15	1								
		ZTR_TEST1-SLOC	I/O	5	23	4	4	1	☐	CHAR	✓	✓	☐	✓		➡ Properties
		ZTR_TEST1-CHANGED_BY	Text	6	2	18	18	1						✓	2	➡ Properties
		ZTR_TEST1-CHANGED_BY	I/O	6	23	12	12	1		CHAR	☐	✓	☐	✓		➡ Properties
		ZTR_TEST1-CHANGED_ON	Text	7	2	20	20	1						✓	2	➡ Properties
		ZTR_TEST1-CHANGED_ON	I/O	7	23	10	10	1	☐	DATS	✓	✓	☐	✓		➡ Properties
		ZTR_TEST1-CHANGED_AT	Text	8	2	10	10	1						✓	2	➡ Properties
		ZTR_TEST1-CHANGED_AT	I/O	8	23	8	8	1		TMS	☐	✓	☐	☐		➡ Properties

Check the Output Only flag to make a field as output only.

Uncheck the Input flag to make a field as display field.

Figure 7.18 Making a Field Non-Editable from the Element List Tab

2. Click the LAYOUT (➡ Layout) icon, select the corresponding input/output field box, and select the checkbox as OUTPUT ONLY (see Figure 7.19).

The fields become non-editable as required.

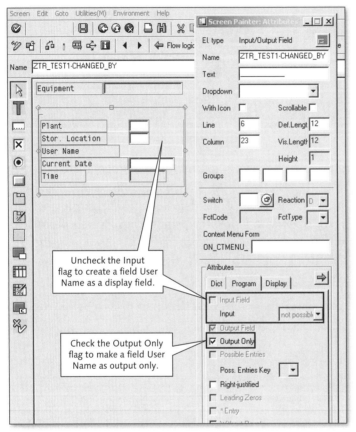

Figure 7.19 Making a Field Non-Editable from the Screen Painter

Data in these fields can be maintained programmatically by creating a new form with the help of events. Let us learn more about events.

Events

The Table Maintenance Generator can be modified with events. Events get triggered whenever certain actions are executed. Events include before saving the data, after saving the data, creating a new entry, and before deleting the data. These events are useful whenever certain new functionality or logic is required. Events are also useful for validating the data with respect to the requirement. The events can be classified as additional or replacement events. The following events are present in the Table Maintenance Generator:

▶ **Additional events**

  ▶ 01: Before saving the data in the database

  ▶ 02: After saving the data in the database

  ▶ 03: Before deleting the data displayed

  ▶ 04: After deleting the data displayed

  ▶ 05: Creating a new entry

  ▶ 06: After completely performing the function GET ORIGINAL

  ▶ 07: Before correcting the contents of a selected field

  ▶ 08: After correcting the contents of a selected field

  ▶ 09: After getting the original of an entry

  ▶ 10: After creating the header entries for the change task (E071)

  ▶ 11: After changing a key entry for the change task (E071K)

  ▶ 12: After changing the key entries for the change task (E071K)

  ▶ 13: Exit editing (exit main function module)

  ▶ 14: After lock/unlock in the main function module

  ▶ 15: Before retrieving deleted entries

  ▶ 16: After retrieving deleted entries

  ▶ 17: Do not use. Before print: Event 26

  ▶ 18: After checking whether the data has changed

  ▶ 19: After initializing global variables, field symbols, etc.

  ▶ 20: After input in date subscreen (time-dependent tables/views)

  ▶ 21: Fill hidden fields

  ▶ 22: Go to long-text maintenance for other languages

  ▶ 23: Before calling address maintenance screen

  ▶ 24: After restricting an entry (time-dependent tables/views)

  ▶ 25: Individual authorization checks

- ▶ 26: Before creating a list
- ▶ 27: After creation or copying a GUID (not a key field)
- ▶ 28: After entering a date restriction for time-dependent views
- ▶ **Replacement events**
  - ▶ AA: Instead of the standard data read routine
  - ▶ AB: Instead of the standard database change routine
  - ▶ AC: Instead of the standard GET ORIGINAL routine
  - ▶ AD: Instead of the standard RO field read routine
  - ▶ AE: Instead of standard positioning coding
  - ▶ AF: Instead of reading texts in other languages
  - ▶ AG: Instead of GET ORIGINAL for texts in other languages
  - ▶ AH: Instead of DB change for texts in other languages
  - ▶ ST: GUI menu main program name
  - ▶ AI: Internal use only

Before discussing the events themselves, let us describe the internal tables and field symbols used during the event maintenance.

Internal Tables Used During Events Maintenance

The internal table TOTAL contains all the data that is created, changed, and read in the extended Table Maintenance Generator. The data present in TOTAL is sorted in ascending order. This internal table is a formal parameter of a generated function module (see Figure 7.20).

For views or tables without text tables, the internal table TOTAL contains the structure of the view or table along with a processing and a selection flag. Listing 7.1 shows the structure of the internal table TOTAL, and Listing 7.2 shows the structure of the internal table TOTAL that is associated with the text table.

```
INCLUDE STRUCTURE <view name> or <table name>
INCLUDE STRUCTURE VIMTBFLAGS
```

Listing 7.1 Structure of Internal Table TOTAL

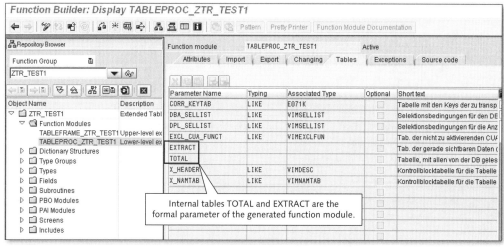

Figure 7.20 TOTAL and EXTRACT are Parameters of a Generated Function Module

For tables with text tables, the internal table TOTAL contains the structure of the table along with the structure of text table, two processing flags, and a selection flag.

```
INCLUDE STRUCTURE <view name>
INCLUDE STRUCTURE <text table name>
INCLUDE STRUCTURE VIMTBFLAGS
```

Listing 7.2 Structure of Internal Table TOTAL with Text Table

The structure of the table TOTAL is not transparent. To access the table fields, the record should be defined with this structure. The fields can be accessed via the structure when the header line of the table TOTAL is assigned to the structure. Processing and selection flags are contained in each record of the table and can be read in the loop for each record over the table.

The processing flag can be accessed via the field symbol <ACTION>. It indicates whether the table record is changed, unchanged (original), new, or flagged for deletion. If the maintenance dialog of the table also contains its text table, which is linked with the table by the foreign key relationship TEXT, the field symbol <ACTION> refers only to the entity table and not to the text table. The text table has its own processing flag with the same semantics, which can be accessed via the field symbol <ACTION_TEXT>. The selection flag can be accessed via the field symbol <MARK>. It indicates whether the record is selected for action or not.

EXTRACT

The internal table EXTRACT is the data display work table; that is, data that will be displayed in the screen should be present in this table. During runtime, it contains all the data that was selected from the table TOTAL in the extended table maintenance. The data present in TOTAL is sorted in ascending order. This internal table is a formal parameter of a generated function module. The user selects the data from EXTRACT by calling functions such as ALL READ ENTRIES, ALL SELECTED ENTRIES, or ALL CHANGED ENTRIES.

Structure of EXTRACT

Like the structure of TOTAL, the internal table EXTRACT also contains the structure of the view or table along with a processing and a selection flag for views or tables without text tables, as shown in Listing 7.3.

```
INCLUDE STRUCTURE <view name> or <table name>
INCLUDE STRUCTURE VIMTBFLAGS
```

Listing 7.3 Structure of Internal Table EXTRACT

Like the structure of TOTAL, the internal table EXTRACT also contains the structure of the table, along with the structure of the text table, two processing flags, and a selection flag for tables with the text table (Listing 7.4).

```
INCLUDE STRUCTURE <view name>
INCLUDE STRUCTURE <text table name>
INCLUDE STRUCTURE VIMTBFLAGS
```

Listing 7.4 Structure of Internal Table EXTRACT with Text Table

The structure of the table EXTRACT is not transparent. To access the table fields, a record should be defined with this structure. The fields can be accessed via the structure when the header line of the table EXTRACT is assigned to the structure. Processing and selection flags are contained in each record of the table and can be read in the loop for each record over the table. The processing flag can be accessed via the field symbol <XACT>. This indicates whether the table record is changed, unchanged (original), new, or flagged for deletion.

If the maintenance dialog of the table also contains its text table, which is linked with the table by the foreign key relationship TEXT, the field symbol <XACT> refers only to the entity table and not to the text table. The text table has its own processing flag with the same semantics, which can be accessed via the field symbol <XACT_TEXT>.

The selection flag can be accessed via the field symbol <MARK>. It indicates whether the record is selected for action or not.

Field Symbols Used During Events Maintenance

The processing and selection flag in the internal tables TOTAL and EXTRACT is populated by the field symbols. Let us discuss the following field symbols:

- ▶ <Action>
  Returns the processing status of individual table records. It is used as a processing status in the internal table TOTAL.

- ▶ <Action_text>
  Returns the processing status of individual table records for the text table read. It is used for the processing status for the text table in internal table TOTAL. This field symbol is used only when the maintenance dialog was created for a table with a text table and not for a maintenance dialog based on a view.

- ▶ <Xact>
  Returns the processing status of individual table records. It is used as a processing status in internal table EXTRACT.

- ▶ <Xact_text>
  Returns the processing status of individual table records for the text table read. It is used for the processing status for the text table in internal table EXTRACT. This field symbol is used only when the maintenance dialog was created for a table with a text table and not for a maintenance dialog based on a view.

- ▶ <Mark>
  The selection flag can be accessed via the field symbol <MARK>. It indicates whether the record is selected for action.

Constants for Field Symbols <ACTION>, <ACTION_TEXT>, <XACT> and <XACT_TEXT>

The entries in the internal tables TOTAL and EXTRACT can have one of the following values for the processing status:

- ▶ GELOESCHT: Flagged for deletion

- ▶ NEUER_EINTRAG: New entry

- ▶ AENDERN: Changed entry

- ▶ UPDATE_GELOESCHT: Entry first changed and then flagged for deletion

▶ NEUER_GELOESCHT: Entry first newly created, not yet saved, and then flagged for deletion

▶ ORIGINAL: The same as the database status

Constants for Field Symbols <MARK>
The entries in the internal tables TOTAL and EXTRACT can have one of the following values for the selection status:

▶ MARKIERT: Selected

▶ UEBERGEHEN: Skipped

▶ NICHT_MARKIERT: Not selected and not skipped

Now, let's discuss the events present in the Table Maintenance Generator.

▶ **Event 01: Before saving the data in the database**
This event is triggered before saving the entries to the database. Entries can be new, changed, or deleted. Other activities that can be performed with this event include hidden entry processing, filling hidden fields, and flagging data to be written to hidden tables after the database change.

▶ **Event 02: After saving the data in the database**
This event is triggered just after saving the entries to the database. Other activities such as maintaining hidden tables and links to application logs can also be performed with this event.

▶ **Event 03: Before deleting the display data**
This event is triggered before deleting the selected entries. Entries can be deleted with the DELETE function. Other activities such as checking whether the entries can be deleted can be performed with this event.

▶ **Event 04: After deleting the display data**
This event is triggered just after deleting the selected entries. Other activities such as filling hidden fields, adjusting user internal data, and sending a user message can be performed with this event.

▶ **Event 05: When creating a new entry**
This event is triggered when a new entry is made with the function NEW ENTRY or COPY. Other activities such as plausibility checks, hidden field handling, and updating user internal tables can be performed with this event.

▶ **Event 06: After the Get Original function**
This event is triggered after the GET ORIGINAL function for all selected entries.

Other activities such as filling hidden fields, initializing hidden fields, and updating user internal tables can be performed with this event.

▶ **Event 07: Before correcting the contents of the selected fields**
This event is triggered when the CHANGE FIELD CONTENTS function is called. Other activities such as checking the entries field, filling the hidden fields, and updating the user internal tables can be performed with this event.

▶ **Event 08: After correcting the contents of the selected fields**
This event is triggered after the execution of the CHANGE FIELD CONTENTS function. Other activities such as filling the hidden fields and updating the user internal tables can be performed with this event.

▶ **Event 09: After Get Original for one entry**
This event is triggered after the execution of the GET ORIGINAL function for each of the selected entries. Other activities such as filling the hidden fields, initializing the hidden fields, and updating the user internal tables can be performed with this event. Only one entry is handled at a time. This entry is returned in the header line of the internal tables (TOTAL and EXTRACT) and in the field symbol <TABLE1>.

▶ **Event 10: After creating the change request header entries (E071)**
This event is triggered after the creation of the standard change request header entry.

▶ **Event 11: After changing the key entry in the change request (E071K)**
This event is triggered after an entry was made in the change request key list by choosing SAVE.

▶ **Event 12: After changing the key entry in the change request (E071K)**
This event is triggered after entries have been made in the change request key list by choosing SAVE.

▶ **Event 13: End processing**
This event occurs when exiting the maintenance dialog. Other activities such as resetting user flags, initializing user fields and internal tables, and initializing the function group local memory can be performed with this event.

▶ **Event 14: After locking/unlocking in the main function module**
This event is triggered when the processing mode changes (display to change or change to display) and after the maintenance dialog tables have been locked according to the ABAP Data Dictionary information. Other activities such as locking/unlocking other hidden tables can also be performed.

▶ **Event 15: Before retrieving deleted entries**
This event occurs before entries are retrieved from the trash with the function RETRIEVE. Other activities can also be performed, such as checking whether the entries are prevented from being retrieved by other dependencies.

▶ **Event 16: After retrieving deleted entries**
This event occurs after entries have been retrieved from the trash with the RETRIEVE function. Other activities such as filling hidden fields, updating user internal tables, and sending a user message can be performed with this event.

▶ **Event 17: Before printing entries**
This event occurs before the PRINT function. Other activities such as changing the format of table or view fields for printing, including hidden fields for printing, and not printing fields that are not flagged as hidden in the ABAP Data Dictionary can be performed with this event. Avoid using this event; instead, use Event 26.

▶ **Event 18: After the data change check**
This event occurs after security-relevant changes have been made in the internal table TOTAL. Other activities such as checking user internal tables for security-relevant changes can also be performed with this event.

▶ **Event 19: After initializing global variables, field symbols, etc.**
This event occurs when a Table Maintenance Dialog is called. The function group local memory is initialized at each entry. Other activities such as initializing user global data or internal tables, changing the maintenance screen title bar, and deactivating interface functions in the internal table EXCL_CUA_FUNC can be performed with this event.

▶ **Event 20: After date subscreen input (time-dependent tables/views)**
This event is only used in association with time-dependent tables/views. It runs as soon as an input is made in the date subscreen. Other activities can be performed, such as filling hidden fields and updating user internal tables.

▶ **Event 21: Fill hidden fields**
This event occurs when fields that are flagged in the Data Dictionary as HIDDEN are to be filled.

▶ **Event 22: Go to long text maintenance for other languages**
This event allows long-text maintenance from the translation. In contrast to other events, this event affects the maintenance screen. When the event is assigned to the maintenance dialog, a button with the DISPLAY/CHANGE OTHERS icon appears after each entry in the TEXTS IN OTHER LANGUAGES maintenance

screen. This event occurs when the user presses the button to go to the long text of the current entry.

▶ **Event 23: Before the Address Maintenance screen call**
This event occurs before the Address Maintenance screen is displayed; that is, before the `ADDR_DIALOG_PREPARE` function module call. The module is usually only used to set the address maintenance screen title. If the standard address maintenance screen does not satisfy your specific requirements, the maintenance screen can be configured context-dependently.

▶ **Event 25: At the start of the maintenance dialog**
This event calls an additional authorization check.

▶ **Event 26: Before displayed data is output in a list**
The function module `REUSE_ALV_LIST_DISPLAY` outputs the list. Other activities can be performed such as changing table or view field display format, printing hidden fields, and not printing fields that are not flagged as hidden in the ABAP Data Dictionary.

▶ **Event 27: After filling a GUID field**
This event occurs if the current table or view has a GUID and the GUID field has a new value. GUID values can be entered by the NEW ENTRY or COPY functions. Even if a maintenance dialog is processed in the background—such as when importing a BC set or comparing tables—GUID fields are given new values. Activities such as filling other tables in the background, linking the new GUID to other objects, and checking whether the field is to have a new or an existing GUID are possible for this event after filling a GUID field.

▶ **Event AA: Instead of the standard data read routine**
This event occurs when the data to be maintained is read in. Non-standard logic can be run, such as reading in additional data, changing the data read in, and reading in the data differently from in the standard. The views or table/text table data must be read in the internal table TOTAL.

▶ **Event AB: Instead of the standard database changes routine**
This event occurs at the SAVE function. Non-standard logic can be run, such as also changing hidden tables in the database.

▶ **Event AC: Instead of the standard cancel changes routine**
This event occurs at the CANCEL CHANGES function. Non-standard logic can be run, such as also processing fields that are not in the view/table, but are displayed in the overview or detail screens.

233

▶ **Event AD: Instead of the standard RO field read routine**
This event is only relevant for views, and only if the view contains fields from referred tables. It occurs when the contents of the referred fields must be changed. Non-standard logic can be run, such as reading display values from a table other than the assigned one. The read-only field in the view must come from a referred table.

▶ **Event AE: Instead of the standard positioning code**
This event occurs at the POSITION function. Non-standard logic can be run, such as having the internal table EXTRACT key not sorted in ascending order.

▶ **Event AF: Instead of reading texts in other languages**
This event occurs at the TRANSLATION function. Texts are read in and made available for translation according to the selected languages. Non-standard logic can be run; for example, changing the data read in, or reading in the data differently from the standard (performance, dependencies), possibly with additional checks. This event also occurs if time-dependent entries are restricted by time-dependent texts. In this case, the language-dependent texts must be read in all languages.

▶ **Event AG: Instead of Get Original for texts in other languages**
This event occurs at the GET ORIGINAL function, which retrieves the language-dependent texts as well as the original texts from the database. Non-standard logic can be run, such as also processing text fields that are not in the table or view but are displayed on the maintenance screen.

▶ **Event AH: Instead of database changes for texts in other languages**
This event occurs at the SAVE function. Non-standard logic can be run, such as also changing hidden tables in the database.

▶ **Event ST: GUI Menu Main Program Name**
This event occurs at every PBO. The function group interface can now be set for the table or view maintenance dialog at runtime instead of the standard interface. The program name of the function group `SAPL<fugr>` is entered here, not a form routine name as in all other events.

Maintain Events

Let us discuss how to maintain events.

1. Follow the path ENVIRONMENT • MODIFICATION • EVENTS. A dialog box will appear with an information message. Click on the checkmark icon to confirm (see Figure 7.21).

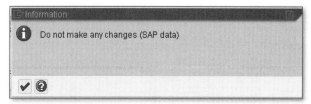

Figure 7.21 Dialog Box While Maintaining Events

2. On the next screen, click on NEW ENTRIES to create a new event.

3. In the next screen, write the name of the event and form. F4 help can be selected for defining the event name (see Figure 7.22).

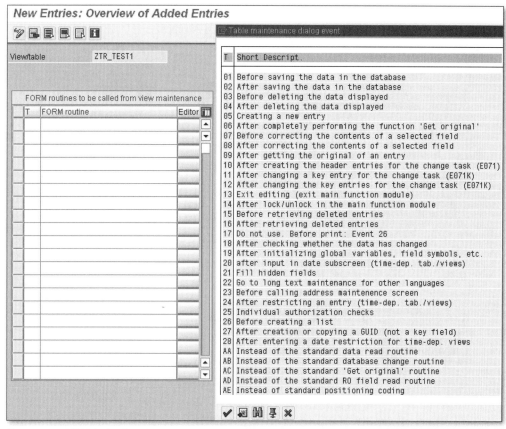

Figure 7.22 F4 Help for Events

4. Save the entries, and click on the EDITOR (📄) icon (see Figure 7.23).

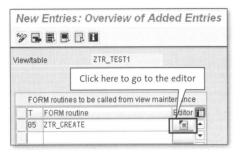

Figure 7.23 Enter Event and Form Name

5. A dialog box will appear that will ask you to specify the `Include` file in which this event's subroutine will reside. Upon clicking on the checkmark icon (see Figure 7.24), another dialog box will appear that will give the warning that a new `include` will be inserted in the main program. Once the checkmark icon is clicked (see Figure 7.25), a newly created include will be inserted.

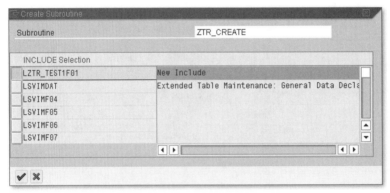

Figure 7.24 Inserting New Subroutine in Main Program

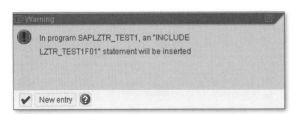

Figure 7.25 Dialog Box While Creating Event Form

6. Write the coding and validation that is required in the FORM routine of this INCLUDE file (see Figure 7.26).

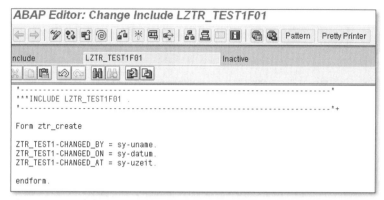

Figure 7.26 Validating Requirement in Event's Form Component

7. Save and activate the `include` by clicking on the ACTIVATE (✱) icon. Because the event is 05 (creating a new entry), this event will be triggered whenever a new entry is created and the SAVE button is pressed. CHANGED_BY, CHANGED_ON, AND CHANGED_AT fields will automatically get populated by the logic present in the FORM routine of the INCLUDE.

Maintain Parameter Transaction Code

Parameter transactions can be created for the maintenance dialog. With this transaction, the maintenance dialog can be called from the program. Let us discuss the procedure for creating the parameter transaction.

1. Go to MAINTAIN TRANSACTION INITIAL SCREEN (Transaction SE93) or follow the path ENVIRONMENT • TRANSACTION CODE. Enter the transaction code to be maintained and choose the CREATE button (see Figure 7.27).

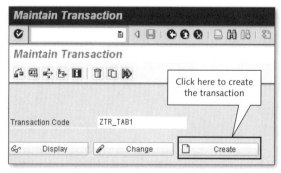

Figure 7.27 Maintain Transaction Initial Screen

2. A dialog box will appear, and you enter the SHORT TEXT and choose the radio button TRANSACTION WITH PARAMETERS (PARAMETER TRANSACTION). Click on the CHECKMARK icon (see Figure 7.28).

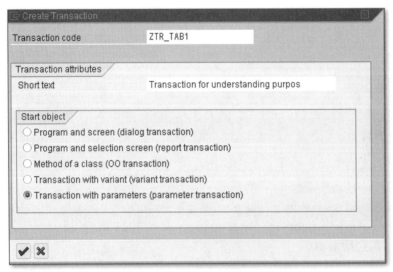

Figure 7.28 Dialog Box to Enter Short Text and Start Object

3. The CREATE PARAMETER TRANSACTION maintenance screen will be displayed. Enter Transaction SM30 in THE DEFAULT VALUE FOR TRANSACTION FIELD. Choose SKIP INITIAL SCREEN if you want to skip the initial screen of SM30 and directly call the maintenance screen of the table. Enter the required parameter in the DEFAULT VALUES box. Selecting F4 will give you a list of all the values that the SCREEN FIELD can have. Select the name of the screen field and give it a value X to perform that action (see Figure 7.29).

4. Save and test the transaction by entering the transaction code in the command box. This created transaction can be used for maintaining the entries for the table.

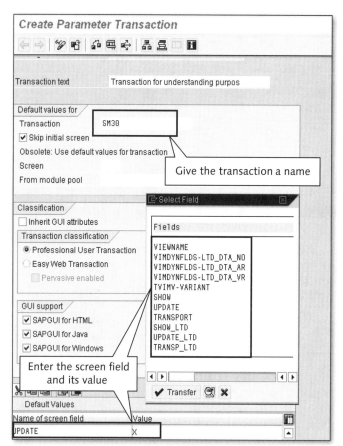

Figure 7.29 Creating Parameter Transaction

7.3 Maintaining Authorization Groups

Authorization groups for tables and views can be maintained either by executing Transaction SE54 and choosing the radio button AUTHORIZATION GROUPS or by following the path ENVIRONMENT • AUTHORIZATIONS • AUTHORIZATION GROUPS from the maintenance screen of a table or view. Follow this procedure to maintain an authorization group:

1. Choose the radio button AUTHORIZATIONS GROUP in the GENERATE TABLE MAINTENANCE DIALOG: INITIAL TABLE/VIEW SCREEN (Transaction SE54). Click on the CREATE/CHANGE button (see Figure 7.30).

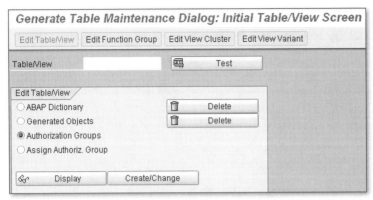

Figure 7.30 Transaction SE54 to Create Authorization Group

2. In the OVERVIEW screen, click on the NEW ENTRIES button (see Figure 7.31).

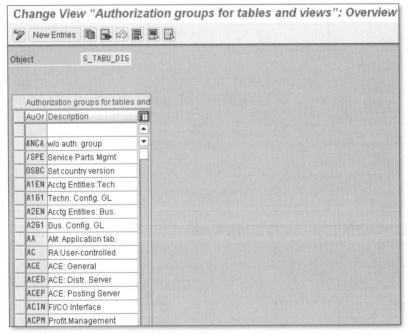

Figure 7.31 Creating New Authorization Group

3. The NEW ENTRIES: OVERVIEW OF ADDED ENTRIES screen will be displayed for adding a new authorization group. Enter the name of the new entry for an authorization group (see Figure 7.32).

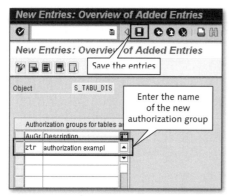

Figure 7.32 Maintaining New Entry to Create New Authorization Group

4. Save the entry by clicking on the SAVE (▣) icon and activating the authorization. For an authorization to be activated, an activity for an authorization group must be maintained in the authorization object.

Tables or views are assigned to an authorization group when their maintenance dialogs are generated. With the ASSIGN AUTHORIZATION GROUP, multiple assignments can be maintained or deleted, and several views and tables can be combined into a new authorization group. Let us discuss the procedure for maintaining the authorization group assignment.

1. Choose the ASSIGN AUTHORIZATIONS GROUP radio button in the GENERATE TABLE MAINTENANCE DIALOG: INITIAL TABLE/VIEW SCREEN (Transaction SE54). Click on the CREATE/CHANGE button.

2. A dialog box will appear for the selection criteria. Mark the criteria as required and choose the checkmark icon (see Figure 7.33).

Figure 7.33 Dialog Box for Selection Criteria While Assigning Authorization Group

3. A dialog box will appear that you can use to determine the work area. Enter the work area for restricting the number of entries, and choose the checkmark icon (see Figure 7.34).

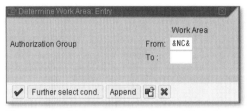

Figure 7.34 Dialog Box for Assigning Work Area

4. Change an authorization group's assignments of the displayed tables and views according to your requirement. Choose NEW ENTRIES to create new assignments (see Figure 7.35).

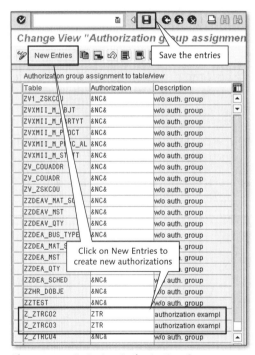

Figure 7.35 Assigning Authorization Groups

5. Save the entry by clicking on the SAVE icon.

7.4 Maintaining Function Group

The function group of the generated maintenance dialog can be maintained by choosing the EDIT FUNCTION GROUPS button in GENERATE TABLE MAINTENANCE DIALOG: INITIAL SCREEN (Transaction SE54) (see Figure 7.36).

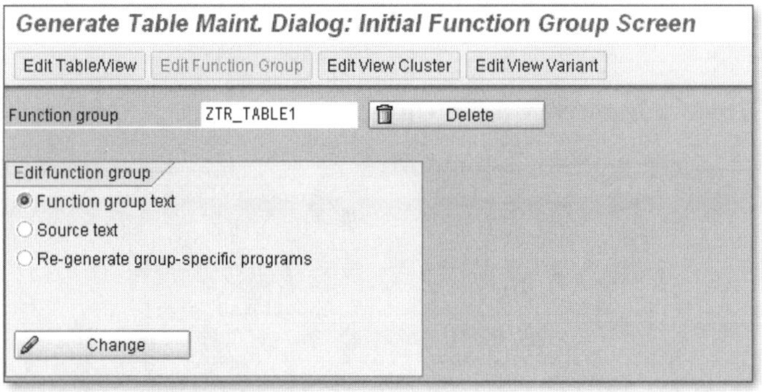

Figure 7.36 Maintaining Function Group

The following maintenance options are offered by the system:

▸ FUNCTION GROUP TEXT
  If you click on this radio button and choose the CHANGE icon, another dialog box will be displayed. In this dialog box, function group text such as SHORT TEXT, PERSON RESPONSIBLE, APPLICATION, and PROGRAM STATUS can be changed. Click on the SAVE button to save the changes (see Figure 7.37). You will be directed to the main program of the maintenance dialog if you choose the MAIN PROGRAM button.

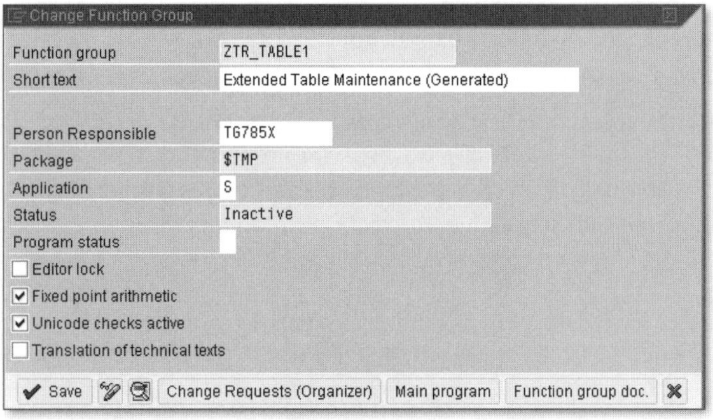

Figure 7.37 Maintaining Function Group Text

▶ SOURCE TEXT

If this radio button is selected, a dialog box will appear. This dialog box will contain the list of the program components in the function group that can be changed. However, this list doesn't contain the generated program components, as these cannot be changed. When a program component is selected and the checkmark icon is clicked, the ABAP editor for the chosen program component is displayed (see Figure 7.38).

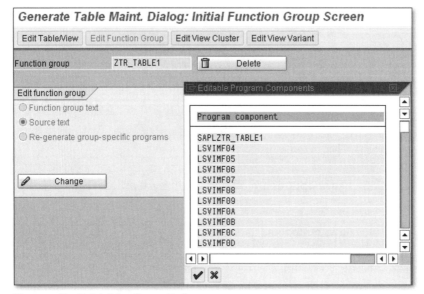

Figure 7.38 Maintaining Source Text

▶ RE-GENERATED GROUP-SPECIFIC PROGRAMS

If this radio button is clicked, a dialog box will appear. This dialog box can have the values STRUCTURE-SPEC. RENEWAL PAI MODULE, STRUCTURE SPEC. DATA DECLARATION RENEWAL, REFRESH STRUCTURE-SPECIFIC FORM ROUTINES, UPDATE GENERAL DATA DECLARATIONS, or UPDATE FUNCTION GROUP MAIN PROGRAM. Check the desired checkboxes as required and click on the checkmark icon. Group-specific programs will be regenerated (see Figure 7.39).

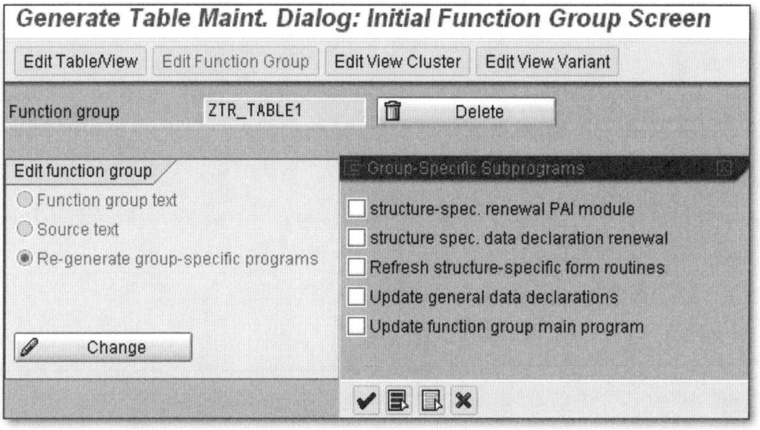

Figure 7.39 Regenerating Function Group

7.5   View Variants

Maintenance view variants represent a partial view of the generated maintenance dialog. Maintenance view variants restrict the maintenance dialog on which they are based. A maintenance view variant may select fewer maintenance fields or implement more restrictive database selection than the initial maintenance dialog. For example, suppose a maintenance dialog is created for the total number of students present in a class. A certain set of rules is required for boys and another set of rules for girls. These rules can be implemented by creating a maintenance view variant from the generated maintenance dialog. The maintenance view variant does not have its own maintenance dialog. It inherits the maintenance dialog, including the maintenance screen and other checks from which it is based.

The maintenance dialog for which you create the maintenance view variant should already exist. Now, let us discuss the procedure for creating a view variant.

1. Go to GENERATE TABLE MAINTENANCE DIALOG: VIEW VARIANT INITIAL SCREEN by selecting the push button EDIT VIEW VARIANT in Transaction SE54. Enter the name of the view variant, select the radio button ABAP DICTIONARY, and click the CREATE button (see Figure 7.40).

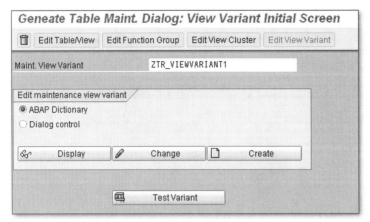

Figure 7.40 Initial Screen to Create View Variant

2. In the maintenance screen of the view variant, enter the short description. This will help to identify the view variant (see Figure 7.41).

3. Under the TABLES column, add the basic maintenance dialog. This maintenance dialog will act as a parent for the view variant. When the maintenance dialog is added, its dependent sub-objects are also added under it in the TABLES column.

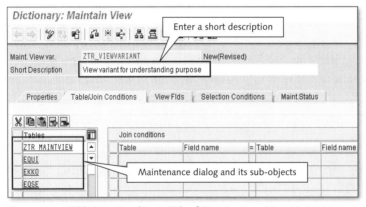

Figure 7.41 Table/Join Conditions Tab of Maintenance View Variant

4. Under the VIEW FIELDS tab, basic VIEW FIELDS of the maintenance dialog are automatically present in the view variants. However, key fields should not be deleted from the view variants (see Figure 7.42).

5. More fields that are present in the maintenance dialog can be added here. To include more fields, choose the TABLES FIELDS button. A dialog box will appear that contains the list of fields present in the basic maintenance dialog. Select the required field and click on the COPY button.

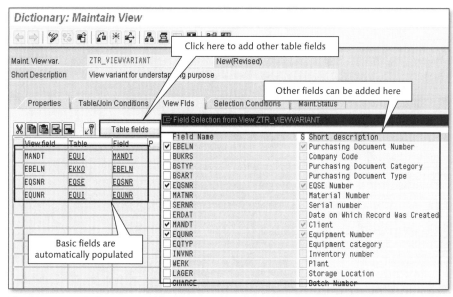

Figure 7.42 Including New Fields in View Variant

6. Enter the value for the MAINTENANCE ATTRIBUTE FOR A VIEW FIELD. Maintenance attributes of the view variant must be compatible with the maintenance attributes specified in the basic dialog (see Figure 7.43). The values shown in Table 7.1 are compatible with the maintenance attributes.

Maintenance Attributes of Basic Dialog	Maintenance Attributes of View Variant
<Space>	R, H
R	R, H
S	S
H	H

Table 7.1 Mapping of Maintenance Attributes of View Variant to Basic Dialog

The compatibility is not checked when the variant is created. At runtime, invalid maintenance attributes are ignored and the original dialog maintenance attributes are used.

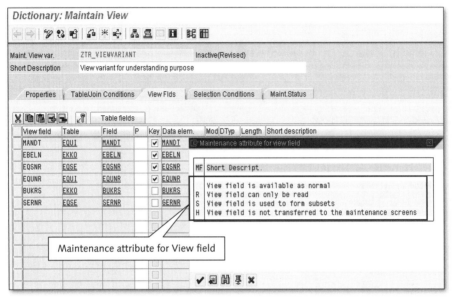

Figure 7.43 Values of Maintenance Attributes for View Field

7. Under the SELECTION CONDITIONS tab, select the conditions for restricting the data records according to requirements (see Figure 7.44). In data maintenance, both the maintenance view selection conditions and the maintenance view variant selection conditions are applied. The maintenance view selection conditions only apply if they were generated in the maintenance dialog. For example, if the selection conditions were put in the ABAP Data Dictionary later and the maintenance dialog was not regenerated, these selection conditions would not apply in the maintenance view variants.

8. Under the MAINTENANCE STATUS tab, enter the value for ACCESS mode and DATA BROWSER/TABLE VIEW MAINT. (see Figure 7.45).

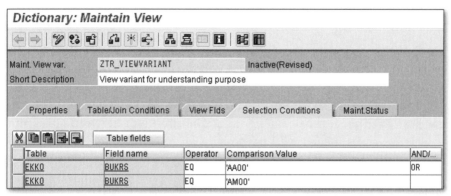

Figure 7.44 Entering Selection Conditions for View Variant

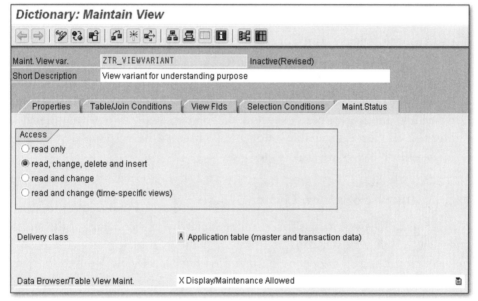

Figure 7.45 Maintaining Status for View Variant

9. Save the view variant by choosing the SAVE icon. Activate the view variant by choosing the ACTIVATE icon. Assign the view variant to the authorization group from the path UTILITIES • ASSIGN AUTHORIZATION GROUP and test your view variant.

7.6 View Clusters

A view cluster is a collection of maintenance dialogs of tables or views that are collected in one maintenance unit for business or technical reasons. Related data from more than one table or view can be maintained consistently with a view cluster. Maintenance views can process only 1:1 relationships between tables. In addition, a view cluster can process key extensions and relationships between tables and views. This means maintenance dialogs with no key or partial key dependency can be processed with view clusters.

Grouping dialogs into single maintenance units with the help of view clusters has the following advantages for data maintenance:

▶ **Navigation**
With standard navigation in a view cluster, navigation between the individual maintenance dialogs is convenient. This simplifies the maintenance of the data in a view cluster.

▶ **Consistency**
Data consistency is maintained in view cluster while deleting, copying, saving, retrieving, and manually transporting data. For example, when an entry in a higher-level view is deleted, it automatically ensures that all dependent entries in lower-level views are also deleted.

7.6.1 Structure of a View Cluster

Navigation in a view cluster is based on the hierarchy of the dialogs of the tables and views. A view cluster consists of one or more root dialogs and at most 14 maintenance dialogs that depend on them. A lower level view has one or more additional fields in its key when compared with its higher-level view. Each data record at a higher level view contains several dependent data records below it at the lower level.

Each maintenance dialog of a view variant is an independent unit consisting of an overview screen or an overview and a single screen, depending on the dialog type. The unit contains the data to be maintained. The overview screen also contains a navigation area used for navigation between lower- or higher-level maintenance dialogs.

A maintenance dialog can be one-level or two-level. One-level maintenance dialogs contain only one screen: the list screen in which all existing data records are displayed in a table. Two-level maintenance dialogs contain two screens. On double-clicking the data records in the list screen, a detailed screen of the selected data record will be displayed.

Before creating the view cluster, a maintenance dialog for each view should be generated. While generating the maintenance dialog, flag with the maintenance attribute S the key fields that are identical in the view and its higher level in the cluster. The system will automatically fill the key fields while navigating from the upper level to the lower level, with the values of the data record selected in the upper level. Transaction SE54 is used for creating and defining a view cluster, and Transaction SM34 is used for maintaining a view cluster.

7.6.2 Creating View Clusters

The maintenance dialogs must be created before defining a view cluster. With that done, proceed as follows to create a view cluster.

1. Go to GENERATE TABLE MAINTENANCE DIALOG: VIEW CLUSTER INITIAL SCREEN by selecting the EDIT VIEW CLUSTER button in Transaction SE54. Enter the name of the view cluster and choose the CREATE/CHANGE button (see Figure 7.46).

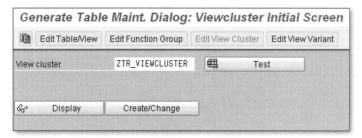

Figure 7.46 Initial Screen for Creating a View Cluster

2. You will be directed to the HEADER ENTRY screen of the view cluster (see Figure 7.47).

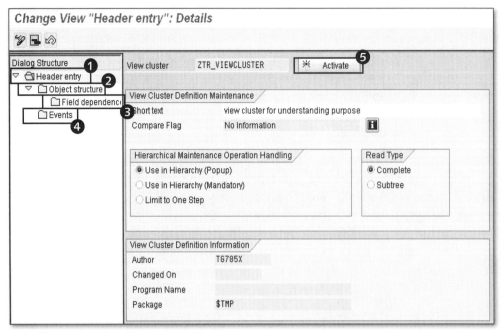

Figure 7.47   View Cluster and Its Steps

The creation of view cluster can be divided into five steps.

Step 1: Header Entry

The header entry specifies the behavior of the view clusters in maintenance operations. It also affects the hierarchy levels and the data read type. The maintenance screen of the header entry comprises three groups:

▶ NAVIGATION
  The navigation group is used to navigate from one maintenance screen to another. This group is present in all the view cluster creation maintenance screens.

▶ VIEW CLUSTER DEFINITION MAINTENANCE
  In the view cluster definition maintenance group, the short text can be maintained. This will help to identify the view cluster later. Apart from short text, technical data such as hierarchical maintenance operation handling and the read type can also be maintained for view cluster under this group (see Figure 7.48). Hierarchical maintenance operation handling can have one of the following values.

► USE IN HIERARCHY (POPUP): This value states that object's changes will affect the superior and dependent objects. The same changes can be made to the superior objects by ignoring the prompt, or the maintenance dialog can be cancelled.

► USE IN HIERARCHY (MANDATORY): If the changes are made to an object and the same changes are required in the superior or dependent objects, the system automatically makes the required changes to the superior or dependent objects.

► LIMIT TO ONE STEP: The system ignores the dependencies and executes the operation for the current object only.

Read type can have one of the following values:

► COMPLETE: Data is transferred to the application server for all view cluster objects.

► SUBTREE: Data of the start object and its dependent objects is only transferred to the application server. Data of other objects is transferred as required.

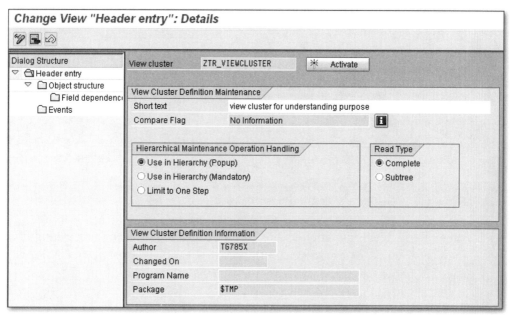

Figure 7.48 View Cluster Header Data

▶ VIEW CLUSTER DEFINITION INFORMATION
The system displays general information such as AUTHOR, CHANGED ON, PROGRAM
NAME, and PACKAGE.

Step 2: Object Structure

Object structure determines the relationships of the view cluster objects on the
table or view level. The navigation subscreen structure and the initial view cluster
maintenance object can also be defined in the object structure. Object structure
contains three components: navigation, object structure, and field dependency. We
discuss navigation and object structure in the list below, and field dependency is
discussed in step 3.

▶ **Navigation**
A navigation group is used to navigate from one maintenance screen to another.
This group is present in all the view cluster creation maintenance screens.

▶ **Object structure (view cluster description maintenance)**
In this group, the object relationship of the tables and the entry format in the
navigation subscreen are entered (see Figure 7.49).

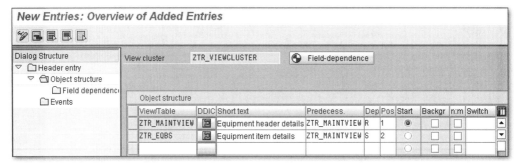

Figure 7.49 View Cluster Object Structure

When these details are entered and ⌨Enter is pressed, a dialog box stating that
the VIEW/TABLE & CAN ALSO BE MAINTAINED INDEPENDENTLY OF VIEW CLUSTER will
appear. Choose the checkmark icon (see Figure 7.50).

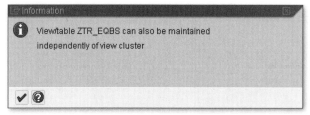

Figure 7.50 Information Dialog While Adding an Abject Structure

Step 3: Field Dependencies

This button is used to automatically generate the field dependencies of the view cluster objects if the corresponding foreign key relationship for these objects exists in the ABAP Data Dictionary. Select the objects and choose the FIELD DEPENDENCE (🌐) icon. A dialog box stating the successful generation of field dependencies will be displayed (see Figure 7.51).

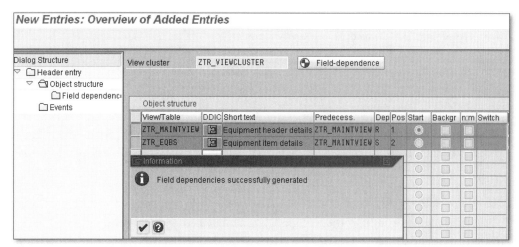

Figure 7.51 Generating Field Dependencies

Field dependencies specify the relationships among the fields present in a dialog. The dependency of a view or table field is generally limited to a field in the higher-level dialog (see Figure 7.52). For the key fields that depend on their predecessors, view definition maintenance attribute S must be assigned. The restrictions from the predecessor of the selected entry are displayed in the maintenance screen header. When new entries are created, the key fields are filled according to these restrictions.

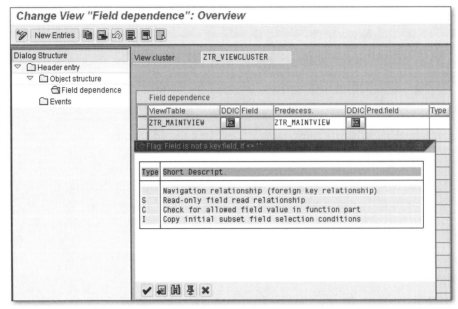

Figure 7.52 Field Dependencies of a View Cluster

Step 4: Events

The standard flow can be modified at the predefined positions in the flow logic with the help of events. Form routines are defined in the module pool (type M) or subroutine pool (type S). The module pool or subroutine pool must contain the include LSVCMCOD for global data transfer. The events can be classified as an additional or replacement event. The following events are present in view clusters.

- ▶ **Additional events**
    - ▶ 01: After initialization of global variables, field symbols, etc.
    - ▶ 02: After reading/specifying selection conditions
    - ▶ 03: Before navigation in another object
    - ▶ 04: Before saving the data in the database
    - ▶ 05: After saving the data in the database
    - ▶ 06: After locking/unlocking in main function module
    - ▶ 07: After leaving the view maintenance module for an object
    - ▶ 08: End of processing (leave the main function module)
    - ▶ 09: In navigation before sending the missing-subsets pop-up

- ► 10: In navigation, after the target object is determined
- ► 11: When determining the dependent entries for a hierarchical view cluster maintenance operation (copy, delete, undo, manual transport)
- ► 12: When determining the superior entries for a hierarchical view cluster maintenance operation
- ► **Replacement events**
  - ► EQ: Instead of locking/unlocking
  - ► GR: Instead of specifying selection conditions
  - ► RE: Instead of reading
  - ► SV: Instead of saving the data in the database
  - ► CK: Instead of checking the values for new/changed entry

Step 5: Activate

View clusters can be activated after maintaining the header entry, the object structure, and the field dependencies. Proceed as follows to activate the view cluster.

1. Go to the header entry screen of the view cluster.

2. Activate the view cluster by choosing the ACTIVATE icon (see Figure 7.53).

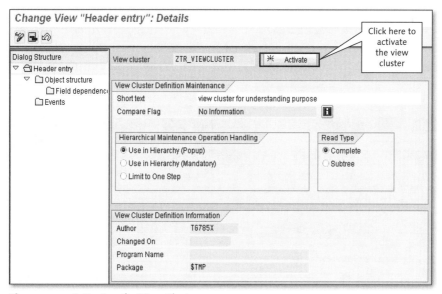

Figure 7.53 Activating the View Cluster

3. The MODIFY SCREEN dialog box will appear. Confirm the dialog box (see Figure 7.54).

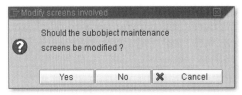

Figure 7.54 Modify Screen Dialog Box

The system saves the view cluster definition and checks its consistency. If errors occur, they are logged and the view cluster is not activated. The system also generates the maintenance object description.

Single dialog maintenance screen can be automatically adjusted. Because the entries must be checked against an internal table and not against a database table, the system deactivates the foreign key checks.

> **Note**
>
> Dialogs used for modifying the view cluster must not be used for maintenance of individual tables or views. This can cause database table inconsistencies because the foreign key check is deactivated when the screens are modified.

If errors occur while activating a view cluster, they are logged in an error log. An overview of all activation errors is displayed on the initial screen. To see additional information on an error message, mark the error message and choose LTEXT (see Figure 7.55).

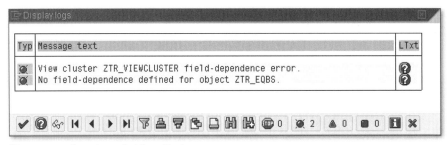

Figure 7.55 Error Log of a View Cluster

4. Remove the error and again activate the view cluster by choosing the ACTIVATE icon. A dialog box will be displayed when the view cluster is activated (see Figure 7.56).

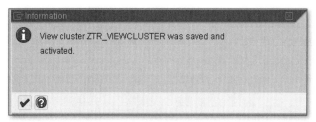

Figure 7.56 Activation Dialog Box

7.6.3 Testing View Clusters

Now that we've created view clusters, let us discuss the procedure to test them.

1. Go to GENERATE TABLE MAINTENANCE DIALOG: VIEW CLUSTER INITIAL SCREEN by selecting the button EDIT VIEW CLUSTER in Transaction SE54. Enter the name of the view cluster and choose the TEST button (see Figure 7.57).

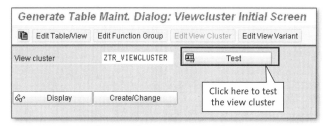

Figure 7.57 Initial Screen for Testing View Cluster

2. You will be directed to the header-level view screen where the HEADER DETAILS are displayed. New entries can be maintained by clicking on the NEW ENTRIES button.

3. Item details of a particular entry can be displayed by selecting an entry and clicking the ITEM DETAILS folder box (see Figure 7.58). The item-details screen will be displayed for a selected header level entry (see Figure 7.59).

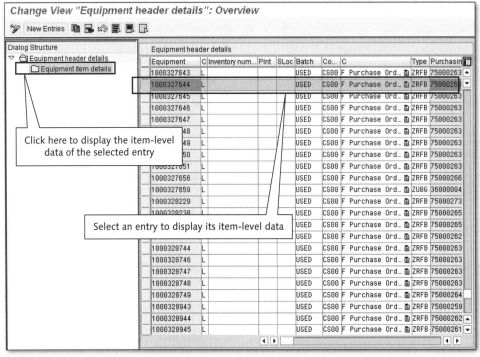

Figure 7.58 Header-Level Screen of View Cluster

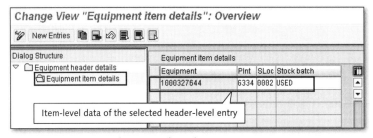

Figure 7.59 Item-Level Screen Selected

4. Existing entries can be modified and new entries can be created with the help of view clusters. Whenever an entry is modified or created, it will be saved automatically to the corresponding table.

7.7   Summary

The Table Maintenance Dialog is a special tool provided by SAP to create user interfaces for tables and views. It is used for customizing and maintaining customer tables and view contents and for enhancing their limited functionality. The Table Maintenance Generator can be activated through Transaction SE54. Authorization is used to assign authorization checks to users. The Table Maintenance Generator can be modified with the help of maintenance screens or events. Events get triggered whenever certain actions are executed. Maintenance view variants provide a partial view of the generated maintenance dialog. Maintenance view variants restrict the maintenance dialog on which they are based. A view cluster is a collection of maintenance dialogs of tables or views, which are collected in one maintenance unit of view clusters for business or technical reasons. Related data from more than one table or view can be maintained consistently with view clusters.

In our next chapter, we will discuss complex data types. We also will learn in detail about structures and table types.

Complex data types can be divided into structures and table types, which are among the most important components of the ABAP Data Dictionary. A structure consists of component or field, while a table type describes the structural and functional attribute of an internal table.

8   Complex Data Types: Structures and Table Types

As discussed in Chapter 2 (Data Types), the ABAP Data Dictionary data types can be classified broadly into two categories: built-in and user-defined data types. User-defined data types can be further divided into elementary, reference, and complex types. We have already discussed built-in data types in Chapter 2 and elementary and reference data types in Chapter 4 (Data Elements). This chapter focuses on complex data types.

Complex types are made up of other types. You can access a complex data type either as a whole or by the individual component. Complex data type groups semantically relate data under a single name, and manage and process it. No predefined complex data types are defined in ABAP. They can either be defined in ABAP programs or in the ABAP Data Dictionary. Structures and table types are considered to be complex data types.

Let us consider some examples of complex data types, presented in ascending order of complexity.

1. A structure consisting of a series of elementary data types of fixed length
2. An internal table whose line type is an elementary type
3. An internal table whose line type is a non-nested structure
4. A structure with structures as components
5. A structure containing internal tables as components
6. An internal table whose line type contains further internal tables

For this chapter's discussion of complex data types, we start with the general introduction of complex types. Next we discuss structures and their types. Later we explain the concept of table types and ranges table types. We also show how structures, table types, and ranges table types are created. Finally, we conclude the chapter with an explanation of how data types are deleted.

8.1   Structures

A structure or structure type consists of components or fields. A component can refer to a built-in type, elementary type, reference type, or complex type. Thus, a component of the structure can refer to a data element, another structure, or a table type. Structures can be nested to any depth.

Structures can be defined either locally in ABAP programs or globally in the ABAP Data Dictionary. It can be used in the interface of the module pools and report programs. It can also be used to define the parameter types of function modules. In this section, we discuss types of structures and the creation of structures.

8.1.1   Types of Structures

Structures can be classified as flat, nested, or deep (see Figure 8.1). Let us discuss the classification in detail:

▶ **Flat structures**
A flat structure is a structure that refers to an elementary type or reference type. In other words, flat structures only refer to the data element or predefined data type. They do not refer to any other structure or table types. In a database table, only flat structures can be included as substructures.

▶ **Nested structures**
A nested structure is a structure that refers to at least one structure. Thus, nested structures can refer to the data element and predefined data type, and to another structure (which is mandatory). They do not refer to the table types.

▶ **Deep structures**
A deep structure is a structure that refers to at least one table type along with data elements, predefined types, and structures.

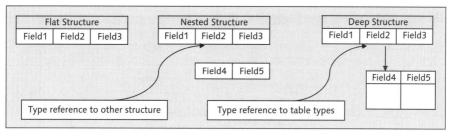

Figure 8.1 Types of Structures

Structures can be nested to any depth. Because a structure is defined globally, it can be used by many objects (programs, screens, and function components). Once the structure is changed and activated, all the objects that use the structure automatically adjust and refer to the newer version of the structure. This ensures the consistency of data definitions for all simple and complex programs.

Let us discuss an example of nested structure, Person (see Figure 8.2), which contains personal information (name, address, and phone number). The Person structure is a nested structure that contains the components Name (structure), Address (structure), and Phone Number (data element). The Name structure contains the First Name (data element) and Last Name (data element) components. The Address structure contains the Flat Number (data element), Building Name (data element), Street (data element), City Name (data element), and Pin Code (data element) components. We can create this scenario in the ABAP Data Dictionary with Transaction SE11. Figure 8.3 shows the hierarchical description of the structure.

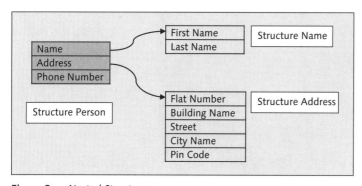

Figure 8.2 Nested Structures

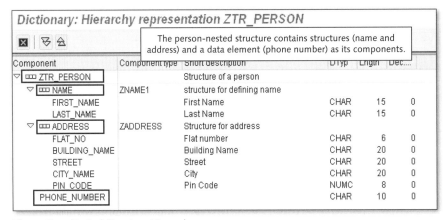

Figure 8.3 Nested Structure Hierarchy

8.1.2 Creating Structures

Let us discuss the procedure for creating structures.

1. Go to Transaction SE11. Select the radio button for DATA TYPE in the initial screen of the ABAP Data Dictionary, and enter the name of the structure.

2. Choose the CREATE button. You can create SAP objects like structures under the customer namespace. The name of the object always starts with "Y" or "Z".

3. Next you see a CREATE TYPE pop-up with three radio buttons. Check the STRUCTURE radio button (see Figure 8.4). Now choose the green checkmark icon, and you are directed to the maintenance screen of the structure (see Figure 8.5).

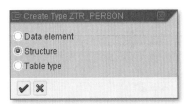

Figure 8.4 Pop-up to Choose Data Type

4. Enter the explanatory short text in the SHORT TEXT field of the maintenance screen of the data element (see Figure 8.5). This is a mandatory attribute, and you cannot enter any other attribute without entering this attribute.

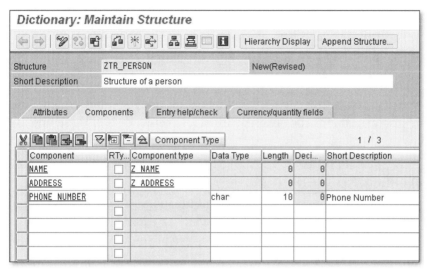

Figure 8.5 Maintenance Screen of Structure

5. Enter the COMPONENT and COMPONENT TYPE. The component type can be a data element, structure, or table type. If the component type does not exist in the data dictionary, you have to create that component. You can create the component by going to Transaction SE11 in another transaction and following these steps, or you can create the component by double-clicking on COMPONENT TYPE. Once you double-click on COMPONENT TYPE, you get the dialog box as defined in Step 2. Follow the instructons in Step 2 to create the component (DATA ELEMENT, STRUCTURE, or TABLE TYPE).

   You can also specify a predefined type. Once you click on the PREDEFINED button, you can enter the data type, length, decimal places, and short text for the component that refer to the predefined type. If you want to use your structure as an include in a table, the component name should not be more than 16 places.

6. For types CURR (Currency) and QUAN (Quantity), REFERENCE FIELD and REFERENCE TABLE must be defined. You can define these fields in the CURRENCY/QUANTITY FIELD tab. For more details about currency/quantity refer to Chapter 5, Tables.

7. Maintain the FOREIGN KEY entry for the components of the structure. For more details on how to create and maintain foreign keys, refer to the Append Structures section of Chapter 5, Tables.

8. Save your entries. You are asked to assign the development class. You can change the development class later from the path GOTO • OBJECT DIRECTORY ENTRY.

9. Activate your data element. Click on the ACTIVATE button (※) or press ⌈Ctrl⌉+⌈F3⌉ to activate the structure.

Other options such as activation log, enhancements, include structures, and runtime objects are also available while creating structures. Let us discuss these options one by one.

Activation Log

The activation log gives you activation flow information. All warning and error messages are displayed in the activation log, which is automatically displayed if errors occur during activation. The activation log can be found via the path UTILITIES • ACTIVATION LOG (see Figure 8.6).

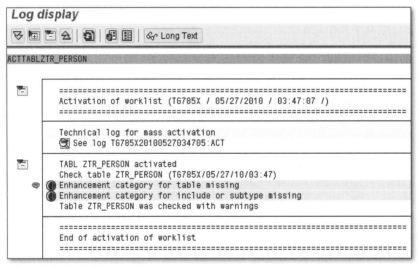

Figure 8.6 Activation Log

Create Documentation

Documentation is used to create a text that describes the use of a table and maintenance of the table data. You can create documentation by following the path GOTO • DOCUMENTATION.

Assign Activation Type

An activation type can be assigned to the structure by following the path Extras • Activation type. This option is relevant for the structures in the runtime environment. For more details about activation types, refer to the Activation Types section in Chapter 5, Tables.

Enhancements

As with tables, you can enhance your structure from the path Extras • Enhancement Categories. You get a dialog box where you can choose the enhancement category for structure (see Figure 8.7). After choosing the enhancement category, press the Copy button (✔ Copy). For more details about enhancement categories, refer to the Enhancements in Tables section of Chapter 5, Tables.

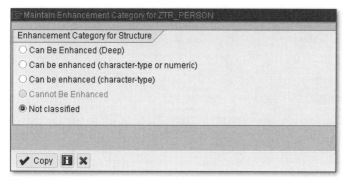

Figure 8.7 *Maintain Enhancement Category*

Append Structures

As with tables, you can add an append structure to your structure from the path Goto • Append Structure or by directly clicking on the Append Structure button. For more details about append structures refer to the Append Structures section of Chapter 5, Tables.

Includes

As with tables, you can add an include structure to your structure from the path Edit • Include • Insert. For more details about includes and named includes, refer to the Components of a Table section of Chapter 5, Tables.

Transfer Fields

As with tab, fields can be copied to the structure from other structure or tables from the path EDIT • TRANSFER FIELDS. To learn how to copy the fields from other structure/tables refer to the Copying Fields from Another Table section in Chapter 5, Tables.

Runtime Objects

During activation, the runtime object for the structure is also created. You can display the runtime object via UTILITIES • RUNTIME OBJECT • DISPLAY (see Figure 8.8).

Display: Active runtime object for ZTR_PERSON

Struct.					Timestamp runtime object								
ZTR_PERSON					05/27/2010 03:47:05								
Timestamp ABAP					Timestamp DYNP								
05/27/2010 03:47:06					05/27/2010 03:47:06								

Header of active runtime object

Obj...	Dat...	No....	Tabl...	No....	Key...	Po...	Alig...	Buff...	Nu...	Len...	Flag 1	P...	DB	Flag 2	Flag 3
J	J	10	114	0	0	0	0		0	3	00010000		B	00000000	00000001

Fields of active runtime object

Field Name	Fiel...	De...	Data ...	ABA...	DB len...	De...	Field...	Out...	Fiel...	AB...	ABA...	Dict...	Flag 1
NAME	1	0	STR1	30	30	0	0	30	204	14	u	0	00000000
FIRST_NAME	2	1	CHAR	15	15	0	0	15	40	0	C	0	00000000
LAST_NAME	3	1	CHAR	15	15	0	15	15	40	0	C	0	00000000
ADDRESS	4	0	STR1	74	74	0	30	74	204	14	u	0	00000000
FLAT_NO	5	1	CHAR	6	6	0	30	6	40	0	C	0	00000000
BUILDING_NAME	6	1	CHAR	20	20	0	36	20	40	0	C	0	00000000
STREET	7	1	CHAR	20	20	0	56	20	40	0	C	0	00000000
CITY_NAME	8	1	CHAR	20	20	0	76	20	40	0	C	0	00000000
PIN_CODE	9	1	NUMC	8	8	0	96	8	176	6	N	0	00000000
PHONE_NUMBER	10	0	CHAR	10	10	0	104	10	40	0	C	0	00000000

Figure 8.8 Display Runtime Object

8.2   Table Types

Internal tables can be defined locally in ABAP programs with the help of a data statement or globally in the ABAP Data Dictionary with the help of table types. The table type describes the structural and functional attribute of an internal table. A table type in the data dictionary is defined by the following attributes.

▸ **Line type or row type**
  The line type defines attributes such as the structure and data type of the line of the internal table. You can define your table type with line types, predefined types, or reference types. This means that your table type can have the structure of an existing data element, table, view, structure, or other table type. A table type can be referred to by a predefined type (by specifying data types, length, and number of decimal places) or by any reference type. All of the lines in the internal table have the fully specified technical attributes of the specified data type defined in the line type.

▸ **Access**
  This attribute defines how data is managed and accessed in the internal table when key operations (read table, insert table, modify table, collect) are performed. The access mode can be a standard table, sorted table, hashed table, or index table.

▸ **Key**
  This attribute defines the key definition and key category of the internal table. The key category defines whether the internal table defined by the table type can contain only unique records or duplicate records.

Suppose you have created table type ZTR_TTYP in the ABAP Data Dictionary. This table type refers to the structure ZTR_PERSON (see Figure 8.9).

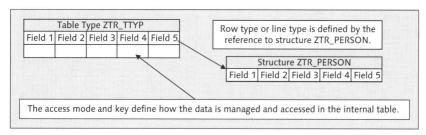

Figure 8.9 Example of Table Type and Its Attributes

The structure can be referred to in ABAP programs with the command:

```
DATA it_table1 type Ztr_ttyp.
```

An internal table, it_table1, is created in the program with an attribute similar to the attributes defined in the table type. In this section, we discuss the attributes of table types in detail.

8.2.1   Access Mode

Access mode defines how data is accessed in an internal table when key operations like read table, insert table, modify table, and collect are performed. Access mode also defines whether key access to the internal table is allowed. It defines which type of search technique is used when a record is read, inserted, or changed in the internal table. The following access modes are possible (see Figure 8.10).

Standard Table

All the records in the internal table are sequentially arranged. Key access to the data record in the internal table is based on the sequential or linear search. The time required to access any entry from the internal table linearly depends on the number of entries in the internal table. A standard table should be accessed with index operations.

Sorted Table

All the records in the internal table are sorted on the basis of the internal table's key and then stored in the internal table. Key access to the data record in the internal table is based on binary search. The time required to access any entry from the internal table logarithmically depends on the number of entries in the internal table. If the key is not unique, the entry with the lowest index is accessed first. A sorted table can be accessed by the index, but access to the sorted table with its key is preferred.

Hash Table

All the records in the internal table are arranged with the hash procedure. In the hash procedure, each entry is determined by the key. Hence, all the entries of the internal table must have a unique key. The time required to access any entry from the internal table does not depend on the number of entries in the internal table.

Hash tables cannot be accessed by an index. Generic key operations like `LOOP`, `SORT`, etc. should be used to access the hash table.

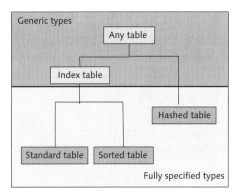

Figure 8.10   Access Modes

Index Table

An index table can be a standard table or a sorted table. Index tables are accessed by indexes. These tables are used to define generic table types. The generic parameter of subroutines and function modules can be defined with the help of an index table.

Not Specified

If the access mode is not specified, the table can be a standard table, sorted table, or hash table. Valid operations for these tables exist at the intersection of the valid operations for standard, sorted, and hash tables. Tables that are not specified cannot be accessed by indexes.

8.2.2   Key Definition

This attribute defines the key used for the table type. It can have the following possible values:

▶ **Standard key**
Standard key depends on the row type category. Let us discuss these categories.

▶ **Structured row type**
If the row type is a structured row type, the standard key consists of all the character-like components of the table row.

▶ **Elementary or reference row type**
If the row type is an elementary or reference row type, the standard key consists of the entire table row; i.e., all the components of the table row.

▶ **Table type row type**
If the row type is a table type row type, the standard key is empty. An empty key is allowed only with standard table access mode. Hence, the table type row type always has standard table access mode.

▶ **Row type**
The key consists of all the fields of the row type. It does not depend on the row type category.

▶ **Key components**
Components of the row type can be selected to specify the key. This value is possible only when the row type is of tables, structures, and view types. This value is not possible for elementary or reference row types because elementary and reference row types refer to only one component (field).

▶ **Key not specified**
A generic table type is defined if the key is not specified.

8.2.3 Key Category

This attribute defines whether the internal table defined by the table type contains unique records or duplicate records. A key category can have the following values:

▶ **Unique**
Records in the internal table are unique with respect to the key definition.

▶ **Non-unique**
Records in the internal table are not unique; that is, the internal table may contain the duplicate records.

▶ **Not specified**
The key category is not specified. Records in the internal table may be unique or non-unique. If a key category is not specified, the generic table type is defined.

Access mode and key category do not combine with each other in all cases. Thus, only certain combinations of access mode and key category are possible. These combinations can be found in Table 8.1.

Access Mode	Key Category
Not specified	Not specified
Index table	Not specified
Standard table	Non-unique
Sorted table	Unique, non-unique or not specified
Hash table	Unique

Table 8.1   Relationship between Access Mode and Key Category

Apart from this, if the key definition of the standard table or hash table is not specified, the key category is not specified.

8.2.4   Generic Table Types

If some of the attributes of the table type are undefined, a generic table type is created. A generic table type does not define all the attributes of an internal table. Because generic table types do not define all the necessary attributes of an internal table, you cannot use generic table types to define data objects (with DATA) or types (with TYPE). Generic table types are used to define the types of generic table parameters in function modules and in sub-routine forms. Sorted tables or standard tables can be passed in the function module or sub-routine call if the access mode of a generic table type is an index table and a generic table type is used as a parameter of the function module.

A table type is generic in the following cases:

- Access mode is either INDEX TABLE or NOT SPECIFIED.
- Key definition is NOT SPECIFIED.
- Key category is NOT SPECIFIED.

8.2.5   Correlation between Table Types and Internal Tables

Now let us correlate the table types of the ABAP Data Dictionary with internal tables of ABAP programs (see Figure 8.11).

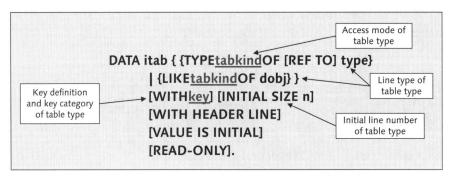

Figure 8.11   Correlation between Table Types and Internal Table

8.2.6   Creating Table Types

1. Go to Transaction SE11. Select the DATA TYPE radio button in the initial screen of the ABAP Data Dictionary, and enter the name of the table type. Choose the CREATE button. You can create SAP objects like table types under the customer namespace. The name of the object always starts with "Y" or "Z".

2. You see a CREATE TYPE pop-up with three radio buttons. Check the TABLE TYPE radio button (see Figure 8.12) and choose the green checkmark icon. You are directed to the maintenance screen of the table type (see Figure 8.13).

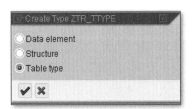

Figure 8.12   Pop-up to Choose Data Type

3. Enter the explanatory short text in the SHORT TEXT field of the maintenance screen of the table type (see Figure 8.13). This is a mandatory attribute, and you cannot enter any other attribute without entering this attribute. This short text acts as the explanatory text when F1 help or list is generated.

4. Under the LINE TYPE tab, enter the line type or row type of the table type. You can either refer to an existing type (data element, structure, table, view, table type) or directly enter the row type by defining the data type, number of characters, and decimal places. You can also refer your row type to an existing reference objects using the REFERENCE TYPE field.

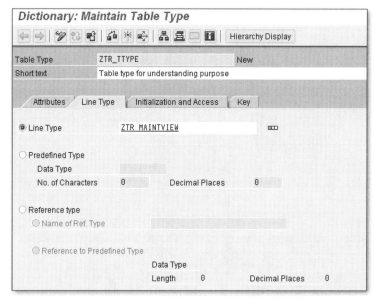

Figure 8.13 Line Type Tab in the Maintenance Screen of Table Type

5. Under the INITIALIZATION AND ACCESS tab, define the initial line number and access mode of your table type (see Figure 8.14). Access mode defines how to access the data in an internal table defined by the table type in ABAP programs. With the initial line number attribute, you can define the memory space allocated to your table type.

6. Underthe KEY tab, define the key definition and key category. If you choose KEY COMPONENT as your key definition, you can select the components that you want to be part of your key. This option is only possible if the row type of the table type is a structure, table, or view. If you choose the KEY COMPONENT radio button, the KEY COMPONENTS AREA and CHOOSE COMPONENTS buttons are enabled. If you click on the CHOOSE COMPONENTS button, you get a dialog box where you can choose components to belong to the key. Select the components and the green checkmark icon (see Figure 8.15).

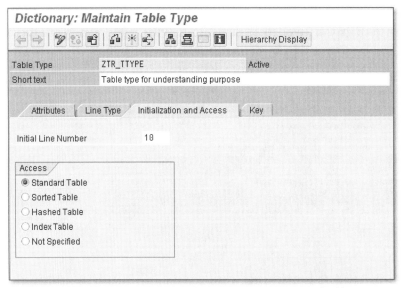

Figure 8.14 Initialization and Access Tab in Maintenance Screen of Table Type

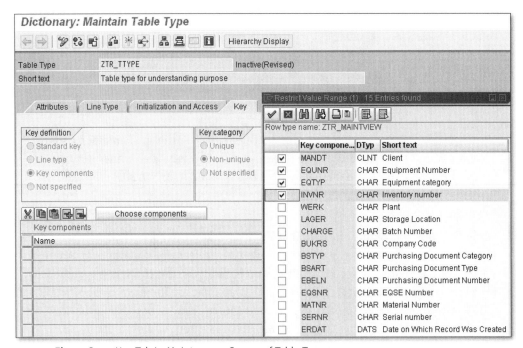

Figure 8.15 Key Tab in Maintenance Screen of Table Type

7. Save your entries. You are asked to assign the development class. You can change the development class later from the path GOTO • OBJECT DIRECTORY ENTRY.

8. Activate your data element. Click on the ACTIVATE button (✳) or press Ctrl + F3 to activate the structure.

Other options such as activation log, documentation, and runtime objects are also available while creating structures. Let us discuss these options one by one.

Activation Log

The activation log gives you the activation flow information. All the warning and error messages are displayed in the activation log, which is automatically displayed if errors occur during activation. The activation log can be found at UTILITIES • ACTIVATION LOG.

Create Documentation

Documentation is used to create a text that describes the use of a table and maintenance of the table data. You can create documentation by following the path GOTO • DOCUMENTATION.

Runtime Objects

During activation, the runtime object for the structure is also created. You can display the runtime object from the path UTILITIES • RUNTIME OBJECT • DISPLAY.

8.2.7 Ranges Table Types

A ranges table type is a special kind of table type used for ranges internal tables. Ranges internal tables are used in the logical conditions (IN operators) of the SELECT, IF, WHILE, and CHECK statements. It is also used to pass the data to selection tables. The row type of a ranges table type has a fixed structure. The row type consists of four components: SIGN (sign), OPTION (comparison operator), LOW (lower limit), and HIGH (upper limit) in this same order (see Figure 8.16).

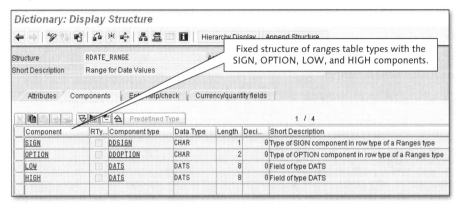

Figure 8.16 Structure of Ranges Table Type

The LOW and HIGH components of ranges table types are defined by an elementary associated type (see Figure 8.17). Ranges table types can be associated with the data element or a predefined type (by specifying the data type, number of characters, and decimal places). A ranges table type always has standard-table access mode and a non-unique standard key.

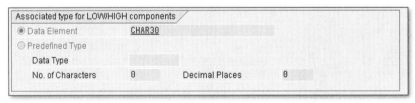

Figure 8.17 Association of Low/High Component of Ranges Table Type

8.2.8 Creating Ranges Table Types

Let us discuss the process for creating ranges table types.

1. Go to Transaction SE11. Select the DATA TYPE radio button in the initial screen of the ABAP Data Dictionary and enter the name of the ranges table type. Choose the CREATE button. You can create SAP objects like table types under the customer namespace. The name of the object always starts with "Y" or "Z".

2. You see a CREATE TYPE pop-up with three radio buttons. Check the TABLE TYPE radio button and choose the green checkmark icon. You are directed to the maintenance screen of the table type (see Figure 8.18).

3. Enter the explanatory short text in the SHORT TEXT field of the maintenance screen of the table type (see Figure 8.18). This is a mandatory attribute, and you cannot enter any other attribute without entering this attribute. This short text acts as the explanatory text when F1 help or list is generated.

4. For creating ranges table types, follow the path EDIT • DEFINE AS RANGES TABLE TYPE. You are directed to the maintenance screen of the ranges table types.

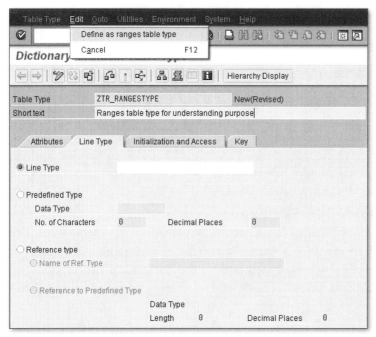

Figure 8.18 Creating Ranges Table Type

5. In the maintenance screen of the ranges table type, the access mode, key definition, and key category are already defined in advance, as these attributes are fixed. A ranges table type always has standard-table access mode and a non-unique standard key.

6. Associate your LOW/HIGH component with a data element or predefined type (by specifying the data type, no. of characters, decimal places).

7. Just like any other type, a ranges type should have a row type. In the STRUCTURED ROW TYPE field, enter the name of the row type for the ranges table type (see Figure 8.19). This structure defines the row type for the ranges type. This structure has fixed components (SIGN, OPTION, LOW, and HIGH).

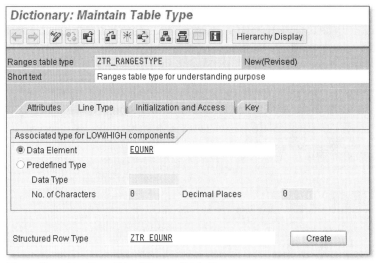

Figure 8.19 Line Type Tab of Ranges Table Type

8. Before defining the structure row type, you get an information message asking you to save your ranges type. After saving your ranges type, click on the CREATE button to create your structure row type.

9. You are directed to the maintenance screen of the structure (see Figure 8.20). The components of the row type are already assigned. This assignment is based on the definition given to the associated type for the LOW and HIGH components. Enter the short description and activate your structure by clicking on the ACTIVATE button (✳) or pressing Ctrl + F3.

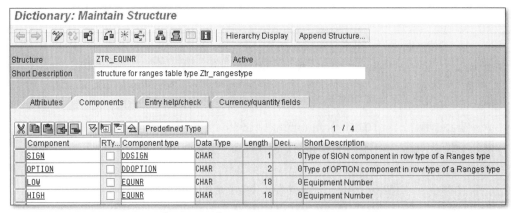

Figure 8.20 Structure of Row Type for Ranges Type

10. Choose the BACK button (), and activate the ranges table type by clicking on the ACTIVATE button or pressing Ctrl + F3 .

8.3 Deleting Data Types

You can only delete data elements if they are not used by any table field or component. Let us discuss the procedure for deleting an existing data element.

1. Go to Transaction SE11. Select the DATA TYPE radio button in the initial screen of the ABAP Data Dictionary. Enter the name of the data type. Choose the WHERE-USED LIST button, and check if the data type is still being used by any component. If the data type is in use and you delete the data type, all the tables and programs become inconsistent. For this reason, never delete a data type that is still in use.

2. Choose the DELETE icon ( ) in Transaction SE11. A dialog box appears for confirmation of the deletion request (see Figure 8.21). Once the deletion request is confirmed, the data type is deleted.

Figure 8.21 Dialog Box to Confirm Deletion Request

8.4 Summary

Complex data types group semantically related data under a single name and manage and process it. Complex data types can be divided into structures and table types. A structure consists of components or fields that can be of the built-in type, elementary type, reference type, or complex type. A table type describes the structural and functional attributes of an internal table. Table types are defined with the help of line types, access modes, key definitions, and key categories. A special category of table type is the ranges table type, which is used for the ranges internal tables. These are used in the logical conditions (IN operators) in the SELECT, IF, WHILE, and CHECK statements. Structures, table types, and ranges table types can be created, changed, or deleted from Transaction SE11.

In our next chapter, we discuss search help. This is a data selection method that provides the possible input value for the screen field. This component of the ABAP Data Dictionary is used in selecting and filtering data according to user selection.

Input help (⌐F4⌐ help) is one of the important functions of the SAP system. Input help for screen fields is activated by search helps. Search helps can be elementary or collective and can be assigned to data elements, table fields, check tables, screens, and other components of the ABAP Data Dictionary.

9   Search Helps

Input help (⌐F4⌐ help) is one of the most important functions of the SAP system, and is provided through *search helps.* Search helps are independent repository objects that are created by the ABAP Data Dictionary. In this chapter's discussion of search helps, we start with a general introduction and then describe the elementary and collective types of search help. Finally, we will explain how to assign search helps to other Data Dictionary components such as data elements, table fields, and tables.

9.1   Introduction to Search Helps

Search helps are independent repository objects that are created by the ABAP Data Dictionary. Thus, search helps represent a data-selection method that provides possible input values for the screen field. The possible input values can be enhanced with further information. Let us discuss the steps involved while calling the input help.

1. To display the possible input values for a search field in the screen template, user starts the input help by pressing ⌐F4⌐.

2. The dialog box appears. This dialog box contains a number of possible search paths. The user selects one of these search paths.

3. The user enters the value in the fields of the selected search path. These values limit the number of possible input values. Finally, the user starts the search (see Figure 9.1).

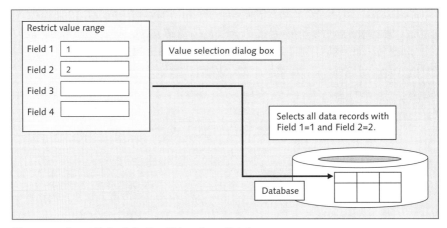

Figure 9.1 Input Help: Selecting Values from Database

4. The system determines the values that satisfy the entered restrictions (hits) and displays them in the form of a list, known as a *hit list* (see Figure 9.2).

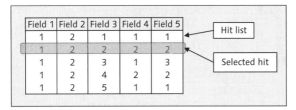

Figure 9.2 Hit List

5. The user selects the value that he wants from the hit list by double-clicking on the value.

6. The selected value is displayed in the screen template.

Steps 2 and 3 are omitted if there is only one search path. In this case, the dialog box for value selection appears immediately. Steps 2 to 4 are omitted if the hit list is displayed directly just after starting input help.

9.2 Types of Search Help

Search help can be broadly divided into two categories: elementary search help and collective search help. An elementary search help describes a search path. It defines the location of the data for the hit list, the way values are exchanged between the screen and the selection method, and the user dialog that occurs when the user chooses input help. A collective search help consists of two or more elementary search helps. A collective search help defines the series of search paths for a field. The collective search help can be considered to be the interface between screens and various elementary search helps.

We discuss both of these types of search helps in this section, and then conclude our discussion with an explanation of search help exit. A search help exit is a function module used to make the input help process described by the search help more flexible than is possible with the standard version, and it is applicable to both elementary and collective search helps.

9.2.1 Elementary Search Help

Elementary search helps describe a search path. They define the standard flow of an input help. The following components of the search help flow can be defined with an elementary search help:

► Selection method

► Search help parameters

► Dialog behavior

Selection Method

Selection method specifies the table or view from which data is read. The selected data is then displayed in the hit list. The possible input values that are displayed for a field in the hit list are selected at runtime. If the data required in the hit list comes from a single table, only this table or a projection view needs to be selected as the selection method. If a text table exists, its fields are also available in the input help. A table entry is linked to the corresponding text with the help of a foreign key.

If all the data required in the hit list comes from more than one table, these tables must be linked with the help of a view (database view or projection view). This view is defined as a selection method. If the underlying tables are client-specific, the client field must be contained in the view. Otherwise, selection for the input help would be applied to all clients.

Search Help Parameters

A search help has an interface consisting of parameters. These parameters define the fields of the selection method that should be used in the input help. Thus, the selection method represents the table or view from which the data is to be selected. The parameters of a search help represent those fields of the selection method (tables or views) that restrict the selection of data or are present in the hit list (see Figure 9.3).

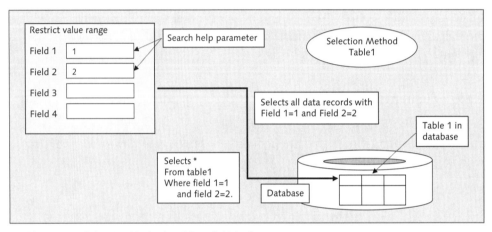

Figure 9.3 Selection Method and Search Help Parameters

The parameters of the search help represent each field in the dialog box for selection and each field of the hit list. The parameters are copied from the corresponding selection method. If the search is restricted with the parameters of the search help, the where condition for the field of the selection method is formulated with the help of search help parameters. Fields of a selection method and parameters of a search help have the same name.

In the input help, selection is automatically processed in the logon client of the user. Therefore, search help should not contain any parameters for the clients. Search help parameters must be assigned to data elements.

Search helps may contain additional parameters that do not correspond to any fields of the selection method. This is only necessary when the standard flow of the input help defined by the search help has to be modified by the search help exit. The search-help parameters have the following attributes (see Figure 9.4):

► **Import parameters**

Import parameters are those parameters with which context information from the processed input template (screen) is copied to the help process. When an input help is called, the entries that the user already made in the input template are accounted for. These entries are responsible for restricting the data in the hit list.

► **Export parameters**

Export parameters are those parameters that help return values from the hit list to the input template (screen). Export parameters cause more than one field of the input template to be populated automatically when one row is selected from the hit list. A parameter can be simultaneously an import and an export parameter. Search helps can also contain parameters that are neither import nor export parameters. Such parameters may be required for the internal input help process.

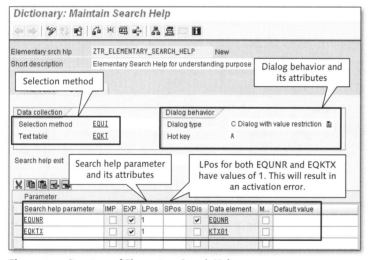

Figure 9.4 Structure of Elementary Search Help

► **LPos**

This attribute specifies the position of the parameter in the hit list. If this attribute is left empty for a particular search help parameter, that parameter does not appear in the hit list. In this attribute, no position number can occur more than once. If it does, an inconsistency error will occur when the search help is activated (see Figure 9.5).

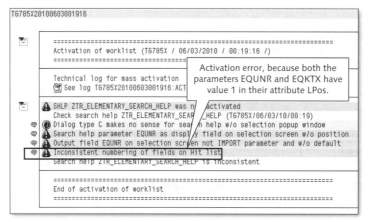

Figure 9.5 Error: LPos Have Same Value for Two Different Parameters

Because gaps do not affect the design of the hit list, they are allowed in this attribute. For example, an elementary search help contains parameters Para1, Para2, Para3, and Para4. Attribute LPos for these parameters and their order in the hit list are defined in Figure 9.6.

Parameter	LPos
Para1	4
Para2	1
Para3	0 or ''
Para4	3

Order in which these parameters appear in the hit list are as follows:

Para2, Para4, Para1 (Para3 does not appear in the hit list).

Figure 9.6 Parameters and Their LPos Positions

In an elementary search help, at least one parameter should appear in the hit list. However, if the display of the hit list is copied from a search help exit, this rule can be ignored.

▶ **SPos**

This attribute specifies the position of the parameter in the dialog box for restricting the hit list. If this attribute is left empty for a particular search help parameter, that parameter does not appear in the dialog box. In this attribute, no position number may occur more than once. Otherwise, an inconsistency error occurs when search help is activated. Because gaps do not affect the design of the dialog box, they are allowed in this attribute. For example, an elementary search help contains parameter Para1, Para2, Para3, and Para4. Attribute SPos for these parameters and their order in the hit list are defined in Figure 9.7.

Parameter	SPos
Para1	4
Para2	1
Para3	0 or ''
Para4	3

Order in which these parameters will appear in the dialog box are as follows:

Para2, Para4, Para1 (Para3 does not appear in the dialog box).

Figure 9.7 Parameters and Their SPos Positions

If this attribute is left blank for all the search help parameters, no dialog box appears. In that case, values A (dialog which depends on sets of values) and C (dialog with value restrictions) of DIALOG TYPE are meaningless. If SPos is left blank for all the search help parameters and the dialog type value is set as A or C, a warning occurs while activating the search help in the activation log.

▶ **SDis**
If this attribute is checked, the search-help parameter that appears in the selection pop-up dialog box for restricting values appears in a display mode. This means the content of the parameter informs the user about the restriction, but the user cannot change the value present in this parameter. This attribute is advisable when the parameter is an import parameter or when it has a default value.

▶ **Data element**
The data element must be assigned to the search help parameter. The data element defines the output attributes and supports the functions of the parameter in the pop-up window and in the hit list for restricting values. Normally, the parameter gets the data element from the field of the selection method having the same name. However, if the data element of this field changes, the search help automatically adjusts itself so that the data element is also changed in the search help.

▶ **Modified**
If the MODIFIED flag is checked, values can be entered in the DATA ELEMENT field. A new data element can be entered, but it must have the same data type, length, and number of decimal places as the previous one. This attribute cancels the link between the data element of the search help parameter and the data element of the corresponding field of the selection method. If this flag is unchecked, the data element of the assigned field of the selection method is re-linked with the

data element of the search help parameter. The MODIFIED flag is not offered for parameters that do not have a field with the same name as in the selection method. These parameters may be needed when a search help is assigned to a search help exit.

▶ **Default value**
This attribute is used to assign a default value to the parameter of a search help. When input help is called, a default value is assigned to the parameter in the following cases:

- ▶ If the parameter is not an import parameter.

- ▶ If nothing is assigned to the parameter in the search-help attachment with which the search help is attached to the screen field.

- ▶ If in the search help attachment a field was assigned to the parameter that does not exist on the screen or in the flow logic (module pool) in the input help process.

- ▶ If a search help is included in a collective search help and the parameter is not linked with any parameter of this collective search help.

The following default values can be assigned to the search-help parameter:

- ▶ Constants: Constants must be enclosed in apostrophes (,). The constant must be specified in internal representation for parameters whose data type has an editing mask, such as date and time. For example, the date 03.06.2010 must be defined as 20100603.

- ▶ System fields: These are the fields of the DDIC structure SYST where the prefix SY- can be used instead of the prefix SYST-.

- ▶ GET parameter ID: This parameter is used to assign values from SAP memory.

Dialog Behavior

The dialog behavior defines the required steps while executing the input help process. It also defines the structure of the dialog box for value selection and the hit list. Dialog behavior has the following attributes:

▶ **Dialog type**
The dialog type defines whether the dialog box for value selection should be displayed. If the dialog box is skipped, the hit list is displayed directly after calling the input help. There are three dialog types:

▶ Display value immediately (D): If this value is set for the dialog type, the hit list is displayed immediately when the input help has been called. If the hit list contains only a few entries, this option is preferable.

▶ Dialog with value restriction (C): If this value is set for the dialog type, the dialog box is displayed immediately. This dialog box is used to restrict the value of the hit list. If the list of possible entries is very large, this option is preferred. Restricting the set of data to be processed increases the clarity of the hit list and reduces the system load during value selection.

▶ Dialog depends on set of values (A): Under this dialog type, if the hit list contains fewer than 100 entries, it is displayed immediately. If the hit list contains more than 100 entries, the dialog box for restricting values is displayed. Thus, this dialog type is a combination of D and C, and its nature depends on the number of entries in the hit list.

▶ **Hot key**
The hot key permits the user to select an elementary search help from the collective search help directly in the input field with the short notation. The restrictions can also be entered directly in the dialog box for restricting values. Thus, the hot key acts as a shortcut for selecting an elementary search help from a collective search help. Only letters and digits are allowed as hot keys. The shortcut must be entered in the input field according to the convention "=<Hot Key>.S1.S2. S3 etc.". Here, S1, S2, S3, etc., represent the restrictions that are entered in this order in the corresponding dialog box. Each entry is considered to be a pattern with a terminating "*". However, restrictions for fields for which no entry could be made in the dialog box are ignored. If S1 consists of more than one character, the first separator "." can be omitted (see Figure 9.8).

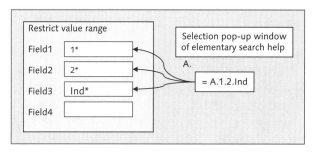

Figure 9.8 Hot Key

Figure 9.9 shows an example of a hot key in collective search help.

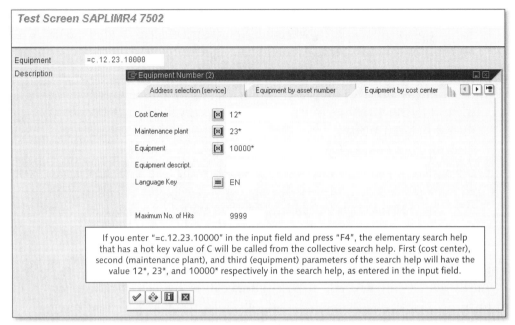

Test Screen SAPLIMR4 7502

Equipment   =c.12.23.10000
Description

Equipment Number (2)

Address selection (service)   Equipment by asset number   Equipment by cost center

Cost Center   12*

Maintenance plant   23*

Equipment   10000*

Equipment descript.

Language Key   =   EN

Maximum No. of Hits   9999

If you enter "=c.12.23.10000" in the input field and press "F4", the elementary search help that has a hot key value of C will be called from the collective search help. First (cost center), second (maintenance plant), and third (equipment) parameters of the search help will have the value 12*, 23*, and 10000* respectively in the search help, as entered in the input field.

Figure 9.9 Example of Hot Key Selection

If only one elementary search help is assigned to the field or if the elementary search help is stored as the standard search help, you don't need to enter the hot key. If the hot key is entered without restrictions (=HK), the dialog box for restricting values appears. If restrictions are defined, the dialog box for restricting values does not appear and the hit list is displayed directly. If exactly one hit is found in the hit list, the hit list is not displayed. In this case, the values of the hits are returned automatically to the screen.

9.2.2 Collective Search Help

A collective search help consists of two or more elementary search helps. It combines several elementary search helps. It defines the series of search paths for a field. The user can select any of these search paths for input help. To define a collective search help, elementary search helps that are to be combined should be defined. In the input help, the values are transported between the elementary search help selected by the user and the input template using the collective search help. Thus, a collective search help has an interface for transporting the values, and elementary search helps are assigned to it. Let us discuss these in detail.

Interface of the Collective Search Help

Like an elementary search help, a collective search help also has an interface of import and export parameters. With the help of this interface, the data is exchanged between the screen template and the parameters of the assigned elementary search helps (see Figure 9.10).

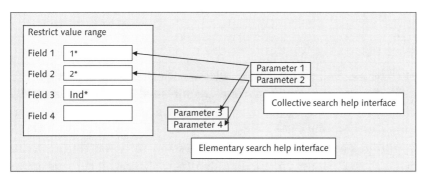

Figure 9.10 Interface of Collective Search Help

Assigned Search Helps

In assigning two or more elementary search helps to form a collective search help, the search paths of the elementary search helps that are meaningful for a field are combined (see Figure 9.11).

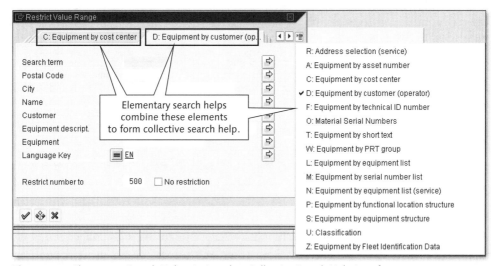

Figure 9.11 Elementary Search Helps Assigned to Collective Search Help Interface

The interface parameters (import and export) of the included elementary search helps must be assigned to the parameters of the collective search help. It is not necessary to assign all the parameters of elementary search helps to the collective search help. This means assignment can be open for some of the parameters of the elementary search helps. If other collective search helps are contained in collective search help, they are expanded to the level of the elementary search helps when the input help is called.

Append Search Helps

Append search helps are used to enhance collective search helps delivered by SAP using customer-specific search paths that don't require modifying the actual collective search help. Like append structures, append search helps can be used in special developments and country versions and work by SAP partners and customers to add search paths to a collective search help in the standard system (Figure 9.12). Thus, append search help is used for modification-free enhancement of a collective search help—one that is not the original in the current system—with inclusion of further search help.

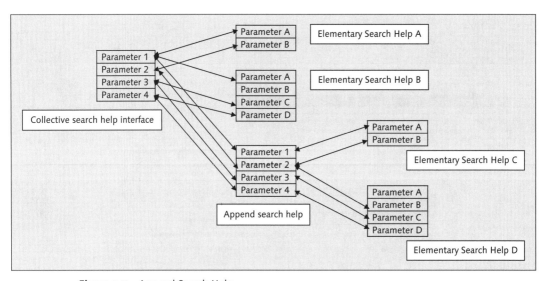

Figure 9.12 Append Search Help

The structure of an append search help corresponds to that of a collective search help. Because the append search help takes on the parameters of its appending object, it cannot be maintained separately. You cannot assign the search help exit to the append search help. An append search help automatically includes itself in its appending object. An append search help can also be used to describe an input help. In that case, they are treated like collective search helps.

With the help of append search helps, modification-free elementary search helps can be hidden from a collective search help. To do this, insert the search help to be hidden in the append search help and then hide the inclusion in the append search help. The search paths defined by this search help are no longer offered in the appending search help. To cancel this, remove the hidden inclusion from the append search help.

If the parameters of the appending object change, this change is not automatically made in the append search help. Instead, you are informed that the parameters of the append search help should be adjusted. In this case you should determine whether you want to change the assignments between the parameters of the append search help and the search helps included in them.

We do not recommend automatically changing the interface of an append object. If the interface of the collective search help changes, some of the elementary search helps present in it need to be adjusted accordingly.

9.2.3   Search Help Exit

A search help describes the standard input help process. In some cases—perhaps to meet some business requirement—this standard input process needs some deviation. Such a deviation from the standard process can be implemented with the help of a search help exit. Thus, search help exit is a function module used to make the input help process described by the search help more flexible than is possible with the standard version.

A search help exit has a predefined interface. The search help exit should follow the interface as defined in function module `F4if_shlp_exit_example` (see Figure 9.13). The search help exit may also include further optional parameters (in particular any exporting parameters). More information about how to use search help exit can be found in the source text and long documentation of the above-specified function module.

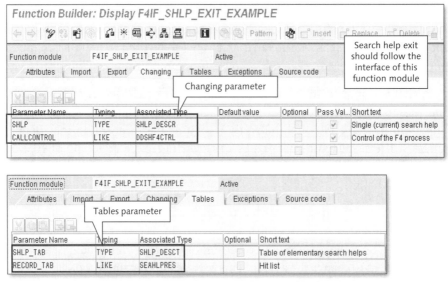

Figure 9.13   Parameters of Function Module F4IF_SHLP_EXIT_EXAMPLE

Some predefined function modules are present in the function library. These function module begin with the prefix F4ut_. These function modules perform frequently executed functions of the search help exit. These function modules can either be used directly as search help exits or used within other search help exits. For example, search help exit F4ut_optimize_colwidth is used to adjust the column width in the hit list to the contents of the column.

Events in Search Help Exit

Input help processes are defined by a number of timepoints. These timepoints define the beginning of an important operation of the input help process. If the input help process is defined with the help of search help exit, this search help exit is called at each of these time points. These timepoints are also known as *events*. The following events are defined.

▶ **Selone**
  This event is called when an elementary search help is selected from a collective search help, and is used to restrict the selection possibilities for elementary search helps. The elementary search helps are already present in Shlp_tab. Shlp_tab is one of the internal table parameters present in function module F4if_shlp_exit_example, which contains the information about the

search help fields and structures. If entries are deleted from Shlp_tab in this step, they are not offered in the elementary search help selection. If only one entry remains in Shlp_tab, the dialog box for selecting elementary search is skipped. The event is not accessed again if another elementary search help is selected during the dialog.

▶ **Presel1**
This event is called after selecting an elementary search help; that is, after event SELONE. Table INTERFACE contains information about how the search help parameters are related to the screen fields. Until this event, Table INTERFACE has not been copied to Table SELOPT. This means that at this event the attachment of the search help to the screen can be changed.

▶ **Presel**
This event is triggered before the display of the dialog box for restricting the values. This event is suitable for predefining the value restriction or for completely suppressing or copying the dialog.

▶ **Select**
This event is triggered before selecting the values. If you do not want the default selection, this event should be copied with a search help exit. After this event, DISP should be selected as the next event. If DISP is not set, standard data selection overrides the customized data selection.

▶ **Disp**
This event is triggered before the display of the hit list. This event is suitable for restricting the values to be displayed in the hit list.

▶ **Return**
This event is called as the next step if a single hit is selected in a search help exit. The sequence of the F4 flow can be changed at this event if control of the process sequence of the transaction depends on the selected value. This can occur, for example, in setting SET/GET parameters.

▶ **Rettop**
This event is triggered only in the case of collective search help. This event directly follows the RETURN event.

▶ **Exit**
This event is triggered only when a user terminates the dialog within the search help exit.

▶ **Create**
This event is triggered only if the user selects the function Create new values. This function is available only if field Custtab of the control string Callcontrol was not already given the value of a space. The Select event should be called after this event so that the newly entered value can be selected and then displayed.

▶ **App1, App2, and App3**
These events are called if further buttons are introduced in the hit list with function module `F4ut_list_exit`. These events are triggered when a user presses the corresponding button.

Note

If the `F4` help is controlled by a collective search help, the search help exit of the collective search help is called at events SELONE and RETTOP. (RETTOP only if the user selects a value.) At all other events, the search help exit of the selected elementary search help is called.

If the `F4` help is controlled by an elementary search help, the event RETTOP is not executed. The search help exit of the elementary search help is called at event SELONE. This search help exit should not do anything at this event. Any preparatory work should be carried out at the event PRESEL1.

9.3 Creating Search Help

As we have explained, search helps represent a data-selection method that provides possible input values for the screen field. They can be divided into two categories: elementary search help and collective search help. In this section, we will discuss the procedure for creating both types of search helps.

9.3.1 Creating Elementary Search Helps

In this section we discuss the procedure for creating elementary search helps.

1. Go to Transaction SE11. Select the Search Help radio button in the initial screen of the ABAP Data Dictionary, and enter the name of the elementary search help that you want to create. Choose the Create button. You can only start the name of the search help with "Y" or "Z" (see Figure 9.14).

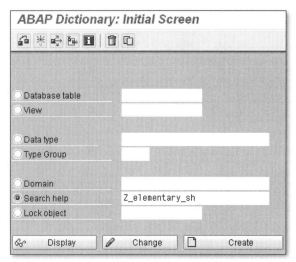

Figure 9.14 ABAP Data Dictionary: Initial Screen for Creating Search Help

2. You get a dialog box that has two radio buttons. Check the ELEMENTARY SEARCH HELP radio button. Click on the checkmark (✔) icon (see Figure 9.15). You are directed to the maintenance screen for elementary search helps.

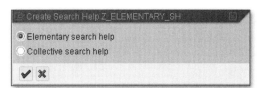

Figure 9.15 Pop-up to Create Elementary Search Help

3. Enter the explanatory short text in the SHORT DESCRIPTION field in the maintenance screen of the search help. With the help of short text, a developer can refer to a particular search help at any time.

4. Under the DEFINITION tab, in the SELECTION METHOD field, enter the name of the table or view (database view, projection view, or help view) from which data needs to be read. If the table entered in the selection method has a text table attached to it, the name of the text table is automatically populated in the TEXT TABLE field (see Figure 9.16).

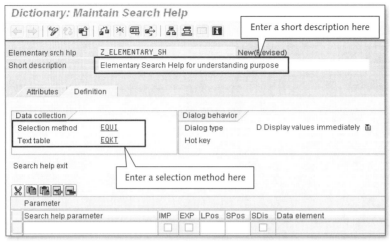

Figure 9.16 Short Text Description and Selection Method under the Definition Tab

5. Under the SEARCH HELP PARAMETER area, enter the name of the parameter. Perform F4 help (input help) on the search help parameter, and select the required fields from the table/view selected in the selection method. Select the fields that should be used in the dialog box for value selection or in the hit list. If the selection method table has a text table, both the fields of the table and the text table are offered in the input help (see Figure 9.17).

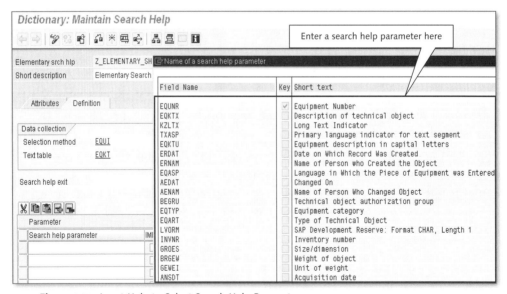

Figure 9.17 Input Help to Select Search Help Parameter

Define the attributes of the search help parameters. Define the import parameter, export parameter, LPos, SPos, SDis, and default values as required (see Figure 9.18). If you want to use any other data element, select the MODIFY flag. The DATA ELEMENT field can now take input. Enter the data element whose data type, length, and number of decimal places are the same as those of the previous data element.

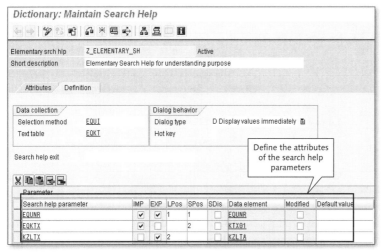

Figure 9.18 Attributes of Search Help Parameters

6. Select the DIALOG TYPE of the search help. The dialog type defines how the hit lists are displayed in the input help (see Figure 9.19).

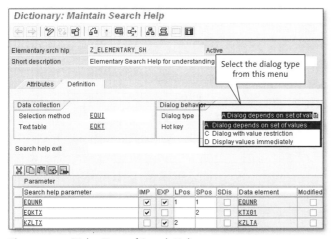

Figure 9.19 Dialog Type of Search Help

7. Save your elementary search help. You are asked to assign the development class. You can change the development class later from the path GOTO • OBJECT DIRECTORY ENTRY (see Figure 9.20).

8. Activate your search help by clicking on the ACTIVATE (✳) icon.

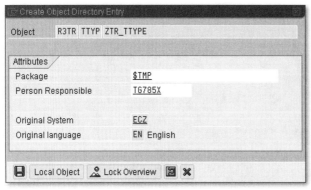

Figure 9.20 Dialog Box While Saving Search Help

Other options, including displaying activation logs and assigning hot keys are also available while creating elementary search helps. Let us discuss these options one by one.

Activation Log

An activation log gives you activation flow information. All the warning and error messages are displayed in the activation log, which is automatically displayed if errors occur during activation. The activation log can be found at UTILITIES • ACTIVATION LOG.

Assigning a Hot Key

If you want to access your elementary search help with a shortcut key when it is attached to a collective search help, define a hot key for it. Note that all the elementary search helps contained in the collective search help should have different shortcut keys.

Assigning a Search Help Exit

Enter the search help exit name if you want to change the standard flow of the search help.

Testing the Search Help

You can test the flow of an input help defined by the elementary search help by selecting the EXECUTE (▤) icon. A dialog box appears in which you can simulate the behavior of the search help under different conditions (see Figure 9.21).

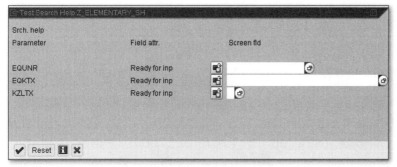

Figure 9.21 Dialog Box While Testing the Search Help

9.3.2 Creating Collective Search Helps

In this section, we discuss the procedure for creating collective search helps.

1. Go to Transaction SE11. Select the SEARCH HELP radio button in the initial screen of the ABAP Data Dictionary, and enter the name of the collective search help that you want to create. Choose the CREATE button. You can only start the name of a search help with "Y" or "Z" (see Figure 9.22).

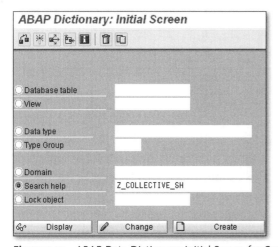

Figure 9.22 ABAP Data Dictionary: Initial Screen for Creating Search Helps

2. You get a dialog box that has two radio buttons. Check the CollectiVE SEARCH HELP radio button. Click on the checkmark icon (see Figure 9.23). You are directed to the maintenance screen for collective search helps.

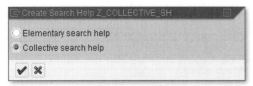

Figure 9.23 Pop-up to Create Collective Search Help

3. Enter the explanatory short text in the SHORT DESCRIPTION field in the maintenance screen of the search help. With the help of the short text, a developer can refer to a particular search help at any time (see Figure 9.24).

4. Under the DEFINITION tab, enter the parameter of the search help. Define the attributes of the parameter such as IMP, EXP, DATA ELEMENT, and DEFAULT VALUE. Enter the search help exit name if you want to change the standard flow of the search help.

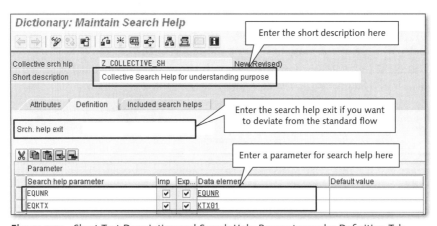

Figure 9.24 Short Text Description and Search Help Parameter under Definition Tab

5. Under the INCLUDED SEARCH HELPS tab, define the search helps that you want to include in the collective search help. Both elementary and collective search helps can be included in the collective search help. If you check the HIDDEN flag, the included search helps do not appear in the dialog box for selecting the elementary search help (see Figure 9.25).

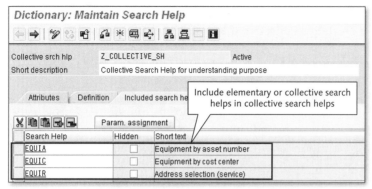

Figure 9.25 Included Search Helps Tab of Collective Search Help

6. Assign the collective search help parameter to the attached elementary search help parameter by clicking on the PARAMETER ASSIGNMENT button. When you click on this button, you get a dialog box. Enter the parameter names of the elementary search help to which the corresponding parameters of the collective search help should be assigned in the REFERENCE PARAMETER field (see Figure 9.26).

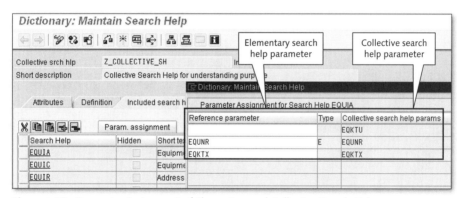

Figure 9.26 Parameter Assignment of Elementary and Collective Search Helps

7. Save your collective search help. You are asked to assign the development class. You can change the development class later from the path GOTO • OBJECT DIRECTORY ENTRY.

8. Activate your search help by clicking on the ACTIVATE icon.

Other options including displaying the activation log and testing search helps are also available while creating a collective search help. Let us discuss these options one by one.

Activation Log

The activation log gives you the activation flow information. All the warning and error messages are displayed in the activation log, which is automatically displayed if errors occur during activation. The activation log can be found via the menu path UTILITIES • ACTIVATION LOG.

Test the Search Help

You can test the flow of an input help defined by the search help by clicking the EXECUTE icon. A dialog box appears in which you can simulate the behavior of the search help under different conditions (see Figure 9.27).

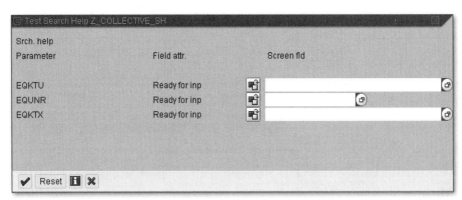

Figure 9.27 Dialog Box While Testing Search Help

Creating an Append Search Help

To create an append search help for a collective search help, follow these steps:

1. Follow the path GOTO • APPEND SEARCH HELP. If you are attaching the append search help to the collective search help for the first time, you get a warning message dialog. Click on the checkmark icon (see Figure 9.28). You get another dialog box where you have to write the name of the append search help. This name should fall in the customer namespace and therefore should start with

"Z" or "Y". Click on the checkmark icon (see Figure 9.29). You are directed to the maintenance screen of the append search help.

Figure 9.28 Information Message Dialog before Creating Append Search Help

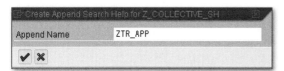

Figure 9.29 Dialog Box While Creating Append Search Help

2. Enter the short text for the append search help in the SHORT DESCRIPTION field (see Figure 9.30). This short text specifies the reason why it is appended in the collective search help.

The append search help always uses the interface of its appending objects. Therefore, entries in the DEFINITION tab cannot be changed.

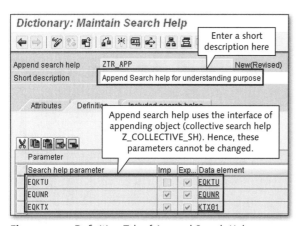

Figure 9.30 Definition Tab of Append Search Help

3. Under the INCLUDED SEARCH HELPS tab, define the search helps that you want to include in the append search help. Both elementary and collective search helps can be included in the collective search help. When you check the HIDDEN flag, included search helps do not appear in the dialog box for selecting elementary search help (see Figure 9.31).

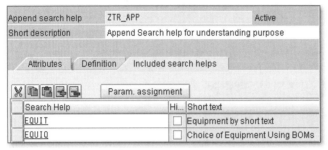

Figure 9.31 Included Search Helps Tab of Append Search Help

4. Assign the collective search help parameter to the attached elementary search help parameter by clicking on the PARAMETER ASSIGNMENT button. When you click on this button, you get a dialog box. In the REFERENCE PARAMETER field, enter the parameter names of the elementary search help to which the corresponding parameters of the collective search help should be assigned (see Figure 9.32).

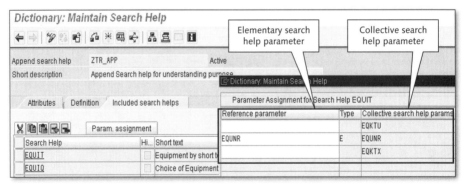

Figure 9.32 Parameter Assignment of Append and Collective Search Help

5. Save your elementary search help. You are asked to assign the development class. You can change the development class later from the path GOTO • OBJECT DIRECTORY ENTRY.

6. Activate your search help by clicking on the ACTIVATE icon.

9.4 Value Transport for Input Helps

When the input help is called and when a line of the hit list is selected, values are transported between the field contents on the screen and the interface of the search help. The values entered in the screen are used as a restriction for a selection from the hit list. Only those hits are displayed that are consistent with the values entered in the screen.

For example, suppose that screen fields A, B, and C are linked with parameters of the search help. Therefore, values can only be transported between the screen and the search help for these three fields. Because screen fields A and B are linked to import parameters A and B of the search help, these fields are used to restrict the selection from the hit list. Similarly, A and C are the export parameters of the search help, and the values of these fields are returned to the screen from the hit list (see Figure 9.33).

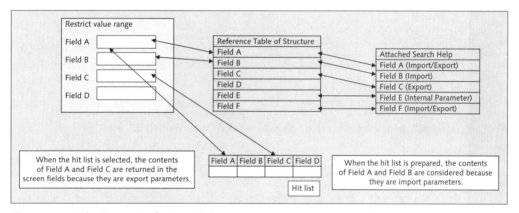

Figure 9.33 Value Transports for Input Help

9.4.1 Parameterizing the Import Parameters

When the input help is called, the system tries to find a field with the same name on the screen for each import parameter of the search help that is attached to a table or structure field. If such a field is found, the contents of the screen field are copied to the search help parameter. Let us suppose input help is called from a step loop. The system searches the screen fields with the same name in the following manner (see Figure 9.34):

- First, the field with the same name is searched in the calling step loop.

- If the step loop does not contain a field with the same name, the corresponding subscreen is searched.

- If the subscreen does not contain a field with the same name, the main screen is searched.

- Finally, the module pool of the corresponding screen is searched, if the main screen does not contain a field with the same name.

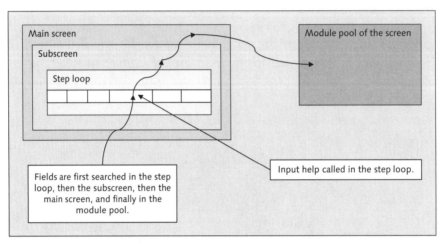

Figure 9.34 Steps While Searching Screen Field When Input Help Is Called

9.4.2 Returning the Values from the Hit List

Values are returned only at the level from where the input help was called. For example, if the input help was called within a step loop, the values are returned from the hit list in fields of the corresponding line of this step loop. Values are never returned from the hit list to the component pool of the screen. The values of the hit list are returned in input fields and in fields that are linked with export parameters of the search help.

9.5   Search Help Attachment

A search help attachment is an assignment of a search help to various components such as tables, structures, or data elements. When these components (which have search helps attached) are used in the screen, the input help process is defined automatically by the attached search help. Search helps can be attached to the following components:

- ▶ Data element
- ▶ Check table
- ▶ Table or structure field
- ▶ Screen field

If the search help is attached to the screen field with a data element or directly with screen fields, only one search help parameter can be assigned to this field. Thus, the value transport can take place only between the screen field and the search help parameter. However, if the search help is attached to the table field or to the check table of the field, the value transport can take place for all the screen fields that are linked with the search help parameter of the search help.

Let us discuss in detail the ways search helps can be attached to the various components.

9.5.1   Search Help Attachment to a Data Element

When the search help is attached to the data element, the attached search help is available for all screen fields that refer to the data element. An export parameter of the search help must be assigned to the data element. If the user chooses a row of the hit list in the input help, the contents of this parameter are returned in the corresponding screen field. However, only one value is returned when a search help is attached to a data element. If the parameter that is assigned to the data element is also an import parameter of the search help, the content of the screen fields can be used for selection.

Let us discuss the procedure of attaching search help to a data element. Remember that you can only attach the search help to a data element that already exists.

1. In the MAINTENANCE SCREEN of the data element, go to the FURTHER CHARACTERISTICS tab. In the SEARCH HELP area, enter the name and the parameter of the search help that you want to attach to the data element in the NAME and PARAMETERS fields, respectively (see Figure 9.35).

2. Activate your data element by clicking on the ACTIVATE icon.

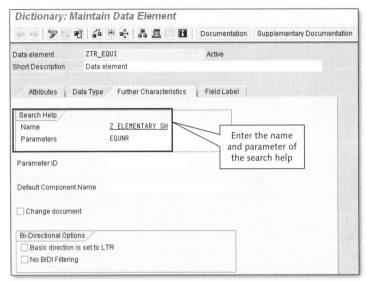

Figure 9.35 Attaching Search Help to Data Element

Once the search help is attached to the data element, the attached search help is available to all screen fields that refer to the data element. For example, in the ABAP program parameter, EQUNR refers to the data element ZTR_EQUI (see Figure 9.36) which is attached to the search help Z_ELEMENTARY_SH. When this program is executed and input help is taken (by pressing F4), a dialog box with the hit list appears (see Figure 9.37).

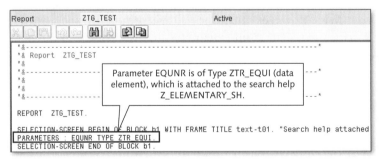

Figure 9.36 Parameters Refer to Data Elements in Programs

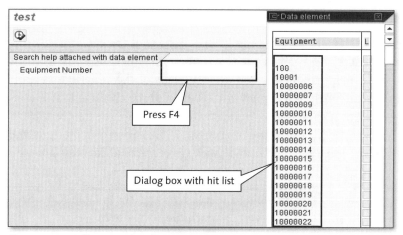

Figure 9.37 Calling Search Help Attached to Data Element from ABAP Program

EQUNR refers to both import and export parameters in the search help Z_ELE-MENTARY_SH. Therefore, the content of the screen field is also used to restrict the selection for the hit list (see Figure 9.38). Also, when any entry on the hit is selected and the checkmark icon is pressed, the contents of the hit list are copied to the screen field.

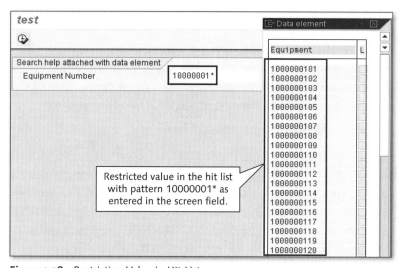

Figure 9.38 Restriction Value in Hit List

9.5.2 Search Help Attachment to a Check Table

When the search help is attached to a check table, it displays the data contained in the check table. For the check table assignment, there also must be an assignment between the search help parameters and the key fields of the table. If an export parameter of the search help is assigned to a key field of the check table, the contents of this parameter are returned to the corresponding screen field when the user selects a line of the hit list in the input help. If an import parameter of the search help is assigned to a key field of the check table, the field contents are used for the value selection.

Let us discuss the procedure of attaching a search help to a check table. The check table must already exist in order for you to attach the search help.

1. In the maintenance screen of the table, follow the path EXTRAS • SEARCH HELP FOR TABLE. You get a dialog box for attaching a search help to a table. Enter the name of the search help that you want to attach to the table and press the checkmark icon (see Figure 9.39).

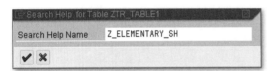

Figure 9.39 Attaching Search Help to Table

2. You are directed to another dialog box. You can generate the proposal and assign the search help parameter with the key fields of the table. When you press the COPY button, the search help gets attached to the table (see Figure 9.40).

3. Activate your table by clicking on the ACTIVATE icon.

Once the search help is attached to the check table, the attached search help is available for all screen fields that are checked against this table. For example, in an ABAP program the parameter EQUNR refers to the table field ZTR_TABLE2-EQUNR (see Figure 9.41) whose check table is ZTR_TABLE1 (see Figure 9.42). Because Table ZTR_TABLE1 is attached to the search help Z_ELEMENTARY_SH, the parameter EQUNR also automatically gets attached to this search help. When this program is executed and input help is taken (by pressing F4), a dialog box with the hit list appears (similar to Figure 9.37).

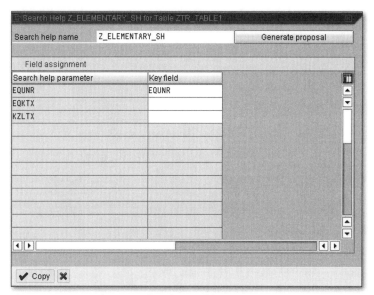

Figure 9.40 Attaching Search Help to Table

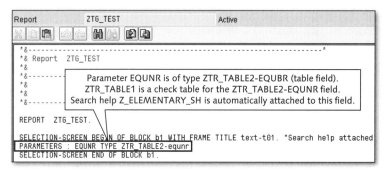

Figure 9.41 Search Help Attached to a Check Table

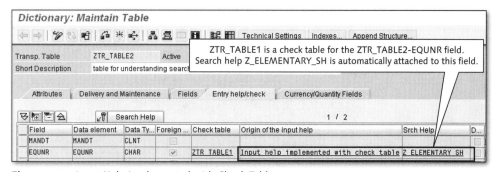

Figure 9.42 Input Help Implemented with Check Table

EQUNR refers to both import and export parameters in the search help Z_ELEMEN-TARY_SH. Therefore, the content of the screen field is also used to restrict the selection for the hit list (similar to Figure 9.38). Also, when any content of the hit is selected and the checkmark icon is pressed, the content of the hit gets copied to the screen field.

9.5.3 Search Help Attached to a Table or Structure Field

The search help can be used by all the screen fields that refer to the table or structure field. For this type of attachment, there must be an assignment between the interface parameters of the search help and the fields of the table or structure. In the input help process, this assignment results in a value transport between the corresponding fields and the search help parameters. If an export parameter of the search help is assigned to a key field of the table or structure, the contents of this parameter are returned to the corresponding screen field when the user selects a line of the hit list in the input help. If an import parameter of the search help is assigned to a key field of the table or structure, the field contents are used for the value selection.

Let us discuss the procedure for attaching search helps to a table or structure field. You can only attach the search help to a table or structure field that already exists.

1. In the maintenance screen of the table, click on the SRCH HELP button that is present under the FIELDS tab of the table maintenance screen. You get a dialog box to attach a search help to a table (see Figure 9.43). Enter the name of the search help that you want to attach to the table and click the checkmark icon.

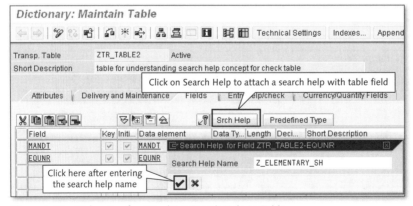

Figure 9.43 Dialog Box for Attaching Search Help to Table

2. You are directed to another dialog box. You can generate the proposal and assign the search help parameter with the key fields of the table. When you press the COPY button, the search help gets attached to the table/structure field (see Figure 9.44).

3. Activate your table by clicking on the ACTIVATE icon.

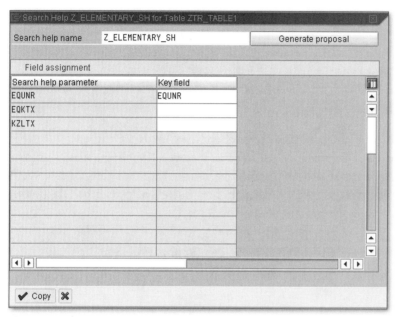

Figure 9.44 Attaching Search Help to Table or Structure Field

Once the search help is attached to the table or structure field, the attached search help is available for all screen fields that refer to that particular field of the table or structure. For example, in the ABAP program, parameter EQUNR refers to the table field ZTR_TABLE2-EQUNR (see Figure 9.45). Because the search help Z_ELEMENTARY_SH is attached to the same table field, the parameter EQUNR of the screen field is attached to this search help. When this program is executed and input help is taken (by pressing F4), a dialog box with the hit list appears (similar to Figure 9.37).

EQUNR refers to both import and export parameters in the search help Z_ELEMENTARY_SH. Therefore, the content of the screen field is also used to restrict the selection for the hit list (similar to Figure 9.38). Also, when any content of the hit is selected and the checkmark icon is pressed, the content of the hit gets copied to the screen field.

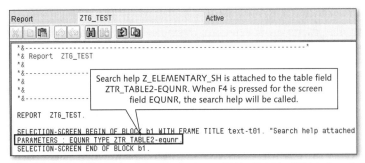

Figure 9.45 Defining Parameter Referring to Table Field for Which Search Help is Attached

9.5.4 Search Help Attached to a Screen Field

Search helps can be assigned directly to the screen fields. In this case, a search help is only available for the attached screen. However, if the same field is used in several screens, then a search help should be attached to the reference table field or data field. The next subsections explain how search helps can be attached in both report program screens and module pool screens.

Attaching a Search Help to a Selection Screen (Report Program)

Let us discuss the procedure for attaching search help to a report program's selection screen.

1. You can create ABAP report program from Transaction SE38. While defining the selection screen, the name of the search help can be defined for selection screens in the `Parameters` or `Select-Options` statement. This can be done by adding a supplement such as `As Search Pattern or Matchcode Objects` (see Figure 9.46).

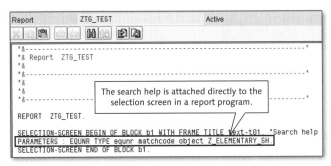

Figure 9.46 Search Help Attachment to Selection Screen

2. When the program is executed by pressing the EXECUTE icon, the input help can be called by pressing ⎡F4⎤. The dialog box appears with the possible values in the hit list (similar to Figure 9.37).

Attaching a Search Help to a Screen Painter (Module Pool Program)

Let us discuss the procedure for attaching a search help to a screen of a module pool program.

1. The module pool program can be created in Transaction SE80.

2. After creating the screen, click on the LAYOUT button and go to the SCREEN PAINTER of the screen.

3. Double-click on the field in which you want to assign the search help. You get the Screen Painter attributes. Define your search help there (see Figure 9.47).

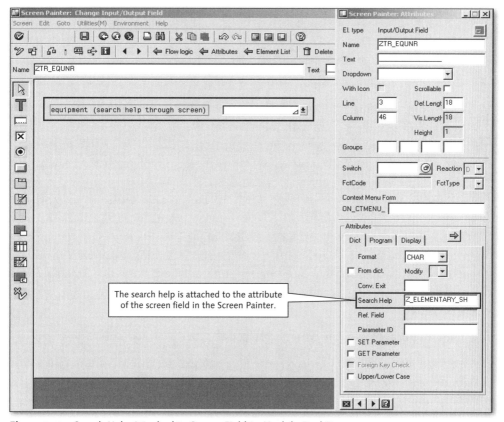

Figure 9.47 Search Help Attached to Screen Field in Module Pool Program

4. After defining the search help for the screen field, activate your screen and your module pool program by clicking on the ACTIVATE icon. Once the module pool program is activated, use a transaction code to execute the program (see Figure 9.48).

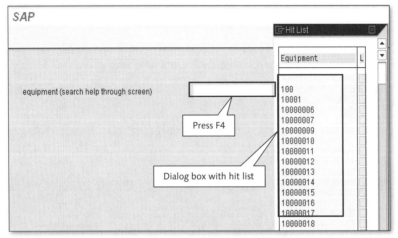

Figure 9.48 Calling Search Help Attached to Screen Painter

Apart from attaching to a screen field from Screen Painter, a search help can also be attached to a screen field with the mechanism of a process on value-request in the flow logic of the screen. A process on value-request is one of the events of a module pool program, which is used to implement the search help on the screen field. Field...select and field...value mechanisms can also be used in the flow logic of the field to attach the field with the search help. Field...Select and Field...Values are ABAP statements that can be used in the process after input (PAI) event block of the Dynpro flow logic. It compares the content of the screen field either with entries in a value list or with the result of a database access. In this case, the input help behaves as if the table specified under Select were assigned to the field as a check table.

9.5.5 Hierarchy of the Search Help Call

We have seen that search helps can be attached to screen fields in different ways. Sometimes, several search helps are assigned to one single screen field. This leads to conflicts, which can be resolved with a hierarchy of different types of search help attachments. Let us discuss this hierarchy.

When the input help for a screen field is called, the field is first checked to determine whether the input search help is attached to it. A search help can be attached to a screen field in three ways:

▶ Search help attachment through a `process on value-request` mechanism

▶ Search help attachment to a screen field through Screen Painter

▶ Search help attachment through field select and field value mechanisms

Conflicts are resolved in the order stated above. If a search help is attached in an ABAP program through a `process on value-request`, it is called. If not, search help attachment to the screen field through Screen Painter is checked. If such a search help attachment is found, it is executed; otherwise a search help attachment through field select and field value mechanisms is checked.

If no input help is defined for the fields on the screen, the system tries to call the search help attached to the table or structure field. If there is no search help attached here, it tries to display the search help attachment through a check table. There are two possible outcomes here. If a search help is attached to the check table, it is displayed. Otherwise, only the key values of the check table are displayed. If the check table also contains a text table, the text for the key value is also added in the user's logon language.

If there is no check table defined for the screen field, the system tries to call the search help from the data element. If there is no search help present in the data element either, the existing domain is checked for fixed values. If the domain contains fixed values, it is displayed. If the domain does not contain fixed values but is of data type DATS or TIMS, the input helps that are assigned to these types are automatically available for the input help. Otherwise there are no input helps available for the field (see Figure 9.49).

A search help attachment always belongs to the definition of the object to which the attachment is made (structure, table, or data element). It is also maintained in the maintenance transaction for this object and transported with this object.

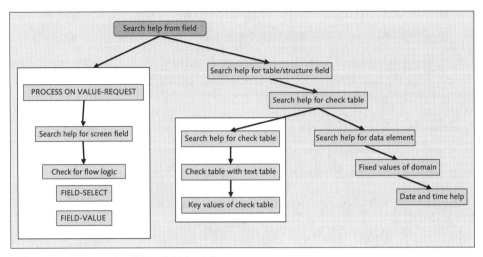

Figure 9.49 Hierarchy of Search Help Call

9.6 Summary

The input help ([F4] help) is one of the most important functions of the SAP system. Input helps for screen fields are presented by the search helps. Search helps are independent repository objects that are created by the ABAP Data Dictionary. Search helps represent a data selection method that provides the possible input values for the screen field and can be elementary or collective. Elementary search helps describe a search path. They define the standard flow of an input help. Collective search helps consist of two or more elementary search helps. They define the series of search paths for a field. The user can select any of these search paths for an input help. Deviation from the standard process can be implemented with the help of search help exits. Append search helps are used to enhance collective search helps. Append search helps can be used in special developments, country versions, SAP partners and customers to add search paths to a collective search help of the standard system. A search help can be attached to a data element, check table, table field, screens of module pool, and report programs, among other system elements.

In the next chapter, we discuss lock objects. A lock is needed when multiple users want to access a database concurrently. A lock authorizes the user to change the data record. This means that the user can change or update the data record only if he or she has locked that particular record.

Lock objects provide authorization for a user to change a data record and to avoid inconsistency. When a lock object is created, the system automatically creates two function modules with the names ENQUEUE_<LOCK OBJECT NAME> and DEQUEUE_<LOCK OBJECT NAME>.

10 Lock Objects

The lock object is an important concept in SAP because it authorizes a user to change a data record. The user first locks the data record and then changes it. Meanwhile, no other user can change the record that is locked. We start the chapter with a general introduction of the topic. Next, we discuss various attributes in lock mechanisms. We also describe the creation of lock objects. We end our discussion with the deletion of lock objects.

10.1 An Introduction to Locks

A lock is needed when multiple users want to access a database concurrently. A lock gives the authorization to the user to change the data record. This means that the user can change or update the data record only if he or she has locked that particular record. In the SAP system, multiple users can access a particular record simultaneously. This may cause inconsistency in the data record if two different users want to change the data record at the same time. For this reason, lock mechanisms are used to maintain data consistency.

Let us consider an example where User1 and User2 want to change the data record at the same time. Without a lock mechanism, the final balance may result in inconsistent values. Figure 10.1 shows the account statement of a company. User1 enters a sales order for the company, while User2 enters an account payment of the company. User1 wants to credit $500 that the company has gained after selling its item to the customer. At the same time, User2 wants to debit $500 that the company has expensed in procuring the raw material from his vendor. User1 accesses the account balance, but before he commits or saves his transaction, User2 accesses the account balance.

As a result, User2 access the initial balance ($10,000) and does not know that User1 is making changes to the account balance. User1 commits his changes, and then User2 commits his changes. Thus, the final account balance is inconsistent.

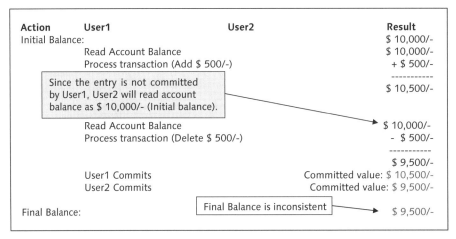

Figure 10.1 Scenario without Lock Mechanism

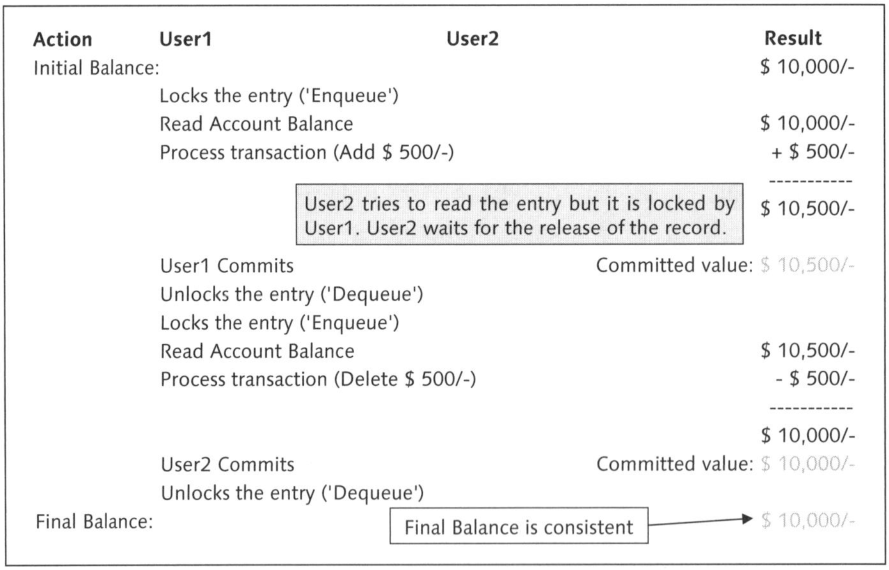

Figure 10.2 Scenario with Lock Mechanism

Now, let us discuss the same example with a lock mechanism in use. When User2 tries to access the data record, his request is refused, as the data record is already locked by User1. User2 waits until User1 releases the lock. User1 releases the lock when he completes his processing and commits his changes. When User1 releases the lock, User2 locks the record and reads the latest account balance: $10,500. User2 completes his processing and releases the record. Thus, the final account balance is consistent (see Figure 10.2).

10.2   Lock Mechanisms and Their Attributes

Whenever a database receives the change statements (`insert`, `update`, `modify`, `delete`) from a program, it sets the database lock on the data record. Database locks are physical locks that are set on the database entries whenever data records are affected by these change statements. The database uses a lock flag that can be set only for the existing entries. This lock flag is automatically deleted after each database commits. Consequently, database locks cannot be set for longer than a single database LUW (logical unit of work) or a single dialog step.

Physical locks or database locks in the database system are therefore insufficient for the requirements of SAP transactions. Locks must remain set for the entire duration of an SAP LUW; that is, over several dialog steps. Different work processes and different application servers must also be handled by locks. Also, each lock must apply to all servers in that system.

Let us describe the various terms and attributes involved in lock mechanisms.

10.2.1   Lock Objects

In order to fulfill the above discussed requirement, the SAP system provides its own logical lock concept, known as *SAP locks*. SAP locks complement the SAP LUW concept, in which bundled database changes are made in a single database LUW. SAP locks are fully independent of database locks. SAP locks span several dialog steps. SAP locks are logical locks, whereas database locks are physical locks.

SAP locks are created with the help of *lock objects*. A lock object sets an SAP lock for an entire application object. An application object consists of one or more entries in a database table, or entries from more than one database table that are linked using foreign key relationships.

Thus, a lock object contains the tables (whose data record should be locked) along with their keys. One table is selected as a primary table for the lock object. Further secondary tables are added with the help of a foreign key relationship.

When a lock object is created, the system automatically generates two function modules with the names ENQUEUE_<LOCK OBJECT NAME> and DEQUEUE_<LOCK OBJECT NAME>. These function modules are called from the ABAP program and are responsible for setting or releasing the lock.

10.2.2 Lock Arguments

The lock argument of a table in the lock object contains the key field of the table (see Figure 10.3). These lock arguments are used as input parameters in the function module generated by the lock object for setting and releasing locks. Values are passed in these fields. Data records having these values are locked or unlocked. Generic values can also be passed. Thus, this field defines the rows that should be locked.

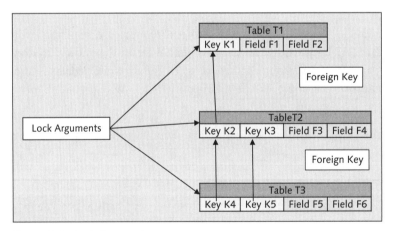

Figure 10.3 Lock Arguments

A lock request can lock an entire logical object, not only a record of a table. It can lock a single table (primary table) or a number of secondary tables with the help of a foreign key mechanism (see Figure 10.4). Locks can also be set from programs in other systems with the corresponding interfaces if the lock objects are defined with RFC (remote function call) authorization.

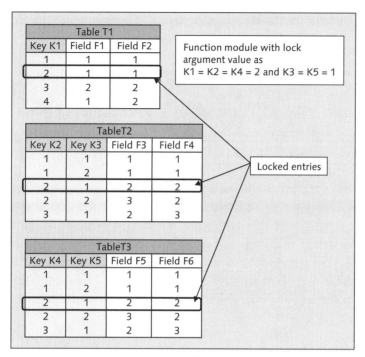

Table T1		
Key K1	Field F1	Field F2
1	1	1
2	1	1
3	2	2
4	1	2

Function module with lock argument value as
K1 = K2 = K4 = 2 and K3 = K5 = 1

TableT2			
Key K2	Key K3	Field F3	Field F4
1	1	1	1
1	2	1	1
2	1	2	2
2	2	3	2
3	1	2	3

Locked entries

TableT3			
Key K4	Key K5	Field F5	Field F6
1	1	1	1
1	2	1	1
2	1	2	2
2	2	3	2
3	1	2	3

Figure 10.4 Entries Locked by a Lock Object

10.2.3 Lock Mode

Lock mode is used to synchronize access by more than one user; that is, to determine whether several users can access a data record at the same time. Lock mode can be used with the following access modes:

▶ **Exclusive mode**
If the data record is locked in exclusive mode, the data record can only be edited or displayed by a single user. Another request of exclusive lock or shared lock is rejected.

▶ **Shared mode**
If the data record is locked in shared mode, a locked data record can be accessed by other users in display mode. Another request for a shared lock is accepted (even if it comes from another user). However, a request of exclusive lock is rejected. This is because only one user can edit or display the record in exclusive lock mode.

▶ **Exclusive but not cumulative mode**
An exclusive lock can be requested and processed successfully several times from the same transaction. In contrast, an exclusive but not cumulative lock can be called only once from the same transaction. If it is called again from the same transaction, the lock request is rejected.

The lock mode can be assigned separately for each table in a lock object. This means that if the primary table of the lock object is locked in exclusive mode, it is not necessary that secondary tables of the lock object also be locked in exclusive mode.

10.2.4 Lock Server

The lock server, also known as an *enqueue server*, administers or manages the lock table. The enqueue server receives a lock request. It checks the lock table and determines whether the lock request conflicts with an existing lock. If it does, the enqueue server rejects the lock request. Otherwise, the enqueue server sets the lock and makes the entry in the lock table.

The enqueue server runs on a central instance. There is only one enqueue server in a distributed SAP system. To ensure high availability for the enqueue server, a stand-alone enqueue server with replication service can be implemented. This is useful when the lock server is a single point of failure in the SAP system.

> **Note**
>
> Locks are saved to the disk when they are inherited by the update task; that is, when `Commit Work` is executed after calling the function module in update task mode `Call Function... In Update Task`. When the lock server is restarted, all the locks are lost if they are not saved to the disk. The lock entries saved on the disk are reloaded to the lock table when the enqueue server is restarted. If the enqueue replication service is used as part of a high availability solution, locks are not lost if the enqueue server fails or is restarted.

A lock server can be used in the following communication models:

▶ The ABAP work processes and the Java server processes communicate directly with the enqueue server, when the stand-alone enqueue server or a Java cluster is used in the SAP Web AS.

▶ In the classical ABAP system having one central instance and several dialog instances, a lock request is sent by the local dispatcher and message server to the central instance, which in turn forwards the request to the enqueue work process.

▶ Work processes on the central instance have a direct access to the enqueue server. Therefore, they do not require dispatchers and message servers to send their lock requests.

The lock table is located in the main memory (shared memory) of the lock server. All work processes in the lock server have access to the lock table. External application servers execute their lock operations in the enqueue process on the lock server. Communication takes place via the relevant dispatchers and the message server.

The work processes on the lock server use the lock table directly, not via the enqueue process. Therefore the lock table is still set up, even when no enqueue work process is started on the lock server in the instance profile. The enqueue process is only responsible for lock requests from external application servers (see Figure 10.5).

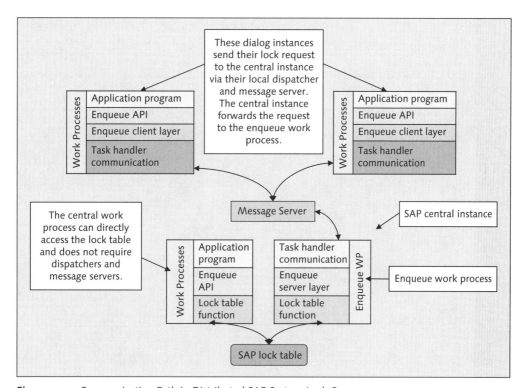

Figure 10.5 Communication Path in Distributed SAP System Lock Owner

The term *lock owner* refers to the person who holds the lock. When the transaction is started, two owners who can request locks are always created. The _SCOPE parameter is used to specify the owner of the lock. A lock can have one or two owners. The SY-MSGV1 field of the function module ENQUEUE_... determines the name of the owner or the user who is currently holding the lock.

An owner is identified by the owner ID. The ID contains the computer name, the work process, and a timestamp. This ID also identifies the SAP LUW. Lock owners are classified as dialog owners or update owners.

Figure 10.6 shows the functionality available to lock owners in a dialog transaction. When the dialog transaction is started, two lock owners (the dialog owner, Owner_1, and the update owner, Owner_2) are created by the system.

Owner_1 requests a lock, and then Owner_2 requests a lock. When the update task is called, the lock and Owner_2 are inherited by the update task. An update work process is started with two new owners, in the same way as a dialog work process. Now there are three owners until the update is completed. All the locks are released with an implicit DEQUEUE_ALL at the end of the update (see Figure 10.6).

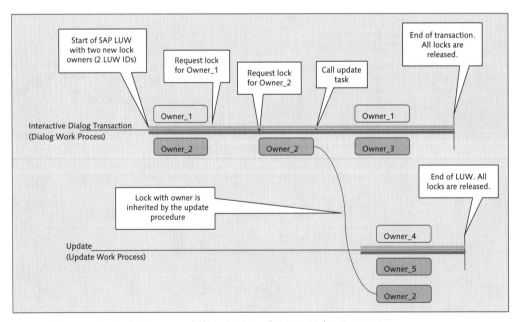

Figure 10.6 Lock Owners and Their Functionality in a Dialog Transaction

10.2.5   _SCOPE Parameter

As described, two lock owners (the dialog owner and update owner) are automatically created for each lock. This parameter determines which of the two owners own the lock. _SCOPE parameters can have the following values:

▶ _SCOPE = 1
  The lock belongs only to the dialog owner (Owner_1); that is, it exists only in the dialog transaction. A dequeue call, the end of the transaction, or ROLLBACK WORK releases the lock.

▶ _SCOPE = 2
  The lock belongs only to the update owner (Owner_2). Therefore, the update inherits the lock when CALL FUNCTION... IN UPDATE TASK and COMMIT WORK are called. The lock is released when the update transaction is complete. You can release the lock before it is transferred to the update using ROLLBACK WORK. COMMIT WORK has no effect, unless CALL FUNCTION... IN UPDATE TASK has been called.

▶ _SCOPE = 3
  The lock belongs to both owners (Owner_1 and Owner_2). It combines the behavior of both the owners. This lock is cancelled when the last of the two owners has released it.

Figure 10.7 shows the locks during the course of an SAP LUW in conjunction with the _SCOPE parameter. The diagram also describes how long the SAP locks are active.

The lock object A is locked by the function module CALL FUNCTION 'ENQUEUE_A'. The _SCOPE parameter of lock object A is set as 1. This means lock object A is not forwarded to the update task. It belongs to the dialog owner E_1 only. This lock is released with the function call DEQUEUE_A, NOT COMMIT WORK, ROLLBACK WORK, or at the end of the dialog transaction.

Later, lock B, which belongs to the update owner (_SCOPE=2), and the lock C, which has two owners (_SCOPE=3), are requested. The CALL FUNCTION '...' IN UPDATE TASK generates an update request. At COMMIT WORK, the update task is called and inherits the locks and the update owner of locks B and C. These locks are released when the update is completed. However, lock C may exist as long as it contains the dialog owner as well. Dialog locks A and C remain set until the end of the dialog transaction. Locks are released if the DEQUEUE function module is called or if the transaction is completed with an implicit DEQUEUE_ALL function module.

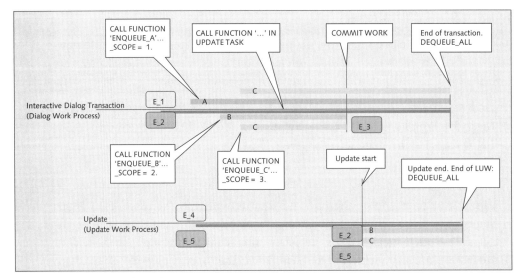

Figure 10.7 Locks with _SCOPE Parameter

> **Note**
>
> If `COMMIT WORK` is called before the `CALL FUNCTION '...' IN UPDATE TASK` and lock is set with `_SCOPE=2`, the lock remains in place as a dialog lock and an update request is not generated. The update request is generated only when `COMMIT WORK` is called after the call of `CALL FUNCTION '...' IN UPDATE TASK`.

10.2.6 Lock Table

The lock table is used to manage locks. It is also used to record the current lock of the system. It is located in the main memory (shared memory) of the lock server. The enqueue server receives a lock request. It checks the lock table and determines whether the lock request collides with an existing lock. If it does, the enqueue server rejects the lock request. Otherwise, the enqueue server sets the lock and makes the entry in the lock table.

For each elementary lock, the table specifies the owner, lock mode, name of the lock table, and lock arguments (see Figure 10.8). Locks written in the lock table are logical locks and are not set at the database level.

Owner_1	Owner_2	Backup ID	Elementary Lock		
			Lock Mode	Name	Argument
• Owner ID • Cumulation counter	• Owner ID • Cumulation counter	• Backup ID • Flag	• X,E,S, or O	• Name of lock table	• Lock arguments

Figure 10.8 Structure of Lock Table

The individual attributes of the lock table have the following meanings:

▶ **Owner_1 and Owner_2**
This attribute specifies the owner ID and cumulation counter of owner_1. The ID contains the computer name, the work process, and a timestamp. It also identifies the SAP LUW. The cumulation counter specifies how often this elementary lock has been set by a particular owner.

▶ **Backup ID**
Backup ID indicates whether the lock entry is to be stored in the backup file. The backup flag can have a value of 0 or 1. A value of 0 indicates no backup, while a value of 1 indicates backup. If the backup indicator is set (value of 1), the system saves the lock to disk. These lock values can be retrieved when the lock server is restarted.

▶ **Lock mode**
Lock mode is used to synchronize the access by more than one user; it determines whether several users can access a data record at the same time. It can have the value S (shared lock), O (optimistic lock), E (exclusive lock), or X (exclusive but not cumulative lock).

▶ **Name**
This attribute specifies the name of the database table whose fields are to be locked.

▶ **Argument**
The lock argument of a table contains the key fields of the table. These fields can also have generic values.

335

10.2.7 Local Lock Containers

A local lock container collects the lock request and lock release request together. All the requests are sent together by calling the function module FLUSH_ENQUEUE. All the lock requests and lock releases are managed together in the local lock container. Lock requests are sent first. Lock release requests are sent only when all the lock requests have been completed; that is, when all the requested locks have been assigned. The lock request and lock release requests are not adjusted in the local lock container. It doesn't matter in what order the individual requests are written.

Using a local lock container has the following advantages over sending the lock request directly:

► The lock server is not accessed again and again, so less communication with the lock server is needed.

► Lock requests and lock release requests are handled as a group, and all the requests are processed as a group. This means that the local lock container is executed and emptied only if all the individual requests are executed successfully; otherwise its contents remain unchanged.

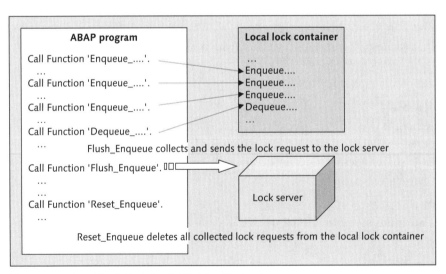

Figure 10.9 Local Lock Container's Working Mechanism

The local lock container is emptied by calling the function module RESET_ENQUEUE (see Figure 10.9). When this function module is called, all the collected lock requests or lock release requests are deleted. The local lock container is automatically emptied if the corresponding internal session ends.

10.2.8 Function Modules for Lock Requests

When a lock object is created, the system automatically generates two function modules with the names `ENQUEUE_<LOCK OBJECT NAME>` and `DEQUEUE_<LOCK OBJECT NAME>`. These function module are called from the ABAP program and are responsible for setting or releasing the locks (see Figure 10.10).

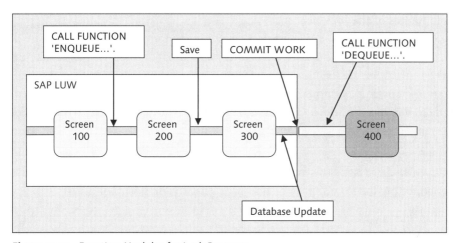

Figure 10.10 Function Modules for Lock Requests

These function modules are executed in the enqueue work process. The enqueue work process runs on a single application server known as an enqueue server. This enqueue server maintains a central lock table in its shared memory for the entire SAP system. The enqueue function module writes the entry in the central lock table. If the requested lock is already locked by an application object, the lock cannot be set. In this case, the value of `SY-MSGV1` reflects the name of the owner who has locked the object.

The generated function modules are automatically assigned to the function groups. Function modules and their assignment to function groups should not be changed. This is because function modules are regenerated each time the lock object is activated, and this may create an error.

Function groups that contain automatically generated function modules should not be transported. The generated function modules of a lock object may reside in a different function group in the target system. Therefore, lock objects should be transported rather than the function group. When a lock object is activated in the target system, the function modules are generated again and correctly assigned to the function group.

Parameters of the Function Modules

The function module ENQUEUE and DEQUEUE have the following parameters:

▶ **Field names of the lock object**
Field names contain the key fields that are to be locked. For each lock field ⟨FIELD⟩, a further parameter X_⟨FIELD⟩ is passed that defines the lock behavior if the initial value of field is passed. If both ⟨FIELD⟩ and X_⟨FIELD⟩ have initial values, a generic lock is initialized with respect to ⟨FIELD⟩. If ⟨FIELD⟩ is assigned with an initial value and X_⟨FIELD⟩ is defined as "X", the lock is set with exactly the same initial value as ⟨FIELD⟩.

▶ **_SCOPE parameters**
As already discussed, this parameter determines whether the parameters are passed to the update program or not. It can have values 1, 2, or 3.

▶ **MODE_⟨TAB⟩**
This parameter exists for each base table of the lock object. With this parameter, the lock mode for the base table can be set dynamically. It can have the values S (shared), E (exclusive), and X (exclusive but not cumulative). The default value of the lock mode that is given during the time of creation of the lock object can be overridden in the function module with this parameter. The lock release request—that is, the DEQUEUE function module—must have the same lock mode value that is passed in the ENQUEUE function module during the lock request.

▶ **_COLLECT**
This parameter decides whether the lock requests or lock release requests are processed individually or whether they are first collected in the local lock container and then processed as a group. This parameter can have an initial value or an X value. With an initial value, lock requests and lock release requests are sent directly to the lock server and these requests are processed individually.

When the value of _Collect is X, then lock requests or lock release requests are placed in the local lock container and these requests are processed as a group by calling the function module FLUSH_ENQUEUE.

▶ **_WAIT**
This parameter is present only with the ENQUEUE function module. This parameter determines the lock behavior during the time of a lock conflict. It can have an initial value or a value of X. An initial value determines that if a lock attempt fails because of the competing lock, the exception FOREIGN_LOCK is triggered. A value of X determines that if a lock attempt fails because there is a competing lock, the lock attempt is repeated after waiting a certain length of time. If the time limit elapses, the exception FOREIGN_LOCK is triggered. The waiting time and the time limit are defined by the profile parameters.

▶ **_SYNCHRON**
This parameter is present only with the DEQUEUE function module. This parameter controls the deletion of the locked entry. If X is passed, the DEQUEUE function waits until the entry has been removed from the lock table. Otherwise, the entry is deleted asynchronously. If the lock table of the system is read directly after the lock is removed, the entry in the lock table may still exist.

▶ **Exceptions**
Please be aware that the ENQUEUE function module can have the following exceptions:

▶ **FOREIGN_LOCK**
This is the competing lock. The name of the user holding the lock can be found in the system variable SY-MSGV1.

▶ **SYSTEM_FAILURE**
If any problem occurs while setting the lock, this exception is triggered. The lock cannot be set if system failure occurs.

▶ **Others**
If the exceptions are not processed by the calling program itself, appropriate messages are issued.

Figures 10.11 and Figure 10.12 define the parameters of the ENQUEUE and DEQUEUE function module respectively when called from an ABAP program.

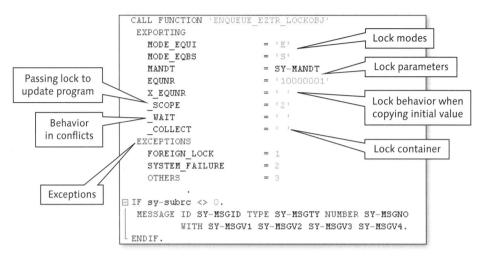

Figure 10.11 ENQUEUE Function Module Call from an ABAP Program

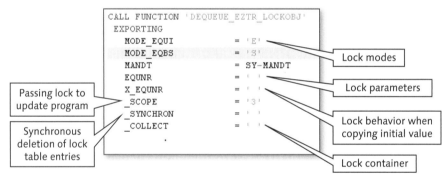

Figure 10.12 DEQUEUE Function Module Call from ABAP Program

Reference Fields for RFC-Enabled Lock Objects

Lock objects can also be defined with RFCs. The type of an RFC-enabled function module must be completely defined. The parameters of the generated function module have the following reference fields for RFC-enabled lock objects, as seen in Table 10.1:

Parameters	Reference Fields
X_<field name>	DDENQ_LIKE-XPARFLAG
_WAIT	DDENQ_LIKE-WAITFLAG
_SCOPE	DDENQ_LIKE-SCOPE
_SYNCHRON	DDENQ_LIKE-SYNCHRON

Table 10.1 Referenced Field for RFC-Enabled Lock Objects

10.2.9 Foreign Keys in Lock Objects

All the secondary tables must be included in the primary table with the help of foreign keys. The following conditions apply to the foreign key relationship:

▶ The foreign key relationships of the tables of the lock object must form a tree. The tables are the nodes of the tree. The links of the tree define the relation "is the check table of." For example, Table EQBS has the key EQUNR. If the foreign key is set for this key EQUNR, Table EQUI is the check table. Thus, the foreign key relationship forms the tree in which the link between the two tables is defined by the relationship "is the check table of."

▶ The foreign key fields must be key fields of the foreign key table.

▶ The foreign key relationships defined between the base tables of the lock object may not include any field that is checked against more than one other field. Therefore, a field may not occur twice as a foreign key field in a relationship and may not be checked against two different fields in two different foreign key relationships.

▶ You must keep one restriction in mind for multi-structured foreign keys. If a field is assigned to a field that is outside the check table, the table containing this field must be in a sub-tree that contains the check table of this foreign key relationship as a root.

These conditions are automatically satisfied if the key of the foreign key table is an extension of the key of the check table. The last three conditions are meaningless if the particular foreign key field was excluded from the assignment to the key fields of the check table. This is done by marking the field as a generic or constant foreign key field. This is also true for multi-structured foreign keys if the foreign key field refers to a table that is not contained in the lock object.

10.2.10 Lock Mechanism

With the logical lock mechanism, the same data can be accessed by several programs in a synchronized manner. To set a lock, a lock object must be defined in the ABAP Data Dictionary. Two function modules are generated with the name `ENQUEUE <LOCKOBJECTNAME>` and `DEQUEUE <LOCKOBJECTNAME>`. To set the lock `ENQUEUE <LOCKOBJECTNAME>` is called. When the lock is set, an entry is made in the lock table. This entry is retained until the lock is removed by the program or the program comes to an end. From this entry, the data record edited by other programs can be identified. If any other program also wants to acquire the lock, that program requests the lock. An entry in the lock table would be checked. If an entry exists, the lock request is rejected by the enqueue server. Otherwise, the enqueue server sets the lock and makes the entry in the lock table (see Figure 10.13).

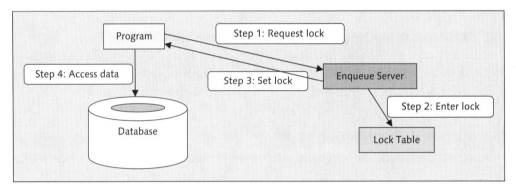

Figure 10.13 Lock Mechanism

Locked data records can be unlocked by calling the function module `DEQUEUE<LOCKOBJECTNAME>`. The key value and lock mode used to set the lock must be passed to this function module.

All the programs should cooperate. Inconsistencies may occur if a program reads or changes data without locking it. When a lock is set, the data records are protected only against changes by another program if this program also requests a lock before accessing the data.

Thus, the lock mechanism fulfils two main functions:

▶ With the help of a lock mechanism, a program can tell another program which data records it is reading or changing.

▶ With the help of a lock mechanism, a program can prevent itself from reading data that is just being changed by another program.

10.3 Creating Lock Objects

Let us discuss the procedure for creating lock objects.

1. Go to Transaction SE11. Select the radio button for LOCK OBJECTS in the initial screen of the ABAP Data Dictionary and enter the name of the lock object. Choose the CREATE button (see Figure 10.14). The name of the lock object should begin with an E (enqueue).

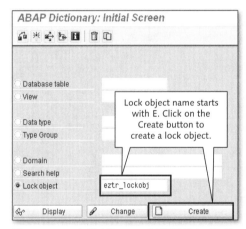

Figure 10.14 Initial Screen of ABAP Data Dictionary to Create Lock Objects

2. Enter the explanatory short text in the SHORT TEXT field of the maintenance screen of the lock object (see Figure 10.15). This is a mandatory attribute and you cannot enter any other attribute without entering this attribute.

3. Enter the name of the primary table of the lock object. Enter the lock mode of the primary table in the LOCK MODE field (see Figure 10.15). The lock mode can have the values S (Shared), E (Exclusive), or X (Exclusive but not cumulative).

4. Other tables (secondary tables) can be linked with the primary table with the help of a foreign key. Click on the ADD button if you want to add a secondary table to the primary table. You get the dialog box that contains the list of tables

that can be added as a secondary table. All the tables in the list have appropriate foreign keys. Select the table and click on the CHOOSE icon (see Figure 10.15). The table is included as a secondary table. The lock mode of the primary table is copied to the lock mode of the secondary table. However, you can change this setting. Further secondary tables can be included from the primary table or from recently added secondary tables. Place the cursor on the name of the table from which you want to add the secondary table and choose ADD. Lock mode should not be assigned if the secondary table is used only to define the path between the primary table and another secondary table with foreign keys.

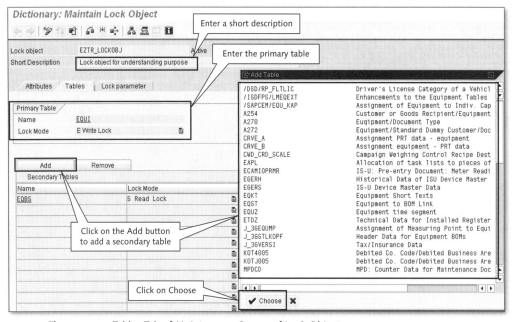

Figure 10.15 Tables Tab of Maintenance Screen of Lock Object

5. All the key fields of the included tables automatically get included under the LOCK PARAMETER tab. However, you can set some of the lock parameters as generic. This can be done by de-selecting the WEIGHT flag of the lock parameter. The lock parameter is excluded from the generated function module. This parameter is then always locked generically (see Figure 10.16).

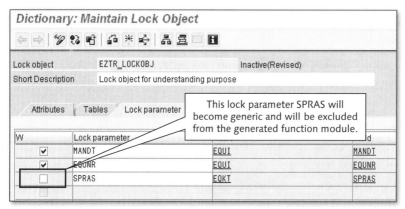

Figure 10.16 Lock Parameter Tab of Lock Object Maintenance Screen

6. Under the ATTRIBUTES TAB, you can define whether function modules generated from lock objects are RFC-enabled. If the ALLOW RFC flag is checked, the generated function module can be called from another system with the help of a remote function call (see Figure 10.17).

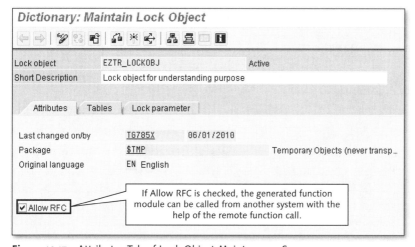

Figure 10.17 Attributes Tab of Lock Object Maintenance Screen

7. Save your changes. A CREATE OBJECT DIRECTORY ENTRY popup appears that asks for a package. Enter the package name in which you are working. If you don't have a package, then you can create one in the Object Navigator (Transaction SE80), or you can save your lock object in the local object in package *$tmp*.

8. Activate your lock object. Click on the ACTIVATE button (✳) or press ⌈Ctrl⌋+⌈F3⌋ to activate the lock object.

The activation log and lock Modules are among the options available while creating lock objects. Let us discuss these options.

Activation Log

The activation log gives you activation flow information. All the warning and error messages are displayed in the activation log. The activation log is automatically displayed if errors occur during activation. The activation log can be found via the menu path UTILITIES • ACTIVATION LOG (see Figure 10.18).

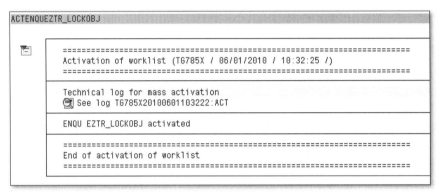

Figure 10.18 Activation Log

Lock Modules

When the lock object is activated, two function modules ENQUEUE_<LOCKOBJECTNAME> and DEQUEUE_<LOCKOBJECTNAME> are generated from its definition. ENQUEUE_<LOCKOBJECTNAME> is used to set (request) the lock, and DEQUEUE_<LOCKOBJECTNAME> is used to release the locks (see Figure 10.19).

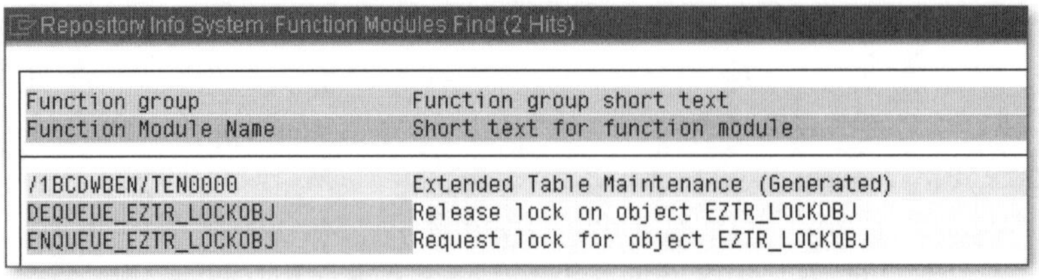

Figure 10.19 Function Module Generated from Lock Objects

10.4   Deleting Lock Objects

When a lock object is deleted, the function modules ENQUEUE_<LOCKOBJECTNAME> and DEQUEUE_<LOCKOBJECTNAME> get automatically deleted as well. These generated function modules might still exist in programs or classes. Therefore, before deleting a lock object, find all programs or classes that contain these function modules and remove the calls to the function modules. Let us discuss the procedure for deleting lock objects.

1. Go to Transaction SE11. Select the LOCK OBJECT radio button in the initial screen of the ABAP Data Dictionary. Enter the name of the lock object that you want to delete.

2. Choose the where-used list by clicking on the WHERE-USED LIST icon (🖪), and check if the lock object and its function modules are still in use by any program or classes (see Figure 10.20). Remove the lock module call from the objects that are using it.

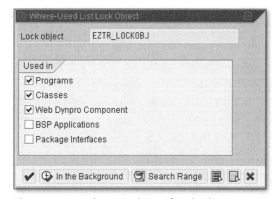

Figure 10.20   Where-Used List of Lock Object

3. Choose the DELETE icon (🗑) in Transaction SE11. A dialog box appears for confirmation of your deletion request (see Figure 10.21). If the function modules belonging to the lock object are still in use by the programs or classes, a warning appears. In this case, you have to adjust the programs or classes affected before deleting the lock object.

Figure 10.21 Pop-up While Deleting Lock Object

4. The lock object along with the function modules generated from this lock object is deleted when you confirm the deletion request. You will see the success message in the status toolbar (see Figure 10.22).

Figure 10.22 Success Message in the Status Toolbar

10.5 Summary

Locks authorize the user to change and modify the data record and provide consistency of data. The SAP system provides its own logical lock concept, which is also known as SAP locks, with the help of lock objects. A lock object sets an SAP lock for an entire application object. An application object consists of one or more entries in a database table, or entries from more than one database table that are linked using foreign key relationships. When a lock object is created, the system automatically generates two function modules with the names ENQUEUE_<LOCK OBJECT NAME> and DEQUEUE_<LOCK OBJECT NAME>. These function module are called from the ABAP program and are responsible for setting or releasing the lock.

Lock mode is used to synchronize access by more than one user, determining whether several users can access data records at the same time. The lock server, also known as the enqueue server, administers or manages the lock table. The term *lock owner* refers to the person who holds the lock. The lock table is used to manage locks. It is also used to record the current lock in the system.

In the next chapter, we discuss database utilities. The database utility acts as an interface between the ABAP Data Dictionary and the underlying relational database of the SAP system. Database objects that are created from the objects of the ABAP Data Dictionary can be edited with the help of the database utility.

The database utility acts as an interface between the ABAP Data Dictionary and the underlying relational database. Database objects created from the ABAP Data Dictionary can be edited from the database utility.

11 Database Utility

The database utility acts as an interface between the ABAP Data Dictionary and the underlying relational database of the SAP system. Database objects created from the objects of the ABAP Data Dictionary can be edited with the help of the database utility. We start our chapter with a general introduction to the topic. Next, we discuss processing types, runtime parameters, activation, storage parameters, and conversion problems. Finally, we see how to edit various Data Dictionary objects such as tables, views, table clusters, and table pools in the database.

11.1 An Introduction to the Database Utility

The ABAP Data Dictionary defines the structure of database objects: tables, views, and indexes. These database objects automatically get created in the underlying database and are defined in the Data Dictionary when the objects are activated (see Figure 11.1).

The database utility provides the following functionality to the database object:

▶ **Editing database objects**
Indexes, database views, matchcode views, matchcode pooled tables, and database tables (generated from transparent tables, physical table pools, or table clusters) can be edited from the database utility. The database utility can be called directly for a particular object from the maintenance screen of that object (Transaction SE11) by following the menu path UTILITIES • DATABASE OBJECT • DATABASE UTILITY. However, the initial screen of the database utility can be displayed with Transaction SE14. You will be directed to the utility screen of a particular database object when you enter the name of the database object and press the EDIT button in Transaction SE14 (see Figure 11.2).

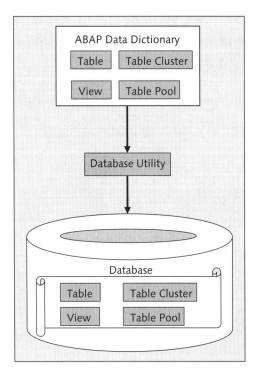

Figure 11.1 Relationship among ABAP Data Dictionary, Database Utility, and Database

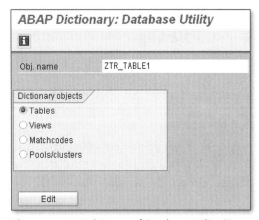

Figure 11.2 Initial Screen of Database Utility (Transaction SE14)

▶ **Analyzing conversion problems**
Problems may occur while converting the database objects. The database utility is

used to find the reason of the conversion problem. You can rectify the conversion error and successfully convert the database object with the database utility.

▶ **Monitoring requests for database modifications**
The database utility also provides a number of options for administering and monitoring requests for database modifications. The following functions are performed by the database utility for monitoring purposes:

  ▶ Scheduling jobs for mass processing

  ▶ Displaying requests for mass processing

  ▶ Displaying logs for mass processing

  ▶ Displaying temporary tables without restart logs

▶ **Incremental conversions**
With the help of incremental table conversion, a table can be reorganized and its structure can be changed. Unlike standard conversion, incremental conversion allows the system to use the table during the data transfer. This means that much more time is available for the data transfer and larger sets of data can be converted in incremental conversion than with the standard conversion method. However, productivity is reduced while initializing the incremental conversion and switching to the new table. The incremental conversion monitor can be displayed from the initial screen of the database utility from the menu path DB REQUESTS • INCREMENTAL. More information about the incremental conversion and incremental request can be found by clicking the INFO (∎) button.

11.2 Processing Types

Processing types are used to modify database objects. With the help of processing types, the database utility schedules the database object for modification. Processing types can have the values shown in Figure 11.3.

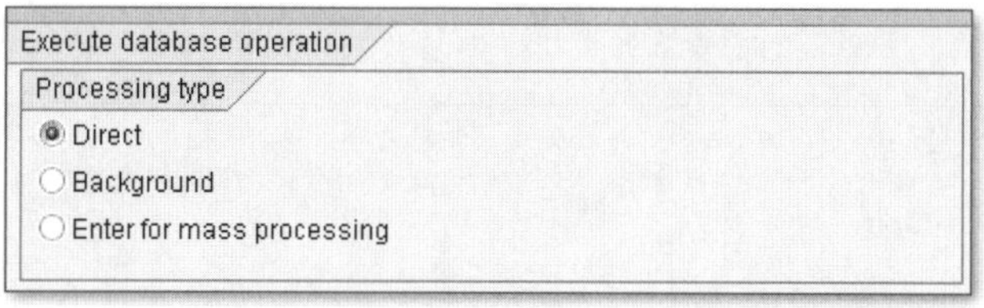

Figure 11.3 Values of Processing Types

11.2.1   Direct

If the value of processing type is DIRECT, the database modifications for the database object are carried out immediately. In this processing type, the conversion process puts a heavy load on the system. Also, runtime restrictions may terminate the conversion process. For these reasons, this processing type is not suitable for converting large tables. For converting large tables, the processing type BACKGROUND should be chosen.

11.2.2   Background

If the processing type value is BACKGROUND, the database modifications for the database object are carried out in background. That means a background job is scheduled for the database modifications. Start date and time should be entered to schedule the background job. The background process will start automatically at this scheduled time. However, if you want to run your job immediately, that can be done by clicking on the IMMEDIATE button (see Figure 11.4).

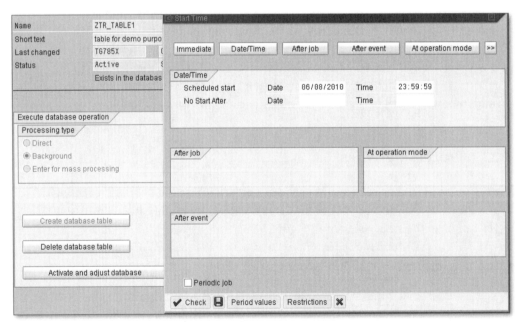

Figure 11.4 Processing Type Background

In this mode, values can also be entered for AFTER JOB, AFTER EVENT, AT OPERATION MODE, and RESTRICTIONS. You can also specify whether the background job is a periodic job or a one-time job. If the job is periodic, you can enter the periodic interval for your job. You can set your job execution period as HOURLY, DAILY, WEEKLY, MONTHLY, or OTHER PERIOD (see Figure 11.5).

The advantage of background type when compared with direct type is that there is no danger of the operation terminating as the result of a runtime restriction.

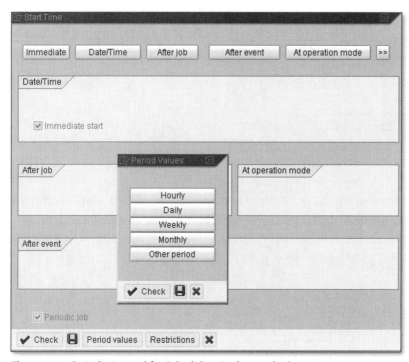

Figure 11.5 Periodic Interval for Scheduling Background Job

11.2.3 Enter for Mass Processing

If the value of the processing type is ENTER FOR MASS PROCESSING, the database modifications for the database object are carried out in the background in mass processing (see Figure 11.6). If this processing type is selected, entries are created with their corresponding functions in system Table TBATG. All the requests are collected and processed from this table in the background at fixed intervals of time. Jobs should be explicitly scheduled for mass processing.

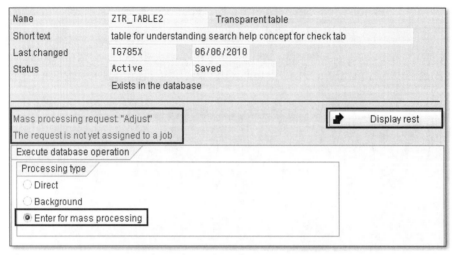

Figure 11.6 Processing a Database Object through Mass Processing

An entry is maintained in Table TBATG when an object is entered in mass- processing mode. The scheduled objects for mass processing can also be displayed from the initial screen of the database utility (Transaction SE14) from the menu path DB REQUESTS • MASS PROCESSING (see Figure 11.7).

Object	Object name	ID	Fct	User	Job status	Start date	Start tim	Job name	Job coun	Date entered	Order
TABL	ZTR_TABLE2		CNV	TG785X						06/08/2010	0

Figure 11.7 List of Mass-Processing Objects

The background program writes messages in a log file. Log files can be displayed with the initial screen of the database utility from the path EXTRAS • LOGS.

Displaying Requests for Mass Processing

Mass-processing requests can be displayed either from the path DB REQUESTS • MASS PROCESSING in the initial screen of the database utility or by choosing the DISPLAY

REST button (see Figure 11.6), which is displayed immediately after choosing the ENTER THE MASS PROCESSING value in the processing type for a database object. This display request will contain all entries for mass processing that are scheduled and not processed by the logged user. This means that requests for which no job has yet been scheduled for processing and those that are still running or have terminated are displayed here.

A list of all requests that are scheduled and not yet processed can be found by choosing the ALL REQUESTS button. A list of all mass-processing entries that arose from an import of objects from another system and which have not yet been processed successfully can be found from the path DB REQUESTS • CREATED WITH IMPORT.

The mass-processing request is processed only when it is scheduled by a job. The job field name present in the display list is blank if no job has been scheduled for the request (see Figure 11.8). Jobs can be scheduled for a particular request by checking the request (first column) and choosing the SCHEDULE SELECTIONS button. Jobs can also be scheduled for mass processing from the path EXTRAS • SCHEDULE JOB.

Object	Object name	ID	Fct	User	Job status	Start date	Start tim	Job name	Job coun	Date entered	Order
TABL	ZTR_TABLE2		CNV	T6785X						06/08/2010	0
TABL	ZTR_TABLE1		CNV	T6785X						06/08/2010	0

ABAP Dictionary: List of Mass Processing Requests

All Requests | Selected | Schedule Selections | Job Overview

The job name is blank since the job has not been scheduled for the request.

User's mass processing requests   T6785X

Figure 11.8 Displaying List of Mass-Processing Requests

Scheduled requests can be deleted by checking the request and choosing the SELECTED (Selected) icon. A dialog box appears for confirmation. The scheduled request is deleted from the list when YES is pressed in the dialog box (see Figure 11.9).

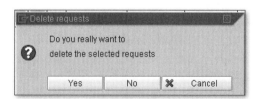

Figure 11.9 Deleting Scheduled Request

Scheduling Jobs for Mass Processing

Let us discuss the procedure for scheduling jobs for mass processing.

1. Jobs for mass processing can be scheduled from the initial screen of the database utility (Transaction SE14) by following the path EXTRAS • SCHEDULE JOB.

2. A dialog box will appear for scheduling a job. A scheduled start date and time should be entered to schedule the job in the background. Background processing will start automatically at this scheduled time. However, if you want to run your job immediately, that can be done by clicking on the IMMEDIATE button (see Figure 11.10).

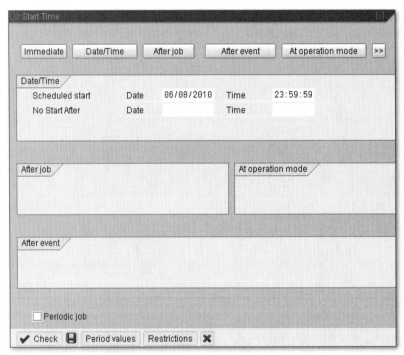

Figure 11.10 Scheduling Jobs for Mass Processing

3. This job can also be started whenever events such as AFTER JOB, AFTER EVENT, and AT OPERATION MODE get triggered. Choose the relevant button and maintain the entry for events.

4. Jobs can also be scheduled periodically. This can be done by checking the PERIODIC JOB flag. Values for periodic intervals should be entered for the periodic job. Periodic jobs can have the values HOURLY, DAILY, WEEKLY, MONTHLY, or OTHER PERIOD (see Figure 11.11).

Figure 11.11 Values for Periodic Jobs

5. Choose the RESTRICTION button if you want to enter any further restrictions regarding the execution of a job. A dialog box will appear (see Figure 11.12). The job will process the entries of Table TBATG only if they satisfy the specified restrictions.

6. Choose the TRANSFER button. You will return to the START TIME dialog box.

Figure 11.12 Restrictions for Scheduling a Job

7. Choose the SAVE (▣) icon in the START TIME dialog box. You are directed to the SCHEDULING TO DD: EXECUTION OF DATABASE OPERATIONS screen (see Figure 11.13).

8. Choose the SCHEDULE IN JOB button to schedule the job (see Figure 11.13).

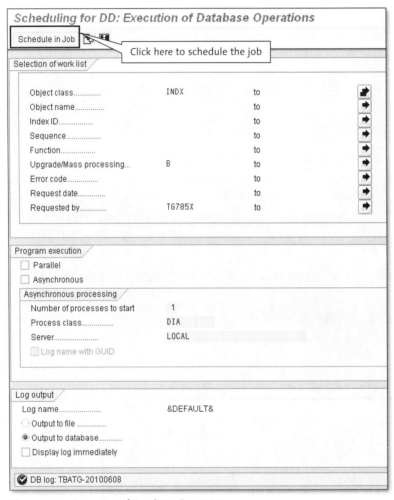

Figure 11.13 Execution of Database Operation

9. A dialog box will appear with the scheduled job name (see Figure 11.14).

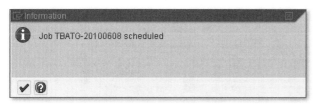

Figure 11.14 Scheduled Job Name

10. The job processes all requests scheduled for mass processing (TBATG entries) that match the selection conditions. Now, you will get the appropriate entry in the display request of the mass processing. You can check it from the path DB REQUEST • MASS PROCESSING (see Figure 11.15).

	Object	Object name	ID	Fct	User	Job status	Start date	Start tim	Job name	Job coun	Date entered	Order
✔	TABL	ZTR_TABLE2		CNV	TG785X	Scheduled	06/08/2010	23:59:59	TBATG-20100608	07011000	06/08/2010	0
✔	TABL	ZTR_TABLE1		CNV	TG785X	Scheduled	06/08/2010	23:59:59	TBATG-20100608	07011000	06/08/2010	0

ABAP Dictionary: List of Mass Processing Requests

All Requests | Selected | Schedule Selections | Job Overview

Value added in job status, start date, start time, job name, and job count field.

User's mass processing requests   TG785X

Figure 11.15 Display Request for Mass Processing

Displaying Logs for Mass Processing

The logs of all the requests for mass processing that have been processed in the background can be displayed from the initial screen of the database utility (Transaction SE14) by following the path EXTRAS • LOGS.

The log list contains the following information (see Figure 11.16):

▶ LOG NAME
The name of the background job.

▶ USER
The name of the user who scheduled the background job.

▶ DATE, TIME
The date and time when the job was started.

▶ LENGTH
The number of lines in the mass-processing log.

► SEVERITY

   The maximum error severity (' ' = no error, W = warning, E = error) for a processing step within the job.

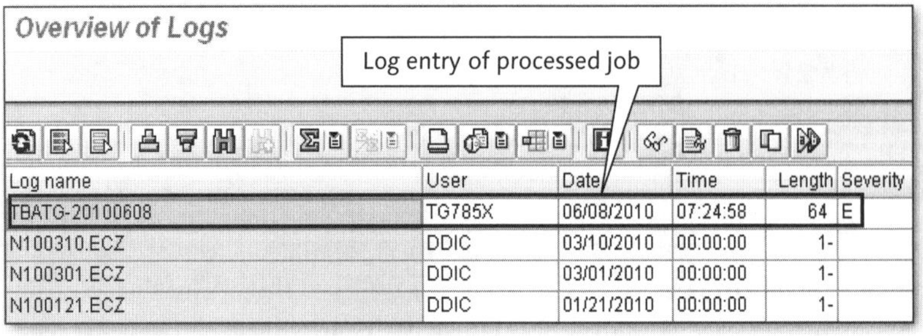

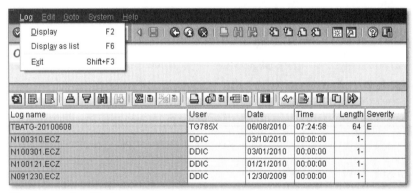

Figure 11.16 Overview of Logs Screen

The following actions can be performed in the log objects list:

► **Display a log**

   To display the log details, follow the path LOG • DISPLAY (see Figure 11.17). If you want to display the log as a list, then follow the path LOG • DISPLAY AS LIST. Figure 11.18 shows the log details.

Figure 11.17 Log Display

► **Change the log name**

   Logs can be renamed with EDIT • RENAME and copied with EDIT • COPY (see Figure 11.19).

► **Deleting a Log**

   Log entries can be deleted by choosing the delete (🗑) icon.

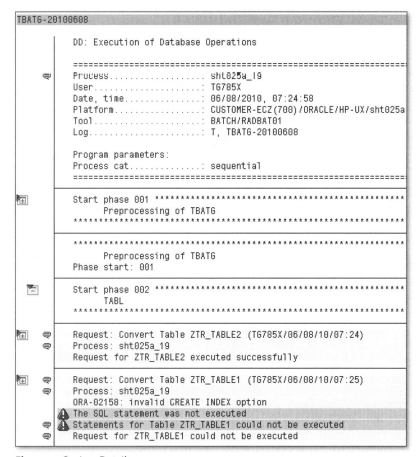

```
TBATG-20100608

            DD: Execution of Database Operations

            ============================================================
            Process.................. sht025a_19
            User.....................: TG785X
            Date, time...............: 06/08/2010, 07:24:58
            Platform.................: CUSTOMER-ECZ(700)/ORACLE/HP-UX/sht025a
            Tool.....................: BATCH/RADBAT01
            Log......................: T, TBATG-20100608

            Program parameters:
            Process cat..............: sequential
            ============================================================

            Start phase 001 ********************************************
                  Preprocessing of TBATG
            ************************************************************

            ************************************************************
                  Preprocessing of TBATG
            Phase start: 001

            Start phase 002 ********************************************
                  TABL
            ************************************************************

            Request: Convert Table ZTR_TABLE2 (TG785X/06/08/10/07:24)
            Process: sht025a_19
            Request for ZTR_TABLE2 executed successfully

            Request: Convert Table ZTR_TABLE1 (TG785X/06/08/10/07:25)
            Process: sht025a_19
            ORA-02158: invalid CREATE INDEX option
            The SQL statement was not executed
            Statements for Table ZTR_TABLE1 could not be executed
            Request for ZTR_TABLE1 could not be executed
```

Figure 11.18 Log Details

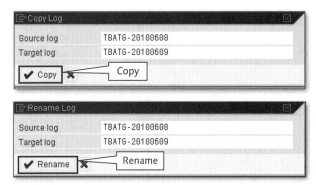

Figure 11.19 Copying and Renaming Log

Displaying Temporary Tables without Restart Logs

Temporary tables present in the system for which there is no restart log can be displayed from the initial screen of the database utility (Transaction SE14) by following the menu path EXTRAS • INVALID TEMP (see Figure 11.20).

Figure 11.20 Temporary Tables Without Restart Log

The temporary tables are created during conversion. During the conversion process, data from the table is saved in the temporary table. The data is reloaded from the temporary table to the actual table once the table is created in the database with the new structure. If the conversion process runs without errors, the temporary table will not be needed.

From SAP R/3 3.0 onward, the temporary table is deleted automatically if the conversion process completes successfully. Prior to SAP R/3 3.0, these temporary tables were retained even if the conversion process ran successfully. Such tables could be deleted manually.

Before deleting the temporary tables, make sure that no terminated conversion was unlocked by mistake. If this is the case, the existing restart log would be deleted. If the conversion is terminated when the data was present only in the temporary table, there is danger of data loss. If you are not sure whether this is the case, you should check whether the original table exists in the database and contains the expected volume of data before you delete the temporary table.

11.3   Storage Parameters

Storage parameters define the creation and handling of the database tables (transparent tables, table pools, and table clusters) in the underlying database. Storage parameters define the tablespace in which the table should be created in the database. They also define the size of each extent; that is, the space allocated to each extent in the database. It also defines the minimum and maximum extents that can be allocated to a table. The storage parameters and the settings that are allowed depend on the database system in use. Storage parameters also define the tablespace and size of extents for database indexes (see Figure 11.21).

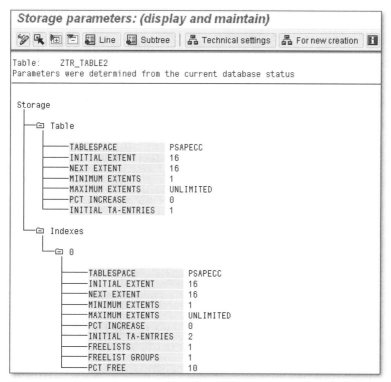

Figure 11.21 Storage Parameters for Database Table

11.3.1   Storage Parameter for a Table

When a table is activated for the first time, the storage parameters for the table are computed from the technical settings of the table and the table is then created in the database with these storage parameters. However, if the table is deleted from the database and again created, the storage parameters are defined on the basis of the fixed hierarchy (see Figure 11.22).

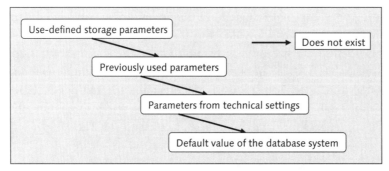

Figure 11.22   Hierarchy for Defining Storage Parameter

As shown in Figure 11.22, user-defined storage parameters are used first if they are present. If there are no user-defined storage parameters, the previously used parameters are used. If there are no such parameters (for example, if the pooled or cluster table is converted to a transparent table), the storage parameters are computed from the technical settings. Finally, the default values of the database system are used to compute the storage parameters if there are no technical settings for a table.

If the technical settings of a table that already exists in the database are changed and activated in the Data Dictionary, the corresponding storage parameters for the table will not be changed automatically in the database. In this case, the storage parameter needs to be changed manually with the help of the database utility.

11.3.2   Maintaining Storage Parameters

Let us discuss the procedure for maintaining the storage parameter.

1. In the initial screen of the database utility (Transaction SE14), enter the name of the object and select the appropriate radio button. Press the EDIT button. You are directed to the maintenance screen of the object.

2. Choose the STORAGE PARAMETERS button (see Figure 11.23). You are directed to the maintenance screen of the storage parameters.

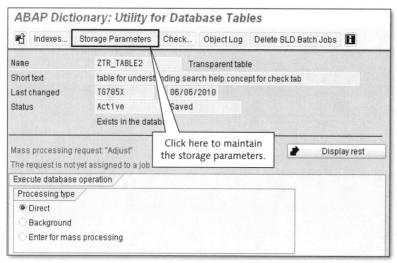

Figure 11.23 Maintenance Screen for Database Objects

3. Storage parameters and indexes are displayed. The parameters displayed depend on the database system used (see Figure 11.24). More information can be found about the parameter and its use by selecting the parameter and pressing F1.

4. Parameters can be changed by choosing the CHANGE (🖉) icon. New entries can be maintained for the changeable parameters (see Figure 11.24).

5. After making the changes, click on the APPLY (🔱 Apply) icon to save your changes. These changes are saved if you have proper authorizations.

6. By clicking on TECHNICAL SETTINGS, storage parameters that are computed from the technical settings of the table are displayed.

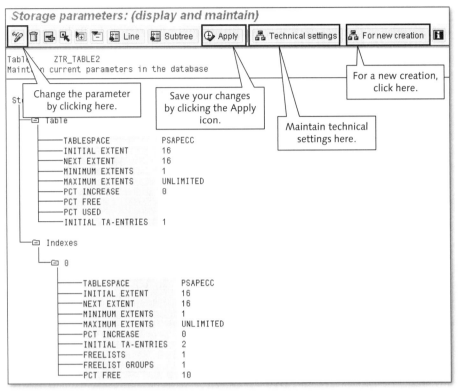

Figure 11.24 Storage Parameters of a Database Table

Storage parameters that are to be used the next time the table or an index of the table is created can be defined explicitly by choosing the FOR NEW CREATION button (see Figure 11.24). You will get a dialog box for selecting the template for computing storage parameters (see Figure 11.25). Storage parameters can be computed through the database parameters, technical settings, and default values of the system and table. Choose the appropriate radio button and press the CHECKMARK (✔) icon.

7. Now, maintain the parameter and save your entries. When the table is created or converted in the database, values entered in newly created parameters are used as storage parameters.

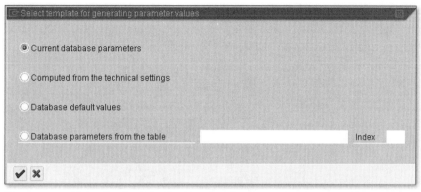

Figure 11.25 Dialog Box for Selecting Template for Generating Parameter Values

11.4 Runtime Objects

Whenever Data Dictionary objects such as tables, types (data element, structure, and table types), and views are activated, they are placed in the runtime environment in the form of runtime objects. These runtime objects contain the information of the activated version of the object that is used optimally when the objects are called by the ABAP programs, screens, classes, function modules, and other ABAP Workbench components. When the object is activated for the first time, a corresponding runtime object (*nametab*) is generated and subsequently is adjusted to the most recent version of the object each time it is activated. The runtime objects are also buffered in the application server so that their information can be accessed quickly by ABAP programs and screens.

A timestamp is used to ensure that ABAP programs and screens always access the most up-to-date information (see Figure 11.26). Whenever an object is activated in the ABAP Data Dictionary, the timestamp of the corresponding runtime object is adjusted. However, the timestamp of dependent programs and screens is adjusted only if there was a change relevant to programs or screens during activation. The next time the program or screen is called or executed, the timestamp source is compared with the timestamp load. If the timestamp source (timestamp of a source program) is greater than the timestamp load (timestamp of previously generated version of the program), the programs or screens are generated again from the timestamp source. This avoids unnecessary delay in generating the object. Also, several consecutive changes to an object can be made in a single generating step.

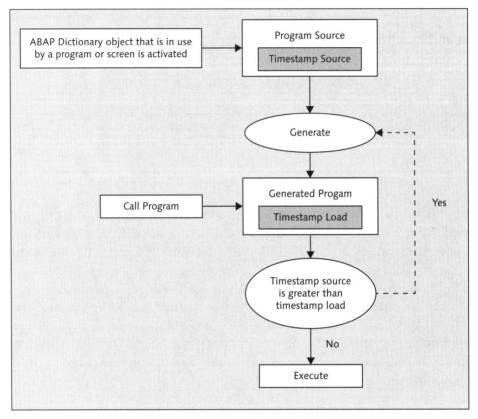

Figure 11.26 Timestamp Mechanism to Compare and Generate Objects

In the maintenance screen of a table, view, or type (data element, structure, table type), the runtime object can be displayed by following the menu path UTILI-TIES • RUNTIME OBJECT • DISPLAY (see Figure 11.27). The consistency of the runtime objects can be checked by UTILITIES • RUNTIME OBJECT • CHECK (see Figure 11.28). The consistency of the runtime objects can be checked recursively by UTILITIES • RUNTIME OBJECT • RECURSIVE CHECK (see Figure 11.29).

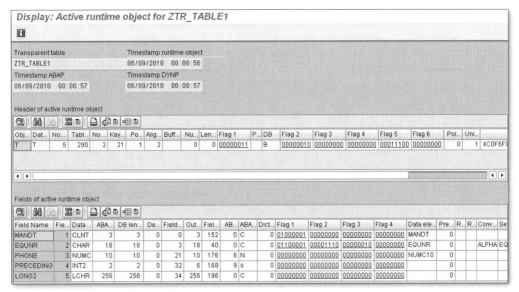

Figure 11.27 Runtime Object Display

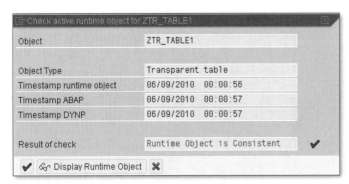

Figure 11.28 Runtime Object Consistency Check

Check Result

Incorrect Objects

	Runtime Ob	Object	Type Cat.	Depth	Msg type	Message	Msg. no.

Figure 11.29 Recursive Check of Runtime Objects

11.5   Activation

The information about a table is divided amongst its associated domains, data elements, field definitions, and the table definitions in the ABAP Data Dictionary. When an object is activated, all the objects dependent on it are reactivated. If a domain associated to the table field is changed and activated—for example if its data type or length is changed—all tables in which this domain is referred must be reactivated. This means that all these tables must be adjusted to the changed technical field information. Thus, activating an object may affect numerous dependent objects. Therefore, before activating any object we always recommend checking the dependent objects by performing a where-used list. This can be done by clicking the WHERE-USED LIST ( ) icon. Objects should be activated in the background if there are many associated dependent objects (see Figure 11.30). Large numbers of objects can be activated simultaneously with the mass-activation program.

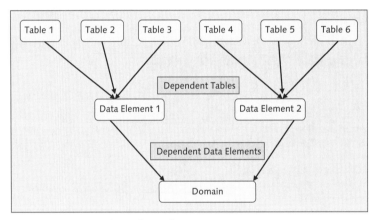

Figure 11.30   Dependent Objects for Domain

11.5.1   Mass Activation

A large set of objects can be activated simultaneously with mass activation. For mass activation, ABAP program RADMASG0 is executed from the ABAP Editor. For example, mass activation can be done when large numbers of programs are transported from one server to another. The mass-activation program is called automatically when a transport request is imported into a system. A list of all the ABAP Data Dictionary objects is input in the mass-activation program RADMASG0 (see Figure 11.31). All objects present in the list are then activated in one action.

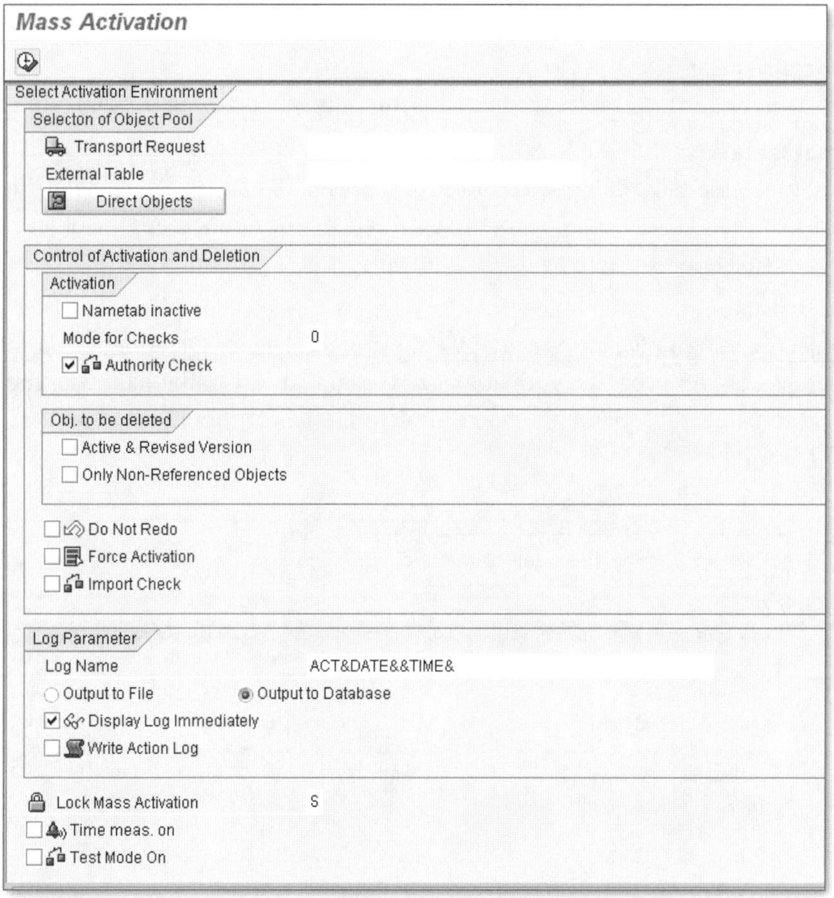

Mass Activation

Select Activation Environment

Selecton of Object Pool

🚚 Transport Request

External Table

▣ Direct Objects

Control of Activation and Deletion

Activation

☐ Nametab inactive

Mode for Checks   0

☑ 🔒 Authority Check

Obj. to be deleted

☐ Active & Revised Version

☐ Only Non-Referenced Objects

☐ ✍ Do Not Redo

☐ 📇 Force Activation

☐ 🔒 Import Check

Log Parameter

Log Name   ACT&DATE&&TIME&

○ Output to File   ◉ Output to Database

☑ 🔍 Display Log Immediately

☐ 📇 Write Action Log

🔒 Lock Mass Activation   S

☐ 🔊 Time meas. on

☐ 🔒 Test Mode On

Figure 11.31 Output Screen of Mass-Activation Program RADMASG0

The mass activation program has the following advantages over activating objects one at a time:

▶ Each table and its associated data element and domain are activated together. Therefore, the dependent tables that are affected by changes to different domains or data elements are reactivated only once.

▶ If objects are activated individually, then the correct sequence needs to follow. There can be an activation error if the sequence is not correct. Mass activation avoids this problem because all the related objects are activated together. For example, a domain and its associated value table can be activated together in mass processing. With one-at-a-time activation, all the domains and data elements referred by the table must be activated before the activation of the table.

Mass activation of Data Dictionary objects can be done in the following way:

▶ **Transport request**
All the data dictionary objects contained in the transport request are activated.

▶ **External table**
The external table must be a pooled table from the ATAB pool and must have the same structure as Table TACOB. Table TACOB can also be defined. All the objects entered in this table are activated automatically in background mode.

▶ **Direct objects**
The objects can be activated directly by choosing the DIRECT OBJECTS button in the mass-activation program. A dialog box will appear. Enter the names of the objects (domains, data elements, tables, indexes, etc.) for them to be activated directly (see Figure 11.32).

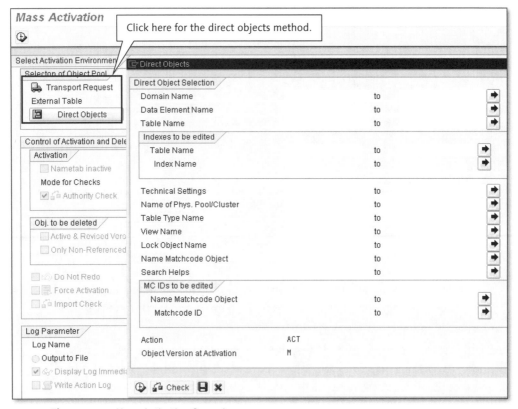

Figure 11.32 Mass-Activation Scenarios

11.5.2 Background Activation

Objects can be activated in the background if large numbers of objects are dependent on the activating object and activation is likely to result in long runtimes. You should select start times when the system is not very busy for the activation of the object. Let us discuss the procedure for background activation.

1. Go to the extended Table Maintenance Generator (Transaction SM30). In the initial screen of SM30, enter the table name "TACOB" and choose the MAINTAIN (Maintain) button (see Figure 11.33).

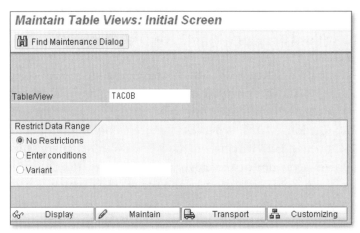

Figure 11.33 Maintaining Table TACOB for Background Activation

2. In the maintenance screen of the table, click on the NEW ENTRIES button and specify the objects to be activated in the background (see Figure 11.34). Choose the F4 help to enter the value and F1 help to learn more about the required parameters of the table.

Type	Name of DD object	Ind	Date	User	Message	
TABL	ZTR_TABLE2		06/09/2010	tg785x	activating tabl	

Figure 11.34 Entries for Background Processing

3. Save your entries and exit from the extended Table Maintenance Generator.

4. Go to the ABAP Editor (Transaction SE38) and execute mass-activation program RADMASG0. Schedule a background job for activating the entries of Table TACOB.

11.6 Adjusting Database Structures

To enable ABAP programs to access database tables correctly, the tables' runtime objects must correspond to the structures of the tables in the database. This means that if the table is changed in the ABAP Data Dictionary, its corresponding database structure must be adjusted (see Figure 11.35). Generally, adjustment is done automatically, but sometimes manual adjustment is required, and this can be done through the database utility (Transaction SE14). The database structure doesn't need to change for certain ABAP Data Dictionary changes. For example, the database table does not need to be adjusted for the field-sequence changes (except for key fields) in the ABAP Data Dictionary. This is because field sequence does not matter in the database structure and field sequence in the ABAP Data Dictionary does not correspond to the field sequence in the database. In this case, the changed structure is activated in the ABAP Data Dictionary and the database structure will remain unchanged.

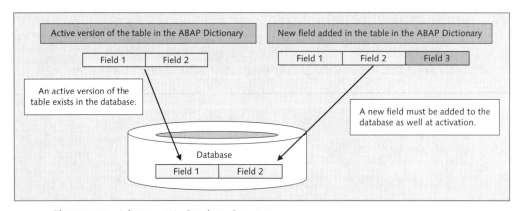

Figure 11.35 Adjustment in Database Structure

The database structure of a table can be adjusted to its changed ABAP Data Dictionary definition in the following ways:

- **Deleting and recreating**
  The database structure can be changed by deleting the table from the database and then recreating it in the database. The table is recreated in the database when the revised version of the table is activated in the ABAP Data Dictionary. However, data present in the table is lost during this process.

- **Changing database catalog**
  The database structure can be changed by changing the database catalog. This can be achieved with the ALTER TABLE command. In this case, only the definition of the table is changed in the database. During this process, data is retained in the table. However, indexes on the table might have to be rebuilt.

- **Converting the table**
  The database structure can be changed by converting the database table. In this case, the database table is renamed and serves as a temporary buffer for the data. The revised version of the table is activated in the ABAP Data Dictionary and created in the database. The data is then loaded from the temporary buffer table to the newly created database table with MOVE CORRESPONDING command. Indexes on the table are also built.

This procedure of adjusting database structure depends on the type of structural change, database system used, and data present in the table. If the table does not contain any data, the existing table is deleted and recreated in the database. If data is present in the table, the system tries to change the structure using an alter table (an SAP DB statement that changes the base table's property). The table is finally converted if the database system used cannot execute the structural change with the alter table method.

Normally, the database structure of production systems should not be adjusted. However, if the adjustment is urgently required, all the applications that access the table should be deactivated during the structural adjustment. The table data is not consistent during the structural adjustment. Programs could behave incorrectly if they access the data during the time.

11.7   Conversion

In this section we will discuss the conversion process, conversion problems, how to continue terminated conversions, and how to find the terminated conversion. Let us begin our discussion with the conversion process.

11.7.1   Conversion Process

Let us consider Table ZTAB1, which contains three fields. Later, it is modified in the Data Dictionary, and one more field is added. Therefore, the ABAP Data Dictionary contains an active version of the table (where the table contains three fields) and a revised version (where the table contains four fields). However, the database only contains the active version of the table; that is, the table with three fields. Let us also suppose that the table contains two secondary indexes, both in the ABAP Data Dictionary and in the database. The table also contains data records. Adding one field in the table will result in a table conversion. Thus, the table is converted in the series of seven steps, which are as follows:

1. **Set lock.**
   The table to be converted (ZTAB1 in this case) is locked in the lock table against the structural changes. With the lock mechanism in place, a new structural change cannot be made before the conversion has finished successfully. However, another structural change could result in a data loss if the conversion terminates after the completion of Step 2 and before the completion of Step 4.

2. **Rename table.**
   The table to be converted is renamed in the database. All indexes on the table are deleted. The name of the new table consists of the prefix QCM and the table name. The name of the temporary table for Table ZTAB1 is thus QCMZTAB1 (see Figure 11.36).

3. **Activate tables.**
   The revised version of the table is activated in the ABAP Data Dictionary. The table is created in the database with its new structure and primary index. The structure of the newly created database table corresponds to the structure of the table in the ABAP Data Dictionary. However, the database table does not contain any data. A database lock is also set for the table to be converted. Thus, during the conversion it is not possible to write into the converting table from the calling application programs (see Figure 11.37).

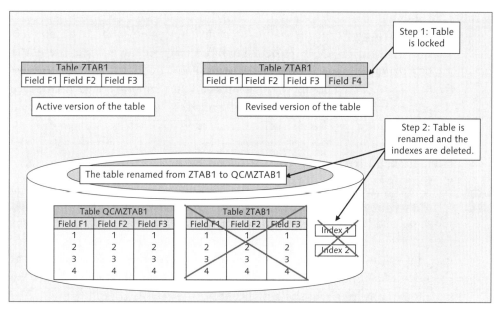

Figure 11.36 Conversion Process (Steps 1 and 2)

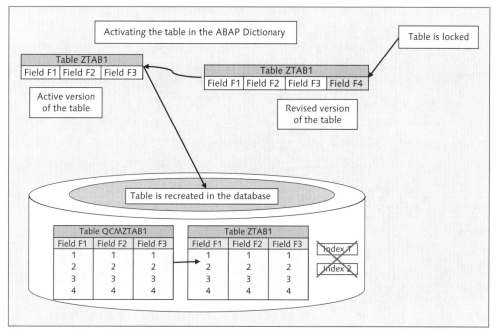

Figure 11.37 Conversion Process (Step 3)

4. **Reload data.**

The data is reloaded from the temporary table (QCM table) to the new table with the ABAP `Move corresponding` command. After this step, the data is present in the original table as well as in the temporary table (see Figure 11.38). Because the data is present in both the original table and the temporary table, more space is required when the conversion is performed. Thus, space in the concerned tablespace should be checked before converting large tables. A database commit is stored after 16 MB when you copy data from the temporary table to the original table. Therefore, the conversion process needs 16 MB of available space in the rollback segment.

The table data is consistent once after the completion of Step 4. For this reason, programs must not access the table while the conversion is running. Programs could behave incorrectly while reading the table, because some of the records may not yet be copied from the temporary table. For this reason, conversions should not be done in the production server. All the applications that use the table to be converted must be deactivated.

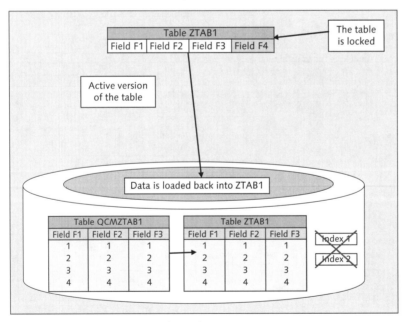

Figure 11.38 Conversion Process (Step 4)

5. **Create a new secondary index for the table.**

   The secondary indexes of the table that is defined in the ABAP Data Dictionary are newly created in the database (see Figure 11.39).

6. **Delete the QCM table.**

   Now, the data present in the temporary table (QCM) is not required at the end of the conversion. Therefore, the temporary table is deleted.

7. **Remove the lock.**

   The lock set at the beginning of the conversion is removed.

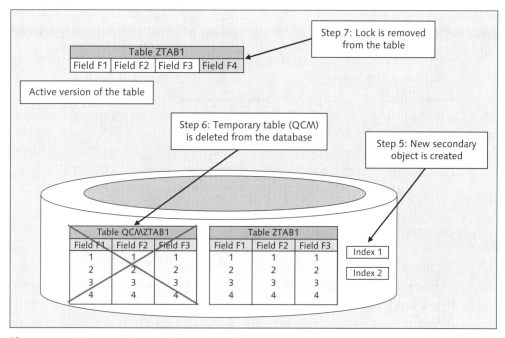

Figure 11.39 Conversion Process (Steps 5, 6, and 7)

The table stays locked and a reset log is written if the conversion process terminates. Successful steps of the conversion are recorded in the reset log. The restart log and the lock are deleted when the conversion is completed. If the conversion terminates during the process, the exact place and reason for termination can be found in the reset log. Terminated conversions should be cleaned. The cause for termination should be found and corrected. Terminated conversion should be re-executed.

> **Note**
>
> In the case of pooled and cluster tables, a temporary database table is created with the name QCM<TABLE_NAME>. Its structure corresponds to the structure of the pooled/ cluster table. The data is also copied from the pooled/cluster table to this table and is then deleted from the physical table pool/cluster. Finally, according to the new table definition, the data is copied from the QCM table back to the physical table pool/table cluster.

11.7.2 Conversion Problems

Problems may occur during the conversion process. Among them are the following:

▸ **Tablespace overflow**
Because the data is present in the original table as well as in the temporary table (QCM table), more space is required during the conversion process. Thus, before converting large tables, space in the affected tablespace must be checked. The conversion will terminate if tablespace overflows. If this happens, tablespace must be extended and the conversion process must be resumed from the database utility. Once the conversion process is resumed, the system will continue the conversion from the point at which it terminated.

▸ **Deletion of a client field**
If the client field is removed from a client-specific table, the system will not be able to distinguish the new key of records from different clients. With the deletion of the client field, the same record may be present in different clients. When data is reloaded from the temporary table, one of these records is reloaded. Which one it is depends on the order in which the records come to the table. Thus, records from other clients can be loaded in the working client. In this case, the table should be cleaned up before conversion.

▸ **Data loss**
Data present in the table may be lost if the key fields are shortened. This is because if the key field is deleted or shortened, the data records can no longer be distinguished. When data is reloaded from the temporary table, only the first record is reloaded into the table, because the database will not allow duplicate records.

▸ **Type conversion problems**
During the conversion process, data is copied from the temporary table back

to the database table using the ABAP command `Move corresponding`. There is no type conversion error if the `Move corresponding` command can be executed with the type change. However, if a field type cannot be changed using `Move corresponding`, the conversion terminates when the data is reloaded into the original table. In this case, the status prior to conversion must be restored. This can be done by the following steps:

▶ In the first step, the database table must be deleted and a temporarily created QCM table must be renamed to its original name.

▶ In the second step, the lock should be removed from the database utility with UNLOCK TABLE.

▶ Runtime objects should be reconstructed using the database utility and the table definition in the ABAP Data Dictionary should be returned to its status prior to the conversion.

▶ Finally, the table should be activated in the ABAP Data Dictionary.

For example, suppose the accuracy of a DECIMAL field (the number of places before the period) is reduced and entries exist for which all positions before the period are used. In this case, termination will occur during conversion when the records are reloaded into the table. If there are no such entries, the records can be reloaded.

▶ **Termination during conversion of pooled or cluster tables**
When a pooled or cluster table is converted, the temporary table (QCM table) is created in the database as a transparent table and the data from the pooled or cluster table is copied to it. There is an upper limit for the number of fields in a database table, depending on the database system used. If the number of fields in the pooled or cluster table exceeds the maximum number of fields possible in a database table, it is not possible to convert pooled and cluster tables.

11.7.3 Continuing Terminated Conversions

If a conversion process terminates, the lock entry set for the table is retained. The table cannot be edited with the ABAP Data Dictionary maintenance tools (Transaction SE11) until the lock entry exists. The table conversion should be corrected; otherwise, the applications accessing this table may not be able to read any data. This may result to the malfunctioning or failure of the application. Let us discuss the process to continue terminated conversions.

1. Go to the initial screen of the database utility from Transaction SE14 or follow the menu path UTILITIES • DATABASE OBJECT • DATABASE UTILITY from the initial screen of the ABAP Data Dictionary (Transaction SE11).

2. Select the TABLES object type, enter the name of the table, and choose EDIT (see Figure 11.40). You are directed to the maintenance screen of the database tables.

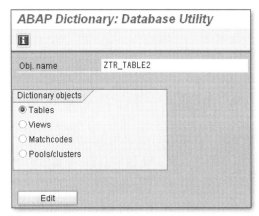

Figure 11.40 Database Utility Initial Screen

3. The browser will start if you choose the ONLINE MANUAL (■) icon. You will see the successful conversion steps that were processed correctly.

4. The exact cause of the termination can be found from the object log by clicking the OBJECT LOG button. The system log or short dumps can be analyzed if the object log does not provide the relevant information. Correct the errors found in the object log, syslog, or short dumps. The conversion can be continued once the error causing the termination is corrected.

5. Go back to the maintenance screen of the database utility and continue the conversion by choosing CONTINUE ADJUSTMENT. The system will try to continue the conversion from the termination point.

Note

The UNLOCK TABLE option only deletes the lock entry that exists for the table. Never choose this option for a terminated conversion if the data only exists in the temporary table; that is, if the conversion is terminated in between Step 2 and Step 4 of the conversion process.

11.7.4 Finding Terminated Conversions

Let us discuss the procedure to find terminated conversions.

1. Go to the initial screen of the Database Utility from Transaction SE14.

2. Choose DB REQUESTS • TERMINATED. A list with all the terminated conversions of the system will appear. The name of the table can be found in the first column of the list. If there is no terminated conversion present, you will get a dialog box stating that there are no restart logs present (see Figure 11.41).

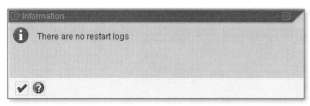

Figure 11.41 Dialog Box When No Terminated Conversion Exists

3. Double-click on the corresponding line to go to the maintenance screen of the database utility for the particular table. Analyze the reason for the termination and continue the terminated conversion.

> **Note**
>
> Table conversions should be corrected; otherwise the applications accessing this table may not be able to read any data. This may result in the malfunctioning or failure of the application.

11.8 Editing Dictionary Objects in the Database

In this section we discuss the procedure for editing various database objects such as tables, indexes, and views. You must edit objects directly in the database when you are not able to edit them in the ABAP Data Dictionary, which happens when a conversion error occurs while activating the object in the ABAP Data Dictionary. Let us discuss this procedure in more detail.

11.8.1 Editing Tables

The database utility provides the following functionality for editing the transparent tables (see Figure 11.42).

▶ **Create database table**
In this case, the active version of the table and its primary index are created in the database. An active secondary index is also created in the database if it is not explicitly excluded when the index is defined.

▶ **Delete database table**
In this case, the table and all its indexes are deleted from the database.

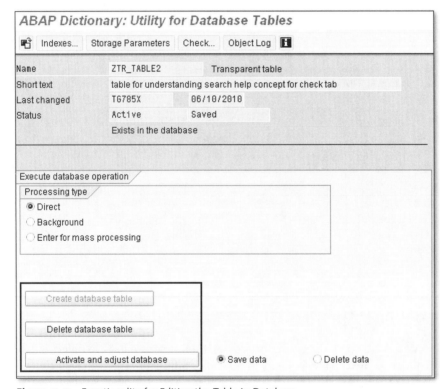

Figure 11.42 Functionality for Editing the Table in Database

▶ **Activate and adjust database**
In this case, the revised version of the table is activated in the database. The table is also adjusted to this modified table definition. Data can be saved or deleted as specified. If the radio button DELETE DATA is checked, the table is deleted

and created again with the revised definition of the table from the ABAP Data Dictionary. However, data is lost in this case. If the radio button KEEP DATA is checked, an attempt is made to perform an adjustment with an ALTER TABLE command. If this is not possible, a table is triggered.

Because pooled and cluster tables are not present separately in the database, the functions CREATE DATABASE TABLE and DELETE DATABASE TABLE are not applicable for pooled/cluster tables. Only DELETE DATABASE TABLE is applicable for these table categories. If DELETE DATABASE TABLE is checked, table data is deleted from the corresponding physical table pool or table cluster.

Apart from these functions, the database utility also provides a number of other check and repair functions for tables. Let us describe these in detail.

Editing Indexes

The maintenance screen of the indexes will appear from the path GOTO • INDEXES in the ABAP DICTIONARY: UTILITY FOR DATABASE TABLES screen. A dialog box with the list of all the table indexes that exist in the ABAP Data Dictionary is displayed (see Figure 11.43).

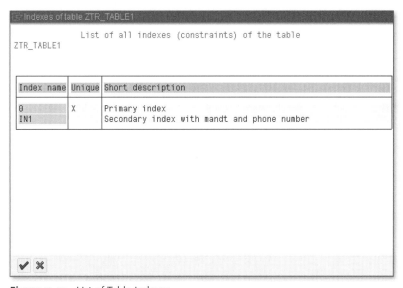

Figure 11.43 List of Table Indexes

Select the required index by double-clicking on it. The maintenance utility for database indexes will appear in the next screen, which has the following functionality (see Figure 11.44):

▶ **Create database index**
In this case, a primary or secondary index can be created in the database.

▶ **Delete database index**
A secondary index of a transparent table is deleted in the database. However, the primary index of a transparent table created in the database cannot be deleted as long as the table exists in the database.

▶ **Activate and adjust database**
First, the index is deleted from the database. The revised version of the index is activated in the Data Dictionary. The index is then created and built again in the database.

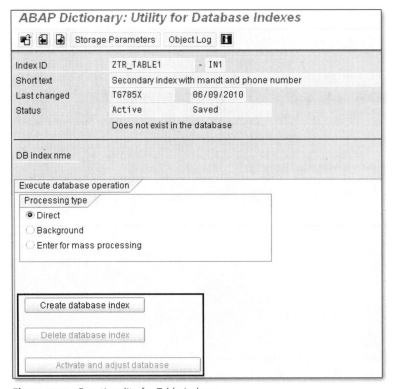

Figure 11.44 Functionality for Table Indexes

Maintain Storage Parameters

Storage parameters influence the database settings for the table, defining the tablespace in which the table should be created in the database. They also define the size of each extent; that is, the space allocated to each extent in database. The storage parameters and the settings that are allowed depend on the database system in use. By clicking on the STORAGE PARAMETER button, storage parameters can be maintained for transparent tables.

Consistency Check

Table definition in the database can be checked with the runtime object of the table by following the path EXTRAS • DATABASE OBJECTS • CHECK. The indexes on the table in the ABAP Data Dictionary are also compared with the indexes on the database. The runtime object of the table can be compared with the information entered in the ABAP Data Dictionary maintenance screen by following the path EXTRAS • RUNTIME OBJECT • CHECK. The database object definition and runtime object definition can be displayed with EXTRAS • DATABASE OBJECTS • DISPLAY (see Figure 11.45) and EXTRAS • RUNTIME OBJECT • DISPLAY, respectively (see Figure 11.46).

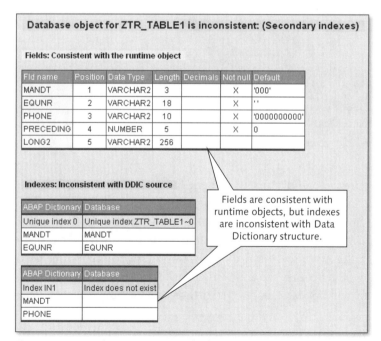

Figure 11.45 Database Consistency Check

Figure 11.46 Runtime Consistency Check

Data Existence Check

By following the path TABLE • DATA EXIST, you can determine whether the table contains data. A dialog box will appear, informing you whether the data is present in the table (see Figure 11.47). Data is selected for all the clients. This function is used to check whether the table is empty prior to the conversion. Data can be displayed from the path TABLE • TABLE CONTENTS.

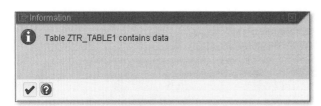

Figure 11.47 Data Existence Check

Force Conversion

Tables can be converted forcefully from the path EXTRAS • FORCE CONVERSION. This function is useful when the storage parameters or technical settings of the table are modified, but the table structure is not changed. This is because some of the modified settings will take effect in the database only if the table has been converted. However, the ACTIVATE AND ADJUST DATABASE function cannot be used to trigger table conversion because the table structure has not changed. The dialog box for confirmation will appear. Choose YES if force conversion is needed (see Figure 11.48).

Figure 11.48 Dialog Box for Force Conversion

Reconstruct

A runtime object for the database table can be created from the path TABLE •
RECONSTRUCT. The created runtime object contains the information about the table
that is available in the database, such as the field name and data types. However,
it does not contain any other information (such as buffering information) about
the table that exists in the ABAP Data Dictionary. This function should be used
only to correct inconsistencies. The table should be adjusted and activated in the
ABAP Data Dictionary.

11.8.2 Editing Views

The database utility provides the following functionality for editing the view in
the database (see Figure 11.49).

▶ **Create database view**
In this case, a database view which is defined in the ABAP Data Dictionary is
created physically in the database.

▶ **Delete database view**
In this case, the database view is deleted from the database.

▶ **Activate and adjust database**
First, the view is deleted from the database and then the revised version of the
view is again created and activated in the database.

Apart from these functions, the database utility also provides a consistency check
for the database view.

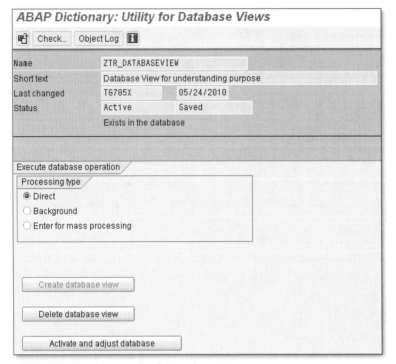

Figure 11.49 Database Utility for Database View

Consistency Check

View definitions in the database can be checked with the runtime object of the view by following the path EXTRAS • DATABASE OBJECTS • CHECK. The runtime object of the view can be compared with the information entered in the ABAP Data Dictionary maintenance screen from the path EXTRAS • RUNTIME OBJECT • CHECK. Both the definitions are displayed and their differences are highlighted. DELTA (only difference) or FULL (all) information can be displayed in both cases. Database object definition and runtime object definition, respectively, can be displayed from the paths EXTRAS • DATABASE OBJECTS • DISPLAY and EXTRAS • RUNTIME OBJECT • DISPLAY.

Editing Pools and Clusters

The database utility provides the following functionality for editing pooled/cluster tables in the database (see Figure 11.50).

▶ **Create database table**
In this case, the physical pool or cluster is created in the database.

▶ **Delete database table**
In this case, the physical pool or cluster is deleted from the database.

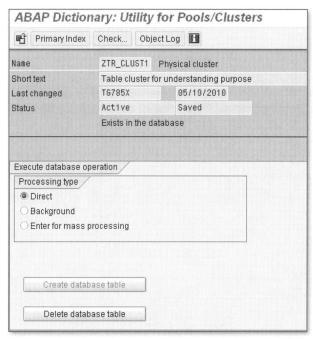

Figure 11.50 Database Utility for Database View

The database utility also provides the following check and repair functions for pools and clusters.

Maintain Storage Parameters

Storage parameter for physical pooled/cluster tables can be maintained from the path GOTO • STORAGE PARAMETER. Storage parameters influence the database settings for the table (see Figure 11.51).

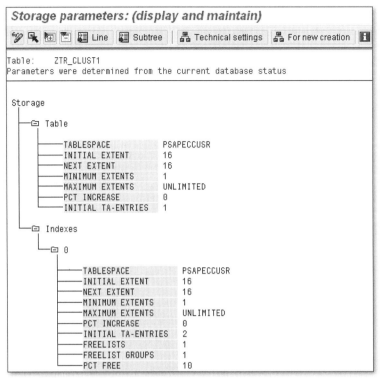

Figure 11.51 Storage Parameter for Physical Pool/Cluster table

Consistency Check

Physical pool/cluster definitions in the database can be checked with the runtime object from the path EXTRAS • DATABASE OBJECTS • CHECK. The runtime object of the physical pool/cluster can be compared with the information entered in the ABAP Data Dictionary maintenance screen from the path EXTRAS • RUNTIME OBJECT • CHECK. Both definitions are displayed and their differences are highlighted. DELTA (only difference) or FULL (all information) differences can be displayed in both cases. Database object definition and runtime object definition, respectively, can be displayed with EXTRAS • DATABASE OBJECTS • DISPLAY (see Figure 11.52) and EXTRAS • RUNTIME OBJECT • DISPLAY (see Figure 11.53).

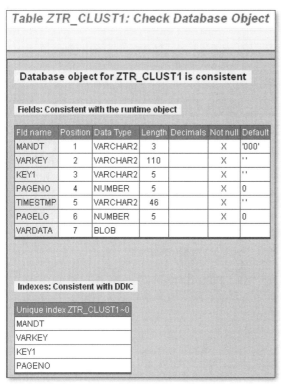

Figure 11.52 Database Consistency Check of Physical Pool/Cluster

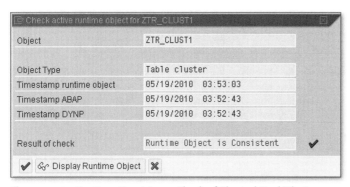

Figure 11.53 Runtime Consistency Check of Physical Pool/Cluster

11.9   Summary

The database utility acts as an interface between the ABAP Data Dictionary and the underlying relational database of the SAP system. Database objects created from the objects of the ABAP Data Dictionary can be edited with the help of the database utility. Processing types are used to modify the database objects. With the help of processing types, the database utility schedules the database object for modification. Storage parameters define the creation and handling of the database tables in the underlying database. Storage parameters also define the tablespace in which the table should be created in the database. Runtime objects contain information about the activated versions of the objects that are used optimally when the objects are called by the ABAP programs, screen, classes, function modules, and other ABAP Workbench components. The database utility can be used to edit the database objects generated from objects of the ABAP Data Dictionary.

In this book, you have learned about the central repository of ABAP, and all its components and functions in detail. You have seen why the ABAP Data Dictionary is one of the most important components of SAP, allowing users to define objects globally in the ABAP Data Dictionary and use them throughout all ABAP programs. You have learned about various dictionary objects and their attributes, classification, creation, modification, and deletion. You have also learned how these objects are related to ABAP programs, and about their significance and importance in the ABAP language. All in all, you have learned new concepts and gained knowledge that will help you to become a talented, skillful ABAP developer and consultant. We hope that you also enjoyed reading, and that this book will serve as a reference guide for years to come.

The Author

Tanmaya Gupta is a Senior Systems Engineer and an SAP ABAP developer working in a well-known software company in India. He has worked on various projects for companies that include John Deere, AT&T, PricewaterhouseCoopers, and Molex. He holds a Bachelor of Technology degree in computer science and engineering and has been involved in many development, implementation, and support projects. He has experience with BDC, dialogue programming, Smart forms, function modules, queries, scripts, LSMW, reports, and the ABAP Data Dictionary. He has published content in the knowledge-share portal and articles in SDN forums.

Index

A

ABAP, 19, 20, 21, 23, 27, 82
Access, 271, 272
Access mode, 277, 281
ACCP, 28, 85
   posting period, 28
Activate, 55, 56, 75, 92, 131, 140, 144, 149,
   151, 152, 153, 155, 162, 164, 187, 190,
   193, 197, 202, 237, 249, 257, 259, 268,
   279, 282, 283, 304, 307, 310, 313, 316,
   319, 322, 346
Activation, 370
   background, 373
   mass, 370
Activation log, 55, 122, 141, 187, 191, 198,
   203, 268, 279, 304, 308, 346
Activation type, 135, 142, 161, 163, 269
ADABAS D, 20
APPEND, 86
Append structure, 83, 128, 130, 131, 296,
   269
Application object, 181
Authorization, 209
Authorization class, 209, 212
Authorization field, 210
Authorization group, 208, 212, 219, 239, 241,
   249
Authorization object, 208, 210, 212, 219

B

Backup ID, 335
BAdI, 21
BAPI, 65
Base table, 185, 190
BIDI filtering, 69
Buffer, 83, 178
Buffering, 113, 116, 117, 143
   full buffering, 118, 119
   generic area buffering, 118
   single record buffering, 119
Byte string, 36

C

Candidate key, 101, 102
Cardinality, 101, 104, 195
Change document, 66, 67, 68, 74
CHAR, 28, 47, 51, 85
Character, 36
Character string, 36
Check field, 93, 98
Check table, 93, 94, 96, 99, 102, 104, 105,
   106, 107, 109, 111, 145, 156, 182, 313,
   316, 323
Client-dependent tables, 134
Client-independent tables, 134
CLNT, 28, 85
Cluster table, 77, 80, 82, 154, 164, 165, 166,
   167, 390
   create, 164
COLLECT, 338
COMMIT WORK, 330, 333
Compare flag, 208, 217
Component, 264, 267
Component name, 64, 65, 74
Consistency check, 387, 390, 392
Constant, 27, 40, 186, 230, 292
Conversion, 376
   process, 376
   terminated, 381, 383
Conversion exit, 30
CONVERSION_EXIT_XXXXX_INPUT, 45
CONVERSION_EXIT_XXXXX_OUTPUT, 45
Conversion problems, 380
   data loss, 380
   deletion of a client field, 380
   pooled or cluster tables, 381
   tablespace overflow, 380
   type conversion, 380
Conversion routine, 39, 40, 45

Ctrl+F1, 153
Ctrl+F3, 55, 56, 75, 92, 187, 190, 193, 197, 202, , 268, 279, 282, 283, 346
CUKY, 29, 85, 87
CURR, 29, 47, 85, 87, 88, 139, 267
Customizing includes, 83, 132, 133

D

DATA, 63, 275
Database, 78, 80, 113
Database interface, 79, 177
Database locks, 327
Database objects, 140, 187
Database optimizer, 123
Database structures
    changing database catalog, 375
Database structures, 374
    converting the table, 375
    deleting and recreating, 375
Database table, 133, 137, 158, 164, 212
Database utility, 349
Data Browser, 136, 164, 202, 248
Data Dictionary, 20, 22, 24, 26, 27, 39, 59, 75, 77, 82, 83, 128, 135, 137, 138, 141, 149, 156, 158, 159, 162, 164, 166, 167, 169, 183, 189, 198, 204, 205, 231, 232, 255, 263, 285
    objects, 24
Data element, 22, 34, 39, 59, 76, 86, 139, 150, 188, 198, 203, 263, 265, 267, 288, 291, 303, 306, 313, 323
    Attributes tab, 60
    create, 71
    Data Type tab, 60, 61
    delete, 75
    Field Label tab, 60, 63, 73
    Further Characteristics tab, 60, 64, 74, 313
Data elements, 285
Data existence check, 388
Data type, 27, 35, 39, 43, 75, 84, 86, 87, 263
    built-in, 27, 28, 263, 264, 266, 283
    complex, 34
    delete, 283

    elementary, 33, 61, 72
    predefined, 61, 62, 72
    reference, 34, 61, 63, 72
    user-defined, 27, 32, 263
Date, 36
DATS, 29, 45, 85, 323
DB02, 20
DBspace, 113
DEC, 29, 47, 51, 85
Decimal place, 39, 40, 44, 47, 87, 281
Default component name, 65
Define maintenance view, 146
Delete, 57
Delivery class, 133, 135, 138, 164, 202
DEQUEUE, 325, 328, 337, 338, 339, 342, 346, 347, 348
DEQUEUE_ALL, 332
Dialog behavior, 287, 292
Dialog type, 292, 303
Dictionary objects, 383
Disp, 299
Dispatcher, 331
Documentation, 52, 69, 142, 161, 164, 187, 188, 191, 198, 203, 268, 279
    document status, 69, 70
    supplementary, 69, 70
Domain, 25, 30, 33, 39, 52, 59, 72, 76, 77, 145, 169, 264, 323
    attributes, 41
    change, 55
    create, 52
    Definition tab, 43, 52
    delete, 56
    Properties tab, 42
    Value Range tab, 50, 53

E

Enhancement, 83, 127, 128, 179, 189, 269
ENQUEUE, 325, 328, 331, 332, 333, 337, 338, 339, 342, 343, 346, 347, 348
Enqueue server, 330, 334, 337, 342
Event, 217, 224, 230, 231, 233, 234, 256
    maintain, 234
EXTRACT, 227, 228, 229, 231

F

F1, 59, 60, 69, 70, 87, 138, 139, 164
F4, 25, 51, 83, 94, 138, 167, 186, 219, 235, 238, 285, 299, 300, 302, 316, 319, 321, 324
F4if_shlp_exit_example, 297, 298
F7, 70
Field, 27, 40, 77, 84, 150, 170, 178, 313
FIELD, 338
Field select, 323, 322
Field symbol, 229
Field value, 322, 323
Financial Accounting (FI), 20
Fixed value, 50, 53
Flat structure, 27
Float, 36
FLTP, 29, 47, 85
FLUSH_ENQUEUE, 336, 339
Force conversion, 388
Foreign key, 51, 82, 92, 93, 96, 98, 101, 104, 105, 106, 107, 109, 111, 128, 131, 139, 144, 145, 146, 170, 173, 180, 182, 184, 194, 228, 267, 327, 328, 341, 344
    constant, 96, 173
    create, 144
    generic, 96, 173
    multi-structured, 98, 341
    semantic attributes, 101
Foreign key field, 93, 104, 145
Foreign key table, 96, 101, 102, 104, 105, 107, 109, 146
FOREIGN_LOCK, 339
Function group, 205, 207, 208, 212, 213, 219, 232, 243
Function module, 212, 226, 233, 347, 348
FUNCTION-POOL, 213

G

Generic key, 118
Get Parameter, 65, 299

H

Hash table, 272
Header details, 259
Help view, 146
Hexadecimal, 36
HIGH, 279, 281
Hit list, 286, 287, 288, 289, 290, 302, 311, 312
Hot key, 293, 294, 304

I

I18N_SET_DATAELEMENTS_FLAGS, 69
Include, 82, 89, 91, 127, 236, 237, 269
INCLUDE, 84, 86, 213
Index, 22, 83, 122, 126, 129, 140, 385, 386
    create, 147
    extended, 149
    ID, 126
    identifier, 126
    primary, 122, 125
    secondary, 122, 147
    unique, 125, 126, 148
Index table, 273, 275
Informix, 20
Initial value, 138
INT, 31
INT1, 29, 51, 85
INT2, 30, 31, 51, 85, 143
INT4, 30, 51, 85
Integer, 36
Internal table, 226, 228, 229, 276, 283, 231, 298
Interval, 50, 53
Item details, 259

J

JAVA, 113, 143
Join, 170, 173, 184, 186, 200
    Cartesian product join, 170, 171
    cross join, 170
    inner join, 170, 171, 172, 177, 180

inner join, *171*
left outer join, *172*
outer join, *171, 172, 181*

K

Key, 84, 93, 138, 162, 271, 316
  category, 274
  component, 277
  definition, 273

L

LANG, 30, 38, 85
LCHR, 31, 47, 85, 129, 143
Lernel, 21
Line type, 271
Literal, 186
Local lock containers, 336
Local object, 54, 220
Lock, 324
Lock argument, 328
Lock container, 336
Lock mechanism, 327, 342
Lock mode, 329, 335, 343, 344, 348
  exclusive, 329
  exclusive but not cumulative, 330
  shared, 329
Lock modules, 346
Lock object, 22, 25, 82, 92, 146, 324, 325, 327, 343, 347
  Attributes tab, 345
  create, 343
  delete, 347
  Lock Parameter tab, 344
Lock owner, 331, 332
Lock parameter, 344
Lock request, 330, 334
Locks, 325, 327
Lock server, 330, 331, 336
Lock table, 330, 334, 337
Log table, 119
LOW, 281, 279
Lower case, 47, 52
LPos, 289, 303

LRAW, 31, 85, 129, 143
LTR, 69, 74
LUW, 327, 332, 335

M

Maintenance dialog, 206
Maintenance screen, 208, 215, 220, 221, 222, 223
  overview, 216
  Overview screen, 240
Maintenance screen
  Overview screen, 221
  Single screen, 216
Maintenance status, 170, 176, 179, 182, 186, 190, 197, 248
MANDT, 125
Mass processing, 353, 354, 356, 359
Materials Management (MM), 20
Message server, 331
MODE_<TAB>, 338
Modified flag, 291
Module pool, 256
Module pool program, 109

N

Native SQL, 21
NOT NULL, 85, 166, 175
NUMC, 31, 51, 85
  numeric text, 31
Numeric character, 36

O

Open SQL, 21
OPTION, 279, 281
Oracle, 20
OS/400, 20
Output length, 40, 44, 45, 52
Owner ID, 335

P

Package, 39, 43, 54, 60, 61, 208, 215, 254, 345
Packed, 36
PAI, 207, 214
Parameter ID, 59, 64, 65, 74
Parameters, 307, 310, 311, 313, 320
Parameter transaction, 237, 238
PBO, 214, 234
Placeholder, 111
Pooled table, 77, 78, 79, 82, 120, 121, 144, 154, 164, 165, 166, 167, 390
  create, 164
PREC, 31
Predefined type, 84, 86, 87
Presel, 299
Presel1, 299, 300
Primary key, 80, 101, 102, 118
Primary table, 181, 182, 195, 199, 200
Process after input, 322
Processing types, 351
  background, 352
Processing types
  direct, 352
Process on value-request, 322, 323
Production Planning and Control (PP), 20
Projection, 170, 173
Projection view, 287

Q

QCM, 376, 378, 379, 380
QUAN, 31, 47, 85, 87, 88, 139, 267

R

R/3, 20
R3TRANS, 136
Ranges table type, 279, 281, 283
  create, 280
RAW, 31, 85
RAWSTRING, 32
Rec/client, 119, 120, 143
Reconstruct, 389

Recording routine, 208, 217, 220
Reference type, 277
Report program, 320
RESET_ENQUEUE, 336
Rettop, 299, 300
Return, 299
RFC, 328, 340, 345
ROLLBACK WORK, 333
Row type, 271, 277
RTL, 69
Runtime object, 187, 191, 198, 203
Runtime objects, 141, 270, 279, 367

S

Sales and Distribution (SD), 20
SAP, 19, 20
SAP ECC, 119, 121
SAP locks, 327, 348
SCOPE parameter, 332, 333, 338, 341
Screen check, 109
Screen field, 238, 323
Screen Painter, 222, 323
SDis, 291, 303
SE11, 41, 52, 57, 59, 71, 75, 100, 123, 136, 149, 158, 159, 162, 164, 183, 189, 194, 198, 202, 204, 205, 206, 265, 266, 276, 280, 283, 300, 305, 343, 347
SE12, 41, 59
SE14, 152, 162
SE16, 123, 136, 190, 202
SE16N, 123
SE37, 46
SE54, 136, 182, 204, 205, 206, 211, 218, 239, 245, 251, 261
SE54, 259
SE80, 54, 74, 220, 321
SE93, 237
Search help, 83, 128, 131, 140, 142, 180, 285, 290, 300, 305, 313, 316, 320
  append, 296, 308
  check table, 316
  collective, 285, 286, 293, 294, 295, 296, 297, 305, 306, 307
  create, 300
  data element, 313

Definition tab, 301, 306, 309
elementary, 285, 286, 287, 293, 294, 297,
  300, 301
hierarchy, 322
Included Search Helps tab, 306, 310
screen field, 320
search help attachment, 312
search help exit, 297
table or structure field, 318
test, 305, 308
types, 286
value transport, 311
Search help exit, 287, 297, 298, 304
  events, 298
Search help parameter, , 287, 288, 295, 296,
  302
  export, 289, 303
  import, 289, 303, 311
Search helps, 22, 25, 64, 74
Secondary table, 173, 181, 182, 195, 199, 200
Select, 299
Selection, 173, 174
Selection condition, 179, 185, 186, 197, 202,
  248
Selection method, 180, 287, 288
Selection screen, 320
Select-Options, 320
Selone, 298, 299, 300
Set Parameter, 65, 299
Shlp_tab, 298
Short description, 42, 60, 87, 138, 139, 147,
  160, 162, 164, 183, 189, 193, 194, 198,
  301, 306, 309
Short text, 72, 73, 130, 145, 238, 243, 266,
  276, 281, 343
Sign, 47, 48
SIGN, 279, 281
SM30, 135, 136, 137, 182, 201, 202, 204,
  210, 238
SM31, 136
SM34, 136, 137, 251
Sorted table, 272
SPos, 290, 303
SQL, 82
SQL server, 20
ST05, 123
Standard table, 272

Status toolbar, 348
Storage area, 115
Storage parameter, 363, 364, 387, 391
STRING, 32
structure, 267, 283
Structure, 22, 34, 89, 90, 127, 132, 154, 228,
  261, 263, 264, 265, 266, 313, 318, 323
  create, 266
  deep, 128, 264
  flat, 90, 264
  nested, 264, 265
Subroutine, 213, 256
SY-MSG, 332, 337, 339
SYNCHRON, 339, 341
SYST, 292
SYSTEM_FAILURE, 339
System field, 292

T

Table, 22, 24, 77, 84, 89, 92, 112, 137, 150,
  152, 158, 167, 169, 193, 206, 211, 285,
  313, 318, 323, 384
  change, 149
  cluster, 179
  components, 82
  create, 137
  delete, 158
  Delivery and Maintenance tab, 138
  Fields tab, 138, 318
  pooled, 179
  primary, 195
  technical settings, 112
Table category, 154, 165
Table cluster, 80, 82, 159, 162, 165, 166
  create, 162
Table field, 82, 84, 148
Table maintenance, 205
Table Maintenance Dialog, 204, 205, 221,
  232, 261
Table Maintenance Generator, 205, 208, 214,
  218, 219, 225, 226, 261
  create, 218
Table pool, 78, 80, 82, 159, 160, 162, 165,
  166
  create, 159

Tables, 246, 250

Table type, 22, 35, 261, 263, 267, 271, 276
  create, 276
  generic, 275
  initialization and access tab, 277
  key tab, 277
  Line Type tab, 277
  ranges table types, 279

Tablespace, 113

Technical settings, 83, 121, 139, 143, 161,
  163, 178, 179, 186
  buffering, 113, 116, 143
  data class, 113, 143
  log data changes, 113, 119, 143
  maintain, 143
  size category, 113, 115, 116, 143, 161

Text table, 99, 100, 101, 102, 228, 229, 301,
  302, 323

Time, 36

Time dependent key, 176

Timestamp, 36, 81, 367

TIMS, 32, 85, 323

TOTAL, 226, 228, 229, 231, 232

Trace list, 124

Transparent table, 77, 113, 120, 121, 144,
  154, 167, 177

Type, 27, 38

TYPE, 275

Types, 22, 25

View cluster, 137, 204, 205, 207, 250, 251,
  252, 258, 259, 260, 261
  create, 251
  field dependencies, 255, 257
  header entry, 252
  object structure, 254
  test, 259

Views, 22, 24, 92, 167, 169, 170, 172, 175,
  183, 184, 189, 193, 194, 198, 204, 211,
  250, 389
  append, 179, 188, 191, 192, 193
  attributes, 170
  create, 182
  database, 169, 170, 176, 177, 178, 179,
    180, 183, 186, 189, 197, 204
  delete, 182
  deleting views, 204
  help, 176, 180, 194
  maintenance, 170, 175, 176, 181, 198,
    200, 250
  Maint. Status tab, 175, 190, 197, 202
  projection, 175, 176, 179, 189, 190
  Selection Conditions tab, 185, 197, 202
  Tables/Join Condition tab, 183, 194, 199
  Time-dependent, 175
  Types, 176
  View Field tab, 184, 190, 195, 200

View variant, 204, 205, 208, 245, 246, 247,
  248, 261

U

UNIT, 31, 32, 85, 87

UNIX, 20

V

Value check, 94

Value range, 39

Value table, 39, 52

VARC, 85, 129
  character field, 32

Variable, 27, 40, 94

W

WAIT, 339, 341

Where-used list, 39, 55, 75, 152, 154, 158,
  166, 204, 283, 347

Windows NT, 20

Work process, 331, 337

X

X_<FIELD>, 338

Presents the most important
ABAP statements comprehensively

Covers key object-oriented
programming concepts

Step-by-step techniques to develop
a working ABAP application

2nd, revised, and updated edition
for ABAP 7.0

Günther Färber, Julia Kirchner

ABAP Basics

In this newly revised and updated book, you will become acquainted
with the most important and commonly used ABAP commands and
terminology. Updated for ABAP version 7.0, you will find all of the
typical tasks and issues that a programmer faces within the fast-paced
SAP environment, which will enable you to write your own ABAP
application.

508 pp., 2. edition 2011, 59,95 Euro / US$ 59.95
ISBN 978-1-59229-369-8

>> www.sap-press.com

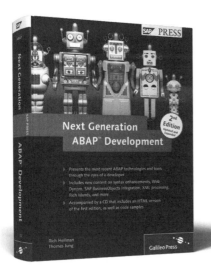

Presents the most recent ABAP technologies and tools through the eyes of a developer

Includes new topics like syntax enhancements, ABAP Test Cockpit, AJAX, SAP BusinessObjects integration, XML processing, Rich Islands, NWBC 3.0, and many more

Rich Heilman, Thomas Jung

Next Generation ABAP Development

After reading this book, you will be able to assess and employ the new tools and features of ABAP within SAP NetWeaver 7.0 to 7.0 EHP2. The updated and revised second edition assumes a scenario where a fictive university has just converted from SAP R/3 4.6C to SAP NetWeaver 7.0 (SAP Business Suite 7.0), this time with the default installation option of EHP2. Readers will experience the entire development process of applications – design, development and testing of all areas – through the eyes of a developer, and will walk away with a firm understanding of many of the newer technologies or design techniques that were not previously available in ABAP.

735 pp., 2. edition 2011, with CD, 69,95 Euro / US$ 69.95
ISBN 978-1-59229-352-0

>> www.sap-press.com

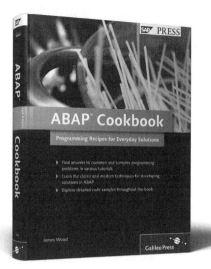

Find answers to common and complex programming problems in various tutorials

Learn the classic and modern techniques for developing solutions in ABAP

Explore detailed code samples throughout the book

James Wood

ABAP Cookbook

Programming Recipes for Everyday Solutions

This book is intended to quickly provide answers to typical ABAP development problems or tasks: persistence programming, interface programming, security and tracing techniques, etc. You'll discover best practices in developing solutions, and you can use this book to broaden your skills and see how to apply ABAP to solve various types of problems. The complexity of the "recipes" ranges from the simple starter plates to the complex main courses – and some sweet desserts, of course! Each chapter is a short tutorial in itself, all organized and consolidated into an easy-to-read format. Many code samples, screenshots, and different icons will help you to follow the best practices provided. Enjoy your ABAP meal!

548 pp., 2010, 69,95 Euro / US$ 69.95
ISBN 978-1-59229-326-1

>> **www.sap-press.com**